Complime

Jo

EU Development Cooperation Policy

Voor papa

EU Development Cooperation Policy

Between Constitutional Strictures and Policy Objectives

Tina Van den Sanden

PhD, Senior Affiliated Researcher, KU Leuven Institute for European Law, Belgium

EE Edward Elgar
PUBLISHING

Cheltenham, UK • Northampton, MA, USA

Cover image: Robert Keane on Unsplash.

Published by
Edward Elgar Publishing Limited
The Lypiatts
15 Lansdown Road
Cheltenham
Glos GL50 2JA
UK

Edward Elgar Publishing, Inc.
William Pratt House
9 Dewey Court
Northampton
Massachusetts 01060
USA

A catalogue record for this book
is available from the British Library

Library of Congress Control Number: 2022934685

This book is available electronically in the **Elgar**online
Law subject collection
http://dx.doi.org/10.4337/9781800881310

Printed on elemental chlorine free (ECF)
recycled paper containing 30% Post-Consumer Waste

ISBN 978 1 80088 130 3 (cased)
ISBN 978 1 80088 131 0 (eBook)

Printed and bound in the USA

Disclaimer: The information and views set out in this book are personal to the author and do not necessarily reflect the official position of the European Commission, where the author is currently professionally active.

Contents

1. Introductory chapter on coherence–conferral and the attainment of the EU's development cooperation policy objectives

This book builds on the premise that EU development cooperation policy suffers from an inherent tension. From a policy perspective, this important area of EU external action is defined in the broadest terms, aiming to ensure an inclusive approach to attaining development cooperation objectives. Legally speaking, the Union's legal structure is also based on the principle of conferral, which means that the Union's legal competences are limited to the boundaries set in the Treaties. These boundaries concern the division of competences between the Union and the Member States, between different areas of Union competence and between different Union actors. This raises the fundamental question that this book addresses: is the EU's legal framework equipped to meet the development cooperation policy aims that the EU sets itself? This introductory chapter is dedicated to further framing this fundamental question. First, it explores EU development cooperation policy as a multidimensional and complementary area of Union action. Second, it discusses the need for coherence, both from a policy and from a legal perspective, which follows directly from the area's characteristics. Third, it goes into the principle of conferral and its consequences and requirements.

1. EU DEVELOPMENT COOPERATION POLICY AS A MULTIDIMENSIONAL POLICY NOTION

EU development cooperation policy is embedded in a strong and well-developed policy framework, which is formed by several policy instruments that lay down different aspects of the Union's development cooperation policy.

The primary policy document on EU development cooperation policy is the European Consensus on Development ('the European Consensus'). The first European Consensus on Development was adopted in 2006[1] and was updated in 2017.[2] The 2017 European Consensus on Development builds further on the principles set in the 2006 Consensus.[3] Central is the objective of poverty eradication in the context of sustainable development as the primary and overarching objective of EU development cooperation. While the 2006 European Consensus linked to the pursuit of the UN Millennium Development Goals, the 2017 European Consensus formulates even more increased links with the international development cooperation policy framework by referring extensively to the Sustainable Development Goals (SDGs) and the 2030 Agenda as well as to the Paris Climate Agreement. In line with this, the 2017 European Consensus frames the Union's development cooperation policy as 'People, Planet, Prosperity and Peace'. Poverty, linked to the primary objective of poverty eradication, is defined as a multidimensional notion, linked to different dimensions of human development and human capabilities. In this respect, the 'People' title of the 2017 Consensus refers to economic, social, environmental, cultural, and political dimensions: ending hunger and all forms of malnutrition, promoting health (coverage), universal access to education and training, and adequate and sustainable social protection and decent work for all, but also demographic growth and shifts, migration issues, addressing inequality, and strengthening resilience.

In line with the multidimensional notion of poverty eradication, the 2017 European Consensus calls even more strongly than the 2006 Consensus to adopt comprehensive approaches by emphasising interlinkages and pursuing

---

1 Joint statement by the Council and the representatives of the governments of the Member States meeting within the Council, the European Parliament and the Commission on European Union Development Policy, The European Consensus, OJ 2006 C46/1 (hereafter: '2006 European Consensus'). On the occasion of the signing of the European Consensus on Development by High Representative Ashton, the European Consensus was confirmed as the guiding document for EU development cooperation: C. Ashton, M. Schultz, Joint Statement on the European Consensus on Development, 3 April 2014.

2 Joint statement by the Council and the representatives of the governments of the Member States meeting within the Council, the European Parliament and the Commission, The New European Consensus on Development: Our World, Our Dignity, Our Future, OJ 2017 C210/1 (hereafter: '2017 European Consensus').

3 It also builds further on the 'Agenda for Change', both as regards the definition of poverty eradication as the primary objective of EU development cooperation policy and the strong links between EU development cooperation policy and other related areas of EU external action (Communication from the Commission to the European Parliament, the Council, the European Economic and Social Committee and the Committee of the Regions, Increasing the impact of European development policy: an Agenda for Change, COM(2011) 637 final) (hereafter: 'An Agenda for Change').

integrated actions (see further below on policy coherence).[4] As such, the Consensus links the attainment of the development cooperation policy objectives to the attainment of the common external action objectives of the Union (see further below). In accordance with the central notions 'People, Planet, Prosperity and Peace', the areas of environmental protection, trade, and security are seen as the core areas with which development cooperation policy is interlinked. The 2017 European Consensus considers that development and environment are strongly connected, as environmental degradation, climate change, and natural disaster are able to reverse development and economic progress, while they increase vulnerabilities and needs.[5] In order to fully align development and environment objectives, environmental issues need to be integrated or mainstreamed in all development cooperation sectors and actions. The 'Prosperity' title of the 2017 European Consensus covers inclusive and sustainable growth and jobs. Creating decent jobs is seen as essential for inclusive and sustainable growth, which in turn is an essential enabler of human development and dignity. The trade title establishes strong links with the 'People' or human development and 'Planet' or environment titles of the Consensus, linking the traditional dimensions of sustainable development.

The 2017 Consensus sees democracy, good governance, the rule of law, and human rights as preconditions for sustainable development and stability. Poverty, conflict, fragility, and forced displacement are deeply interlinked, which leads the Consensus to demand that they are addressed in a coherent and comprehensive way. The Consensus determines that development cooperation helps to prevent, manage, and help resolve conflicts and crises and build lasting peace and good governance. By protecting and further promoting human rights, democracy, the rule of law, and good governance, actions contribute to stability, security, and resilience. On the other hand, peacebuilding and state-building are seen as essential for sustainable development and should therefore be integrated into all actions.

Various other policy instruments emphasise the strong link between EU development cooperation policy and other strongly related areas of EU external action (the so-called 'nexuses'). This book discusses the main nexuses between development cooperation on the one hand, and environment, trade or the common commercial policy (CCP) and security or the common foreign and security policy (CFSP).[6] Following the strong relation between development

---

[4] 2017 European Consensus, 7.

[5] 2017 European Consensus, 19.

[6] See for example also the nexus between development cooperation and disability: T. Van den Sanden, 'Disability in EU development cooperation', in D. Ferri, A. Broderick, *Research Handbook on EU Disability Law*, 2020, Edward Elgar, 379–394.

and environmental protection,[7] the link between development cooperation policy and environment is emphasised in the policy documents on EU development cooperation policy,[8] while several policy instruments focus particularly on the development cooperation policy–environment nexus.[9] The importance of environmental protection is also reflected in the Treaties. The Maastricht Treaty inserted the concept of sustainable development in the Treaties: Article 2 EC Treaty identified sustainable and non-inflationary growth respecting the environment as one of the objectives pursued by the then Community. Further, Article 130r(2) EC Treaty introduced the environmental integration requirement, which is still laid down in the current Treaties in Article 11 TFEU and which demands that environmental protection requirements be integrated into the definition and implementation of the Union's policies and activities, in particular with a view to promoting sustainable development. The environmental integration requirement, that is included in policy instruments and in EU (primary) law, will prove to be essential in explaining the legal delimitation between the development cooperation policy and environmental competence.

From early on, trade and development cooperation policy have been closely linked in the EU's policies vis-à-vis the developing countries[10] and the nexus between development cooperation policy and trade is still essential in the EU's external action. The European Consensus, the Agenda for Change, and

---

[7] Developing countries are often disproportionately impacted by climate change and natural disasters, while at the same time they lack the resources to deal with the negative effects. They are also often particularly dependent on natural resources, aggravating their vulnerability to degradation and depletion of the environment. Moreover, development and growth contribute to prosperity, but they also often cause environmental challenges (Communication from the Commission to the European Parliament, the Council, the European Economic and Social Committee and the Committee of the Regions, A decent life for all: Ending poverty and giving the world a sustainable future, COM(2013) 92 final, 4 (hereafter: A Decent Life for All).

[8] Apart from the European Consensus, also the Agenda For Change (p. 7) and A Decent Life for All (p. 8) determine environmental sustainability to be one of the priority areas of EU development cooperation policy.

[9] Communication from the Commission to the Council and the European Parliament, Integrating environment and sustainable development into economic and development cooperation policy, COM(1999) 499 final; Communication from the Commission to the Council and the European Parliament, EU Strategy for supporting disaster risk reduction in developing countries, COM(2009) 84 final; Communication from the Commission to the Council and the European Parliament, Building a Global Climate Change Alliance between the European Union and poor developing countries most vulnerable to climate change, COM(2007) 540 final; Communication from the Commission, A sustainable Europe for a better world: a European Union Strategy for sustainable development, COM(2001) 264 final.

[10] For an extensive overview and analysis, see: L. Bartels, 'The trade and development policy of the European Union', 4 EJIL, 2007, 715–756.

A Decent Life for All underscore the importance of inclusive and sustainable growth for human development, while several specific policy instruments further focus on the development cooperation policy–trade nexus.[11] The fact that development cooperation policy and trade have been linked from early on and the importance of external trade, as well as the dominance of the competence, affect the legal delimitation between development cooperation policy and the common commercial policy, will be analysed in detail in Chapter 3.

Insecurity and violent conflict are considered to be amongst the biggest obstacles to achieving the development cooperation policy objectives. The 2017 European Consensus maintains a broad interpretation of peaceful and inclusive societies by including democracy, good governance, the rule of law, and human rights, as 'preconditions for sustainable development and stability'.[12] Peace and security and development cannot exist without one another: security is a precondition for development, while development actions are important conflict prevention activities.[13] EU policy documents have addressed the development cooperation–security nexus under notions such as the 'comprehensive approach',[14] the 'whole-of-government-approach'[15] or 'human security'.[16] The Global Strategy for the European Union's Foreign

---

[11] Communication from the Commission to the Council and the European Parliament, Trade and Development: Assisting Developing Countries to Benefit from Trade, COM(2002) 513 final; European Commission Non-Paper, Trade and Sustainable Development Chapters in EU Free Trade Agreements, 11 July 2017; Conclusions of the Council and of the Representatives of the Governments of the Member States meeting within the Council, EU Strategy on Aid for Trade: Enhancing EU support for trade-related needs in developing countries, 29 October 2007; Communication from the Commission to the Council, the European Parliament, the European Economic and Social Committee and the Committee of the Regions: Trade for All – Towards a more responsible trade and investment policy COM(2015) 497 final.

[12] 2017 European Consensus, 31.

[13] European Council, A secure Europe in a better world: European Security Strategy, 12 December 2003.

[14] Joint Communication from the Commission and the High Representative to the European Parliament and the Council, 'The EU's comprehensive approach to external conflict and crises', JOIN(2013) 30 final, 3 (hereafter: The EU's comprehensive approach). For a critical analysis of the EU Global Strategy (from a political science perspective), see for example: M. Smith, 'Institutionalising the "comprehensive approach" to EU security', 4 European Foreign Affairs Review, 2013, 25–44

[15] Conclusions of the Council and the Representatives of the Governments of the Member States meeting within the Council on Security and Development, 15097/07, 20 November 2007.

[16] For an analysis, see for example: S. Ogata, 'Development cooperation and human security', 1 Conflict, Security and Development, 2010, 181–188; S. Breslin, G. Christou, 'Has the human security agenda come of age? Definitions, discourses and debates', 1 Contemporary Politics, 2015, 1–10; A. de Waal, R. Ibreck, 'A human

and Security Policy[17] would address the nexus mainly in relation to 'resilience',[18] which encompasses sustainable development, democracy, and trust in institutions.[19]

2. EU DEVELOPMENT COOPERATION POLICY AS A COMPLEMENTARY POLICY

The EU's development cooperation policy initially developed as a policy that was to complement, and not replace, the Member States' national development cooperation policies. The EU's relations with the developing countries find their origin in the relations of the Member States with their former colonies, mainly in Africa. The Member States therefore held a key (political) role in early EU development cooperation policy. The earliest documents on the emergence of an EU development cooperation policy therefore determine that the Union's development cooperation policy should complement the Member States' development cooperation policies, rather than replace them.[20] The explicit legal basis for development cooperation policy, as inserted by the Treaty of Maastricht, consequently determined that Union policy in the area of development cooperation is to be complementary to the policies pursued by the Member States.[21]

The fact that Union development cooperation policy existed, and continues to exist, as an accumulation of Union and national Member State policies

---

security strategy for the European Union in the Horn of Africa', Security in Transition Working Paper, 2016, 1–42.

[17] For a critical analysis of the EU Global Strategy (from a political science perspective), see for example: T. Buitelaar, J. Larik, A. Matta, B. de Vos, 'The EU's new Global Strategy: its implementation in a troubled international environment', The Hague Institute for Global Justice, 2016; J. Coelmont, 'The EUGS: realistic, but not too modest, please', 3 The International Spectator, 2016, 9–11; M. Smith, 'Implementing the Global Strategy where it matters most: the EU's credibility deficit and the European neighbourhood', 3 Contemporary Security Policy, 2016, 446–460; S. Biscop, 'The lonely strategist: who but the High Representative and the EEAS cares about the EU Global Strategy?', European Foreign Affairs Review, 2021, 25–33.

[18] For a political science analysis of the notion, see: W. Wagner, R. Anholt, 'Resilience as the EU Global Strategy's new leitmotif: pragmatic, problematic or promising?', 3 Contemporary Security Policy, 2016, 1–17.

[19] On concerns regarding the 'securitisation' of development cooperation, see for example: S. Brown, J. Grävingholt (eds), *The securitization of foreign aid*, Palgrave 2016, 267.

[20] Commission Memorandum on a Community policy for development co-operation, 27 July 1971, SEC(71) 2700, 8, 22.

[21] Article 130u EC Treaty.

necessitated the need for cooperation and coordination from early on.[22] The Treaty of Maastricht incorporated therefore not only the complementarity of Union development cooperation policy, but also the need for coherence and coordination into the Treaty framework. The Maastricht Treaty provisions incorporated the so-called triple Cs: (i) coherence between different Union policies that have an impact on developing countries; (ii) complementarity between Union and Member State action in development cooperation policy; and (iii) coordination of Union and Member State actions.[23] Complementarity and coordination are two sides of the same coin: the fact that both the EU and the Member States develop policies in the area of development cooperation policy makes coordination necessary in order to ensure that the development cooperation policy objectives can be attained. On the other hand, coordination makes complementarity possible: well-developed and well-functioning coordination arrangements, in particular division of labour arrangements, make it possible that both the EU and the Member States develop their development cooperation policy in a complementary manner.

From the beginning of the 2000s onwards, a distinct EU development cooperation policy took shape, which reinforced the EU's policy in parallel to that of the Member States. The idea emerged that EU development cooperation policy was fragmented, bilateral, and ad hoc, which negatively influenced the effectiveness of the EU's common development cooperation policy.[24] At the same time, the Member States allowed the EU to play a more important and active role in development cooperation policy. This trend coincided with a new impetus in the development cooperation discourse at international level with the adoption of the MDGs and the Financing for Development Conference, which increased the demand for coordination and cooperation in light of effectiveness concerns. From a policy perspective, coordination efforts are rooted in the idea of aid effectiveness and avoiding aid fragmentation:[25] fragmentation is seen as an important obstacle to the effectiveness of development cooperation.[26] The policy documents on EU development cooperation policy emphasise the added value of the EU's development cooperation policy vis-à-vis

---

22 Memorandum from the Commission on a Community policy on development cooperation, 2 February 1972, SEC(72) 320, 20–21.

23 Article 130u EC Treaty; Article 130v EC Treaty; Article 130x EC Treaty: P. Hoebink (ed.), The Treaty of Maastricht and Europe's development co-operation, Studies in European Development Co-operation Evaluation, 2004.

24 M. Holland, M. Doidge, *Development policy of the European Union*, 2012, Palgrave, 184, 189.

25 Council conclusions, EU Common Position for the Fourth High Level Forum on Aid Effectiveness (Busan Conclusions).

26 OECD Busan Outcome Document, http://www.oecd.org/development/effectiveness/49650173.pdf, para. 25.

that of the Member States. The EU's added value in development cooperation policy would flow from its capacity to ensure coherence and synergies among the development policies and between development cooperation and other areas of external action,[27] its added value in financial terms but also in terms of economic and political weight and influence at international level, including with its presence on the ground and membership of multilateral bodies and its experience in regional integration.[28]

The Treaty of Lisbon has further reinforced the weight of the Union's development cooperation policy vis-à-vis that of the Member States, compared with the previous Treaty provisions, by holding that the Union's and the Member States' development cooperation policies complement and reinforce *each other*. The 2017 European Consensus further emphasises the need to draw on the comparative advantages of the Union and the Member States and to improve effectiveness and impact through stronger coordination and cooperation.[29] Chapter 5 will analyse the two strands of complementarity: the nature of the EU competence in the area of development cooperation policy and the coordination and cooperation between the Union and the Member States in development cooperation policy.

3. THE DEMAND FOR COHERENCE – POLICY COHERENCE FOR DEVELOPMENT

The multidimensional broad scope of development cooperation policy and its complementary nature in relation to Member State development cooperation policy necessitate the need for coherence. The principle of coherence and its relation with the principle of conferral is essential to analyse the EU's legal framework on development cooperation policy. This section will therefore go into the definition of the notion of coherence, both from a policy and a legal perspective.

3.1 Policy Coherence for Development as a Policy Concept

The first documents on the creation of an own Community development cooperation policy already emphasised the importance of coherence and coordina-

---

27 An Agenda for Change, 3.

28 Communication from the Commission to the Council and the European Parliament, The European Community's Development Policy, COM(2000) 212 final, 5 (hereafter: The European Community's Development Policy).

29 2017 European Consensus, 37–40.

tion as conditions for the effectiveness of development cooperation policy.[30] While the early documents on EU development cooperation policy mainly concern coherence and coordination between the Union and the Member States,[31] the 2000 Communication stresses the need for coherence between EU policies as well. It indicates that because of its multidimensional character, a development cooperation policy that fosters poverty reduction requires an integrated approach, touching upon other areas of EU action such as trade, environment, security, and political dialogue.[32]

While policy coherence is arguably a more general requirement, it finds a specific expression in EU development cooperation policy, referred to as 'policy coherence for development' (PCD). The Communication 'Policy Coherence for Development – Accelerating progress towards attaining the Millennium Development Goals' defines PCD as 'the challenge of how non-aid policies can assist developing countries in attaining the MDGs' and 'non-development policies should respect development policy objectives and development cooperation should, where possible, also contribute to reaching objectives of other EU policies'.[33] With this, the following priority areas were identified where synergy with development cooperation objectives is considered to be particularly relevant: trade, environment, security, agriculture, fisheries, the social dimension of globalisation, migration, research and innovation, information society, transport, energy, and climate change.

The 2006 European Consensus on Development defined PCD as 'ensuring that the EU shall take account of the objectives of development cooperation in all policies that it implements which are likely to affect developing countries, and that these policies support development objectives'.[34] On this basis, the notion of PCD would bring about a negative and a positive aspect: other policies may not only have a negative impact on developing cooperation policy,

---

30 Commission Memorandum on a Community policy for development cooperation 1971, 7, 22.

31 Commission Memorandum on a Community policy on development cooperation 1972.

32 The European Community's Development Policy, 16–21.

33 Communication from the Commission to the Council, the European Parliament and the European Economic and Social Committee, Policy Coherence for Development – Accelerating progress towards attaining the Millennium Development Goals, COM(2005) 134 final, 3, 9 (hereafter: Communication 'Policy Coherence for Development'), 3–4. See also: Communication from the Commission to the Council, the European Parliament, the European Economic and Social Committee and the Committee of the Regions, Policy Coherence for Development – Establishing the policy framework for a whole-of-the-Union approach, COM(2009) 458 final and Council conclusions on policy coherence for development (PCD), 17 November 2009.

34 2006 European Consensus, point 35.

they must also support the attainment of the development cooperation policy objectives.[35] The 2017 European Consensus sees PCD as a fundamental part of attaining the SDGs.[36] It refers to PCD applying across all policies and all areas covered by the 2030 Agenda, seeking synergies, notably on trade, finance, environment and climate change, food security, migration, and security, and with particular attention to combating illicit financial flows and tax avoidance, and to promoting trade and responsible investment.

An important mechanism to implement PCD is the EU's Better Regulation Agenda[37] and the corresponding revision of impact assessment guidelines, which is essential for PCD.[38] PCD is embedded in the broader Better Regulation agenda: a specific toolbox for analysing the potential impact of future EU actions on developing countries is included in the Better Regulation Agenda. Tool 34 aims to ensure that impacts on developing countries are taken into account at a very early stage of the preparation of an initiative.[39] The toolbox provides guidelines for assessing systematically the possible effects that different EU policy initiatives generate on developing countries, including the assessment of economic, social, and environmental impacts, from a qualitative and quantitative respect, and the possibility to adopt mitigating measures in order to minimise the negative impact of actions on developing countries.[40]

While policy coherence for development is often used in the horizontal context, in order to attain coherence between different policies and actions that affect development and developing countries, PCD is also relevant in the vertical and the institutional relationship. In the vertical relationship, PCD refers to the complementary nature of EU development cooperation policy: PCD requires the EU and the Member States to pursue mutually reinforcing

---

[35] G. Ashoff, 'Enhancing Policy Coherence for Development: Justification, recognition and approaches to achievement' German Development Institute, 2005, 11.

[36] See also: Communication from the Commission to the Council, the European Parliament, the European Economic and Social Committee and the Committee of the Regions: Next steps for a sustainable European future – European action for sustainability, COM(2016) 739 final. Goal 17.14 of the SDGs focuses particularly on policy coherence for sustainable development.

[37] European Commission Staff Working Document, Better Regulation Guidelines, SWD(2015) 111 final, 5.

[38] For a critical analysis, see: M. Carbone, M. Furness, 'EU policy coherence for development: The challenge of sustainability', European Parliament Directorate-General for External Policies 2016, 1–48.

[39] Council Conclusions Policy Coherence for Development (PCD): 2015 EU Report, 13202/15, 26 October 2015.

[40] European Commission, Better Regulation Toolbox: Tool 34 Developing Countries, at https://ec.europa.eu/info/sites/info/files/file_import/better-regulation-toolbox-34_en_0.pdf.

policies.[41] The same is true for the different actors in development cooperation policy. In line with the universal nature of the Agenda 2030, policy coherence and creating an enabling environment for attaining the sustainable development objectives are a shared responsibility of all stakeholders at all levels.[42]

3.2 The Legal Principle of Coherence

Policy coherence for development is not only an important policy notion in EU development cooperation policy; it is also a legal principle: the general principle of coherence is an important organising legal principle, particularly in EU external action. The principle moreover finds specific expression in the area of development cooperation policy.

Although some authors do not attach legal importance to the principle,[43] the majority of legal scholarship recognises coherence as a constitutional principle because of the multiple references to the principle in the Treaties as a legal obligation.[44] With the Treaty of Lisbon, the need for coherence in external action receives a central role. Article 21(1) TEU[45] lays down the principles which are pursued by EU external action, while paragraph (2) of this article formulates the objectives which are common to EU external action. On the basis of Article 21(3) TEU, these principles and objectives must be respected and pursued in the development and implementation of all different areas of the Union's external action, bringing about the need for coherence: the provision requires the Union to ensure consistency between the different areas of its external action and between these and its other policies. The Council and the Commission, assisted by the High Representative, in particular need to ensure that consistency by cooperating to that effect. As the coherence principle is currently laid down in Article 21(3) TEU in Chapter I of Title V of the TEU on the General Provisions on the Union's External Action, there is no doubt

---

[41] 2017 European Consensus on Development, 51.

[42] 2017 European Consensus on Development, 52.

[43] P. Gauttier, 'Horizontal coherence and the external competences of the European Union', 10 European Law Journal, 2004, 24.

[44] Wessel even refers to the principle as 'a guiding principle of the EU Treaty': R. Wessel, 'The inside looking out: Consistency and delimitation in EU external relations' 37 Common Market Law Review, 2000, 1149. Van Vooren describes it as a principle that 'lies at the heart of EU law': B. Van Vooren, *EU external relations law and the European Neighbourhood Policy: A paradigm for coherence?*, Routledge, 2011, 67; See also: E. Herlin-Karnell, T. Konstadinides, 'The rise and expression of consistency in EU law: Legal and strategic implications for European integration', Cambridge Yearbook of European Legal Studies, 2013, 141.

[45] Article 21 TEU OJ 2016 C202/28.

regarding its general application to the entire field of EU external action and its legal and even constitutional nature in that regard.[46]

A first observation is that the Treaty's English language version refers to the notion of 'consistency' rather than using the term 'coherence'. The French version, on the other hand, refers to 'cohérence' and the German version to 'kohärenz'. In legal scholarship it is generally accepted that the terms consistency and coherence differ in degree: while consistency points to the absence of contradictions between different areas, coherence also brings about a more positive aspect which requires synergy, added value, and complementarity between different areas of EU action.[47]

With reference to case law[48] and following other authors in the area,[49] it has to be concluded that the Treaties would not merely demand the absence of contradictions, but require a higher and more positive degree of synergy between the different areas of Union action. In particular, this book follows the views of *Nutall*,[50] *Cremona*,[51] and *Hillion*,[52] according to whom the principle of coherence is a broad notion that covers several dimensions. First, coherence applies (i) horizontally, requiring coherence between different areas of EU

46 B. Van Vooren, *EU external relations law and the European Neighbourhood Policy: A paradigm for coherence?*, 59.

47 C. Tietje, 'The concept of coherence in the Treaty on European Union and the Common Foreign and Security Policy', 2 European Foreign Affairs Review, 1997, 212; R. Wessel, 'The inside looking out: Consistency and delimitation in EU external relations' 1150; P. Koutrakos, *Trade, foreign policy and defence in EU constitutional law*: the legal regulation of sanctions, exports of dual-use goods and armaments, 2001, Hart, 39; L. den Hertog, S. Stross, 'Coherence in EU external relations: Concepts and legal rooting of an ambiguous term', 3 European Foreign Affairs Review, 2013, 376–377.

48 These cases will be discussed in more detail in the next chapters, in particular in relation to the duty to cooperate: see Case C-266/03 *Commission/Luxembourg*, EU:C:2005:341, para. 60; Case C-433/03, *Commission/Germany*, EU:C:2005:462, para. 66; Case C-263/14, *Parliament/Council*, EU:C:2016:435, para. 72.

49 P. Koutrakos, *Trade, foreign policy and defence in EU constitutional law*, 39; C. Hillion, 'Tous pour un, un pour tous!', in M. Cremona (ed.), *Developments in EU External Relations Law*, OUP, 2008, 13, 17.

50 S. Nutall, 'Coherence and consistency', in C. Hill and M. Smith (eds.) *International relations and the European Union*, OUP, 2005, 91–112.

51 M. Cremona, 'Coherence through law: what difference will the Treaty of Lisbon make?', 3 Hamburg Review of Social Sciences, 2008, 11–36; M. Cremona, 'Coherence in European Union foreign relations law', in P. Koutrakos, *European foreign policy: legal and political perspectives*, Edward Elgar, 2011, 55–92.

52 C. Hillion, 'Tous pour un, un pour tous!', 10–36; C. Hillion, 'Mixity and coherence in EU external relations: the significance of the 'duty of cooperation', in C. Hillion, P. Koutrakos (eds.), *Mixed agreements revisited*, Hart, 2010, 87–115; C. Hillion, 'Cohérence et action extérieure de l'Union européenne', EUI Working Papers 2012/14, 1–21.

action: between the TEU external competences, the TFEU external competences, and the (external aspects of the) internal competences, (ii) vertically, between Union and Member State action, and (iii) institutionally between the EU institutions.[53]

Second, in order to attain these different dimensions, the broad principle of coherence covers also other principles of EU law, in which it finds expression.[54] These in turn apply to the horizontal, vertical, and institutional level. The negative aspect of coherence, or consistency *stricto sensu*, is achieved by avoiding contradictions, gaps, and duplications. This is attained by delimitation rules and by conflict resolution rules. Competence delimitation takes place on the basis of the principle of conferral and the institutional balance, while conflicts are further avoided and resolved by principles such as primacy and exclusivity.[55] These rules apply on the horizontal level, delimiting competence areas from each other, on the vertical level, delimiting Union and Member State competence, and on the institutional level, delimiting the competences of the different actors.[56] This negative aspect of coherence therefore aims to ensure respect for the limits of competences and an effective allocation of tasks between instruments and between actors.[57] The positive aspect of coherence, ensuring synergy and complementarity, is achieved by rules on cooperation and coordination that apply on the basis of the principle of sincere cooperation: in order to achieve coherent action, the different actors should also exercise their competence in cooperation and coordination with each other.[58] The cooperation and coordination rules on the basis of the principle of sincere cooperation apply vertically, between the Union and the Member States, and institutionally, between the different institutions and actors. As such, they affect horizontal coherence as well.[59] Hence, with its different dimensions, coherence also functions as a 'principle of action and organisation'.[60] This will

---

53 S. Nutall, 'Coherence and consistency', 92; C. Hillion, 'Tous pour un, un pour tous!', 17.

54 M. Cremona, 'Coherence through law: What difference will the Treaty of Lisbon make?', 13; C. Hillion, 'Tous pour un, un pour tous!', 18.

55 M. Cremona, 'Coherence through law: What difference will the Treaty of Lisbon make?', 14–16; C. Hillion, 'Tous pour un, un pour tous!', 18–35.

56 C. Hillion, 'Tous pour un, un pour tous!', 18–26.

57 M. Cremona, 'Coherence and EU environmental policy', in E. Morgera (ed.), *The external environmental policy of the European Union*, CUP, 2012, 35.

58 C. Hillion, 'Tous pour un, un pour tous!', 27.

59 C. Hillion, 'Tous pour un, un pour tous!', 27–35; M. Cremona, 'Coherence through law: What difference will the Treaty of Lisbon make?', 13–16; B. Van Vooren, *EU external relations law and the European Neighbourhood Policy: A paradigm for coherence?*, 67–71.

60 P. Gauttier, 40.

prove to be particularly true for the area of development cooperation policy, as demonstrated throughout this book.

The above observations regarding coherence in external action are also present in the specific expression and application of the principle of coherence in the area of development cooperation policy. The principle of coherence is reinforced in the specific Treaty articles on development cooperation policy. In that regard, the Treaty provisions on EU development cooperation policy reflect the policy notion of PCD as defined above. The explicit development cooperation policy legal basis, as introduced by the Maastricht Treaty, formulated the so-called 'triple C-principles',[61] corresponding to the different dimensions of coherence identified above: (i) coherence between policies that have an impact on developing countries and the objectives of development cooperation with the requirement to take the development cooperation objectives into account when implementing these other policies; (ii) complementarity between EU and Member States' policy in development cooperation; (iii) coordination of EU and Member State policy in the field of development cooperation. The specific expression of the principle of coherence in the area of development cooperation policy as PCD can still be found in the current Treaty Articles 208–211 TFEU on development cooperation policy. Article 208(1) TFEU holds that 'The Union shall take account of the objectives of development cooperation in the policies that it implements which are likely to affect developing countries'.

4. THE PRINCIPLE OF CONFERRAL

Like all other Union competences, development cooperation policy is not only to an important extent governed by the principle of coherence but also by the principle of conferral.

The principle of conferral refers to the particular conferment of powers to which the EU is subject.[62] As such, the principle has been referred to as an

---

[61] M. Holland, M. Doidge, 157; M. Carbone, 'Preserving policy autonomy: EU development cooperation from Maastricht to Lisbon', in F. Larusen (ed.), *The EU's Lisbon Treaty. Institutional choices and implementation*, Ashgate, 2012, 231.

[62] For an in-depth analysis of the principle of conferral's influence on the EU legal order and the relationship between the Union and the Member States in general, see: K. Lenaerts, 'Some reflections on the separation of powers in the European Community', 11 Common Market Law Review, 1991, 11–35; N. Emiliou, 'Opening Pandora's box: the legal basis of Community measures before the Court of Justice', 5 European Law Review, 1994, 488–507; P. Craig, 'Competence: clarity, conferral, containment and consideration', 3 European Law Review, 2004, 323–344; S. Weatherill, 'Competence creep and competence control', 1 Yearbook of European Law, 2004, 1–55; L. Azoulai (ed.), *The question of competence in the European Union*, OUP, 2014.

'organising principle of the constitutional order' of the EU, as it expresses the classic characteristic of the EU legal order, namely that it is not so-called 'self-authenticating'.[63] As reflected in Article 5(2) TEU, this entails that competences cannot originate from within the order itself: they necessarily follow from conferment by the Member States through the Treaties. The competences not conferred on the Union remain with the Member States, as confirmed by Article 4(1) TEU. The principle of conferral is therefore the principle that governs the limits of Union competences: the EU only has attributed or derived powers.[64] In *Opinion 2/94*, the Court confirmed that the principle of attributed powers not only applies to the internal EU order but also to EU external action, which means that also in this area the Union has only those powers which have been conferred upon it by the Treaties.[65]

A very concrete consequence of the principle of conferral is the requirement that each EU legal measure has to be based on the correct legal basis included in the Treaties. The theory of the choice of the correct legal basis and its application to the development cooperation policy competence and the related areas of environmental protection, the CCP, and the CFSP will be an important part of the analysis in Chapter 3. As the principle of conferral, and the corresponding theory of the choice of the correct legal basis, is a competence defining principle, the analysis of the correct legal basis is crucial in defining the legal scope of EU development cooperation policy and its delimitation with environmental protection, the CCP, and the CFSP. The analysis of the choice of the correct legal basis is not merely a theoretical or academic exercise. As the EU's competences are defined on the basis of the attribution of competences, the analysis of the choice of legal basis makes it possible to define what constitutes EU development cooperation policy from a legal point of view. The analysis of the choice of the correct legal basis has moreover a broader significance: it also determines the nature of the competence and, therefore, the role of the Member States, the procedure to adopt an act, the institutions involved in the adoption of the act, and their role in the process. These elements are able to influence the content of the act, which demonstrates the importance of the question of the

---

63 A. Dashwood, 'The attribution of external relations competence', in A. Dashwood and C. Hillion, *The General Law of E.C. External Relations*, Sweet & Maxwell, 2000, 116.

64 N. Emiliou, 'Opening Pandora's box: the legal basis of Community measures before the Court of Justice', 489.

65 Opinion 2/94, Accession by the Communities to the Convention for the Protection of Human Rights and Fundamental Freedoms EU:C:1996:140, para. 23–24; Opinion 2/00 Cartagena Protocol on Biosafety EU:C:2001:664, para. 5.

legal basis and the competence applicable.[66] Institutionally, in accordance with Article 13(2) TEU, the principle of conferral is crucial in defining the limits of each actor's competences. The different effects of the choice of a legal basis, particularly the role of the institutions involved, also explain why the choice of the correct legal basis often raises disputes between the institutions, often resulting in cases before the Court in which the legal basis is challenged.[67] Indeed, the main cases discussed in this book to assess the legal scope of EU development cooperation policy follow from inter-institutional disputes.

The literature has argued that the principle of conferral or attribution of competences, as a competence defining principle, can hinder EU external action. External action, particularly in response to an international emergency or crisis situation, often requires quick and flexible responses. It has been argued that the rigid principle of conferral and the flexible external action context do not entirely correspond to each other's needs. *De Baere* has argued that it follows from the principle of conferral that when the EU aims to respond to an international situation, it first has to determine whether and how, on what legal basis, and through which institution, it is competent to act, therefore giving 'precedence to considerations of competence over considerations of effectiveness in its international action'.[68]

From this follows the inherent tension between conferral as competence delimitation and coherence as attaining synergies and cooperation.[69] Article 7 TFEU encapsulates this as follows: 'The Union shall ensure consistency between its policies and activities, taking all of its objectives into account and in accordance with the principle of conferral of powers.' In this Treaty article, the link between coherence, conferral, and the attainment of the objectives of the Union becomes apparent.

The possible tension between delimitation and cooperation seems to be particularly relevant in the area of development cooperation policy. The objectives of the area require a broad scope and approach, including touching upon elements of other strongly related areas, such as trade, environment, and security. However, the legal competence is governed by the principle of conferral, which means that the Union can only act within the limits set by the Treaty. This is also relevant for the division of competences with the Member States: here too the EU must always ask itself whether it is competent to act.

---

[66] J. Heliskoski, 'Small arms and light weapons within the Union's pillar structure: an analysis of Article 47 of the EU Treaty', 6 European Law Review, 2008, 898.

[67] N. Emiliou, 'Opening Pandora's box: the legal basis of Community measures before the Court of Justice', 491–492.

[68] G. De Baere, *Constitutional principles of EU external relations*, OUP, 2008, 10.

[69] M. Cremona, 'Coherence through law: What difference will the Treaty of Lisbon make?', 16.

The same is true for the institutional level: the EU's actors need to cooperate in order to attain coherence but, on the other hand, they always need to take into account that they can only act within the powers conferred upon them, making it difficult for them to meet the requirements of coherence and delimitation at the same time.[70]

This book therefore assesses the interaction between the principle of coherence and conferral in the attainment of the EU's development cooperation policy objectives at the horizontal, vertical, and institutional level of governance. Ultimately, this approach aims to answer the question whether the constitutional and institutional organisation of EU development cooperation policy enables the EU to attain the objectives it sets itself in the area of development cooperation policy.

70 R. Wessel, 'The inside looking out: Consistency and delimitation in EU external relations', 1169.

PART I

The legal scope of EU development cooperation policy and the horizontal division of competences between development cooperation and environment, trade, and security

2. The legal scope of EU development cooperation policy

This chapter examines the legal scope of EU development cooperation policy, first, by assessing the scope of the competence as defined in primary and secondary law as well as case law and, second, by further determining the area's boundaries with other closely linked EU policy and competence areas. These other areas concern environmental protection, the common commercial policy (CCP), and the common foreign and security policy (CFSP). Central to this analysis is the question how the principle of coherence and the principle of conferral affect the legal scope of EU development cooperation policy and its delimitation with areas with which it is strongly linked. Before going into this, it is important to first address the differences in the legal framework that have existed between cooperation with African, Caribbean, and Pacific (ACP) states on the one hand and other developing countries on the other hand.[1]

1. DUAL LEGAL REGIME WITHIN EU DEVELOPMENT COOPERATION POLICY: THE DIFFERENCE BETWEEN AFRICAN, CARIBBEAN, AND PACIFIC STATES AND OTHER DEVELOPING COUNTRIES

EU development cooperation policy is mainly based on concluding international agreements with developing countries, pursuant to Article 209(2) TFEU, and the implementation of this policy by virtue of internal measures, including financing instruments to provide funding, on the basis of Article 209(1) TFEU. The difference between ACP states on the one hand and other developing countries on the other hand has been apparent in both respects.

---

[1] This also entails briefly looking back at the history of EU development cooperation, as in the words of Maresceau: 'The political and historical context in which agreements come into being is essential for the proper understanding of their legal nature, contents and significance.' M. Maresceau, 'Bilateral agreements concluded by the European Community', *Académie de Droit International – Recueil des Cours*, 2006, 313.

The relations between the EU and developing countries, in particular the ones in Africa, go back to the Treaty of Rome: considering the timeframe, this relationship finds its origin in European colonialism.[2] As a consequence, the early relationship with the developing world was mainly focused on African countries in a so-called 'natural partnership between Europe and Africa'.[3] This partnership was mainly based on a trade component and a development aid one.[4] First, the EU opened its internal market to colonial imports by extending the tariff measures that applied among the EU members. Second, the Member States set up a financing mechanism to provide development aid: the European Development Fund (EDF). Therefore, from its origin on, the relationship between the EU and the developing countries was based both on market access and (economic) assistance, in which aid was seen as the natural supplement to trade.[5] As it would mainly concern French colonies who would benefit from EU development aid, other EU Member States and the Netherlands in particular resisted the inclusion of development aid into the Treaty of Rome.[6] As a result, the EDF was created outside the general EU budget as a fund that was financed directly by the Member States on the basis of an internal agreement laying down each Member State's contribution. At the same time, after several colonies gained independence, the EU concluded an encompassing international partnership agreement with this group of countries to establish and frame the renewed cooperation.[7] Over the years and with the continued accession of countries to the EU, these agreements brought about a wider geographical scope.[8] Each agreement was linked to the establishment of a corresponding EDF to fund the cooperation.

---

2 E. Grilli, *The European Community and the developing countries*, CUP, 1993, 331; M. Holland, M. Doidge, *Development policy of the European Union*, 2012, Palgrave, 2; M. Broberg, 'What is the direction for the EU's development cooperation after Lisbon?' 4 *European Foreign Affairs Review*, 2011, 540.

3 E. Grilli, 332.

4 Green Paper on relations between the European Union and the ACP countries on the eve of the 21st century: Challenges and options for a new partnership, COM(96) 570 final, 20 November 1996, 9.

5 M. Broberg, 'What is the direction for the EU's development cooperation after Lisbon? A legal examination', 541; E. Grilli, 340.

6 P. Hoebink, 'European development aid in transition', in O. Babarinde and G. Faber (eds), *The European Union and the developing countries: the Cotonou Agreement*, 2005, 127.

7 M. Carbone, 'Preserving policy autonomy: EU development cooperation from Maastricht to Lisbon', 230.

8 From the First Yaoundé Convention of Association covering the 1964–1969 period, over the Second Yaoundé Convention covering the years 1969–1975, to the establishment of the Lomé (I, II, III and IV) Conventions which went beyond the former French colonies and French-speaking regions of Africa to cover the Africa, Caribbean

By contrast, it is only from the 1970s onwards that the EU's cooperation with non-ACP developing countries starts to take shape.[9] Also here, the cooperation is based on trade arrangements, although less favourable than those for ACP countries,[10] and granting financial aid to Latin American and Asian countries. Only from the 1990s did the EU start to conclude more comprehensive development agreements with countries in Latin America as well as with Asian countries and Central and Eastern European countries.[11] The main difference with the cooperation with ACP states is that the agreements with the non-ACP states were concluded with the countries or regions individually[12] but not with the countries as a group. Further, the financial assistance was financed by the general budget of the Union,[13] instead of by the extra-budgetary EDF.

---

and Pacific countries (established by the Georgetown Agreement on the organization of the African, Caribbean and Pacific group of states, 1975). See further: B. Martenczuk, 'From Lomé to Cotonou: The ACP-EC Partnership Agreement in a legal perspective', 4 European Foreign Affairs Review, 2000; KR Simmonds, 'The Lomé Convention and the New International Economic Order', 13 Common Market Law Review, 1976; M. Broberg, 'From colonial power to human rights promoter: on the legal regulation of the European Union's relations with the developing countries' *Cambridge Review of International Affairs*, 2012; K. Arts, A. Dickson (eds), EU development cooperation: from model to symbol?, Manchester University Press, 2004.

[9] Commission Memorandum on a Community policy for development co-operation, 27 July 1971 SEC(71) 2700, 4.

[10] K. Smith, 'The ACP in the European Union's network of regional relationships: still unique or just one in the crowd?', in K. Arts, A. Dickson (eds), EU development cooperation: from model to symbol?, Manchester University Press, 2004, 62; M. Broberg, 'What is the direction for the EU's development cooperation after Lisbon? A legal examination', 542.

[11] K. Smith, 'The ACP in the European Union's network of regional relationships: still unique or just one in the crowd?', 62; M. Broberg, 'What is the direction for the EU's development cooperation after Lisbon? A legal examination', 542.

[12] For example: Council Decision of 4 October 1999 concerning the conclusion of the Cooperation Agreement between the European Community and the Kingdom of Cambodia, OJ 1999 L269/17; Council Decision of 22 February 1999 concerning the conclusion of a Framework Cooperation Agreement between the European Economic Community and the Republics of Costa Rica, El Salvador, Guatemala, Honduras, Nicaragua and Panama, OJ 1999 L63/38.

[13] Council Regulation 442/81 of 17 February 1981 on financial and technical aid to non-associated developing countries, OJ 1981 L48/8; Council Regulation (EEC) No 443/92 of 25 February 1992 on financial and technical assistance to, and economic cooperation with, the developing countries in Asia and Latin America, OJ 1992 L 52/1), as amended by Council Regulation (EC) No 807/2003 of 14 April 2003, OJ 2003 L122/36.

This dual legal regime existed until very recently.[14] For the period 2014–2020 the 11th EDF was the main source of financing EU–ACP cooperation. It was, like the previous EDFs, set up by an agreement among the Member States: the 11th EDF Internal Agreement.[15] This agreement laid down the financial resources of the 11th EDF, with each Member State's contribution, the provision of loans by the European Investment Bank, and the rules for implementation of the EDF, which were further developed in secondary legislation.[16] The cooperation with the 78 ACP states was governed by the Cotonou Agreement, which was concluded in 2000.[17] While initially concluded for a period of 20 years, its application was extended until the new partnership agreement is in place.[18] Under Cotonou, the extra-budgetary EDF remained the most important financing source for geographic cooperation with ACP states,[19] while the ACP states were also eligible for thematic cooperation under the budget.[20]

Under the newest EU budget for the period 2021–2027,[21] however, the cooperation with ACP states is fully aligned with cooperation with non-ACP states.

---

[14] Although, both legally and policy-wise, the two regimes increasingly aligned over the years to minimise differences.

[15] Internal Agreement between the Representatives of the Governments of the Member States of the European Union, meeting within the Council, on the financing of European Union aid under the multiannual financial framework for the period 2014 to 2020, in accordance with the ACP-EU Partnership Agreement, and on the allocation of financial assistance for the Overseas Countries and Territories to which Part Four of the Treaty on the Functioning of the European Union applies, OJ 2013 L210/1.

[16] Council Regulation (EU) 2015/322 of 2 March 2015 on the implementation of the 11th European Development Fund, OJ 2015 L58/1 and Council Regulation (EU) No 2018/1877 of 26 November 2018 on the financial regulation applicable to the 11th European Development Fund and repealing Regulation (EU) 2015/323, OJ 2018 L307/1.

[17] Agreement amending for the second time the Partnership Agreement between the Members of the African, Caribbean and Pacific Group of States, of the one part, and the European Community and its Member States, of the other part, signed in Cotonou on 23 June 2000, OJ 2000 L317/3; OJ 2005 L287/4; OJ 2010 L287/3.

[18] Decision No 2/2020 of the ACP-EU Committee of Ambassadors of 4 December 2020 to amend Decision No 3/2019 of the ACP EU Committee of Ambassadors to adopt transitional measures pursuant to Article 95(4) of the ACP-EU Partnership Agreement, OJ 2020 L420/32.

[19] Annexes I, IA, IB and IC laid down the Financial Protocols for the respective EDFs.

[20] See for example Article 1 Regulation (EU) No 233/2014 of the European Parliament and of the Council of 11 March 2014 establishing a financing instrument for development cooperation for the period 2014–2020, OJ 2014 L77/44.

[21] Council Regulation (EU, Euratom) 2020/2093 of 17 December 2020 laying down the multiannual financial framework for the years 2021 to 2027, OJ 2020 L433I/11.

After years of proposals to 'budgetise' the EDF,[22] no new EDF is established and, as a result, under the period 2021–2027 also the geographic cooperation with ACP states is financed by the budget.[23] At the same time, the new partnership agreement between the EU and Organisation of African, Caribbean and Pacific States (OACPS) will no longer contain a financial protocol.[24]

2. THE LEGAL SCOPE OF EU DEVELOPMENT COOPERATION POLICY

2.1 The Formulation of the Objectives and Scope of EU Development Cooperation Policy in Primary and Secondary Law

The Maastricht Treaty introduced an explicit legal basis for development cooperation in the Treaties, including a set of specific objectives. Pursuant to Articles 130u–130y TEC (later renumbered as Articles 177–181 TEC), EU development cooperation had to foster:

(i) the sustainable economic and social development of the developing countries, and more particularly the most disadvantaged among them,
(ii) the smooth and gradual integration of the developing countries into the world economy, and
(iii) the campaign against poverty in the developing countries.

---

[22] Communication from the Commission to the Council and the European Parliament. Towards the full integration of co-operation with ACP countries in the EU budget, COM(2003) 590 final; Communication from the Commission to the European Parliament and the Council. Preparation of the multiannual framework regarding the financing of EU cooperation for African, Caribbean and Pacific States and Overseas Countries and Territories for the 2014–2020 period (11th European Development Fund), COM(2011) 837 final, 2. However: Communication from the Commission to the European Parliament, the Council, the European Economic and Social Committee and the Committee of the Regions. A budget for Europe 2020, COM(2011) 500 final, 20–21; European Council on the financial perspective 2007–2013, 19 December 2005, Doc. 15915/05.

[23] Regulation (EU) 2021/947 of 9 June 2021 establishing the Neighbourhood, Development and International Cooperation Instrument – Global Europe, amending and repealing Decision No 466/2014/EU and repealing Regulation (EU) 2017/1601 and Council Regulation (EC, Euratom) No 480/2009, OJ 2021 L209/1.

[24] See the public texts of the negotiating directives and the text as initialled between the parties' chief negotiators on 15 April 2021: https://ec.europa.eu/international-partnerships/acp-eu-partnership_en.

Moreover, Union development cooperation policy had to contribute to the general objective of developing and consolidating democracy and the rule of law, and to that of respecting human rights and fundamental freedoms. The latter also constituted one of the CFSP objectives formulated in ex Article 11(1) TEU, which held the potential to lead to inter-pillar quarrels (see below Chapter 3, Section 3). The objectives in Articles 130u–130y and Articles 177–181 TEC expressed a concept of development cooperation which was not confined to its economic aspect: the trade aspect as well as the environmental, human rights, and peace and security aspect were represented in the Treaty objectives,[25] corresponding to the multidimensional concept of development cooperation policy put forward in the basic policy documents (see Chapter 1).

In the post-Lisbon era, Articles 208–211 TFEU contain the primary legal framework on development cooperation. Reading Article 208(1) TFEU, the following elements would govern the horizontal scope of the development cooperation policy competence: (i) Union policy in the field of development cooperation shall be conducted within the framework of the principles and objectives of the Union's external action; (ii) Union development cooperation policy shall have as its primary objective the reduction and, in the long term, the eradication of poverty; and (iii) the Union shall take account of the objectives of development cooperation in the policies that it implements which are likely to affect developing countries.

Article 208(1) TFEU therefore identifies a primary objective of EU development cooperation: the reduction and, in the long term, the eradication of poverty. Apart from this primary objective, the provisions on EU development cooperation no longer refer to the other development objectives mentioned in the old Articles 130u–130y TEC and Articles 177–181 TEC. Article 208(1) TFEU nevertheless also emphasises that development cooperation has to be conducted within the framework of the principles and objectives of the Union's external action. This has led to the question whether the new formulation of the Treaty articles on development cooperation and its primary objective has limited the scope of the EU development cooperation competence to measures aimed at poverty reduction or eradication.[26] The emergence of common EU external action objectives in Article 21(2) TEU, alongside specific objectives in the TFEU provisions on EU external action, indeed raised questions on the relation between these two types of objectives and on whether a hierarchy

---

[25] K. De Feyter, *World development law. Sharing responsibility for development*, Intersentia, 2001, 128.

[26] Opinion of AG Bot, Case C-658/11, Parliament/Council, EU:C:2014:2025, point 126.

exists between them.[27] It seems that this is *a fortiori* the case as regards development cooperation policy because of the identification of a clear primary aim in Article 208(1) TFEU, while it is also the only objective which has been duplicated both in the general external action objectives and as a specific objective in the field of development cooperation policy.[28]

Arguments that the reformulation of the Treaty objectives and provisions of EU development cooperation policy have limited the competence's scope cannot be supported, in particular the interpretation that the scope of Article 209 TFEU is limited to poverty reduction.[29] Such an interpretation would both neutralise the common EU external action objectives in Article 21(2) TEU and deny Article 208(1) TFEU, which requires that development cooperation be conducted in the framework of the common EU external action objectives.[30] Rather, Article 208 TFEU strongly links the development cooperation objective with the general external action objectives of Article 21(2) TEU, including the duplication of this objective in both articles, which expresses the requirement of policy coherence for development and the broad understanding of EU development cooperation policy. The singling out of the poverty eradication aim in Article 208(1) TFEU would then mainly function as underscoring the importance of poverty eradication as an overarching objective that ensures the steering of the multidimensional development cooperation actions towards the attainment of the primary development cooperation policy objective.[31] As

---

27. For an extensive analysis of the role of external action objectives in European constitutional law, see: J. Larik, *Foreign Policy Objectives in European Constitutional Law*, OUP, 2016, 358p. More generally: E. Neframi, *Objectifs et compétences dans l'Union européenne*, Bruylant, 2015, 438 p.

28. See for example: M. Cremona, 'A reticent court? Policy objectives and the Court of Justice' in M. Cremona, A. Thies (eds), *The European Court of Justice and external relations law*, Hart, 2014, 19.

29. Schutze, who nevertheless nuances his own arguments by indicating that the post-Lisbon scope of EU development cooperation policy will depend on how broadly the Court will interpret the primary aim of poverty reduction and eradication: R. Schutze, 'EU Development Policy: Constitutional and legislative foundations', Cambridge Yearbook of European Legal Studies, 2013, 707.

30. See also Eeckhout and Bartelt, who believe that, on this basis the reformulated Treaty provisions have not limited the scope of EU development cooperation policy: P. Eeckhout, EU external relations law, OUP, 2011, 139–140; S. Bartelt, 'ACP-EU development cooperation at a crossroads? One year after the second revision of the Cotonou Agreement', 1 European Foreign Affairs Review, 2012, 20–21.

31. See also Broberg and Holdgaard, who refer to 'reorganisation' and 'streamlining' of the development cooperation objectives with a much sharper focus on the primary objective of poverty reduction and eradication: M. Broberg, 'What is the direction for the EU's development cooperation after Lisbon?', 546.

such, development cooperation policy actions must always (also) pursue the goal of poverty reduction.[32]

On the other hand, one could follow the reasoning that while Article 208(1) TFEU allows for a broad understanding of development cooperation with multiple components with its link to the objectives in Article 21(2) TEU, development cooperation measures cannot mainly pursue objectives other than the fight against poverty. Otherwise, the development cooperation competence would encroach upon competences and their rules and procedures.[33] As such, the formulation of Article 208(1) TFEU and the primary objective of poverty eradication would both ensure a broad understanding and allow for coherence, while also limiting the scope of the development competence. Also in the secondary legislation, the primary objective of poverty eradication allows that actions are steered towards the primary objective of poverty eradication.[34] As an important consequence, this would entail that assistance in different sub-areas is focused on the poorest and most fragile countries or on the poorest and most vulnerable groups within countries.[35]

The next section will demonstrate that the Court's case law on the interpretation of the Treaty provisions and the notion of poverty reduction and eradication will be crucial to define the scope of EU development cooperation policy. Therein, the balance between allowing a broad and coherent scope, while respecting the principle of conferral, also becomes apparent.

2.2 The Scope Following the Case Law of the ECJ: Finding the Balance

The case law proves to be very important in defining the legal scope of the development cooperation policy competence. While a broad legal scope would support the broad development cooperation policy notion and the attainment of the development cooperation policy objectives, a too broad scope is able to violate the principle of conferral. The Court, however, succeeds in finding the balance between supporting the possibility to adopt a broad development cooperation policy and in respecting the principle of conferral at the same

---

[32] M. Broberg, R. Holdgaard, 'EU development cooperation post-Lisbon: main constitutional challenges', 3 *European Law Review*, 2015, 352.

[33] P. Koutrakos, *The EU Common Security and Defence Policy*, OUP, 2013, 211–212.

[34] Article 1 Regulation 233/2014 of 11 March 2014 establishing a financing instrument for development cooperation for the period 2014–2020, OJ 2014 L77/44.

[35] I. Tannous, 'The programming of EU's external assistance and development aid and the fragile balance of power between EEAS and DG Devco' 3 European Foreign Affairs Review, 2013, 351.

time. It does so by applying a balanced centre of gravity test to the scope of development cooperation policy that balances the different elements of the centre of gravity.[36]

2.2.1 The unfeasibility of applying a mere objectives-based competence delimitation method to development cooperation

Rendered a few years after the entry into force of the Maastricht Treaty, the *Portugal/Council* case[37] was the first to explain the scope of EU development cooperation policy on the basis of its specific legal basis in the Treaty. As will be further discussed below, case law prior to the Maastricht Treaty focused rather on what development cooperation policy *was not* than what it did involve due to the lack of a specific legal basis in the Treaty.[38] Until today, the latter has consequences for the delimitation between development cooperation policy and other competence areas, the CCP in particular (see Chapter 3, Section 2 below on the delimitation with the CCP). In this case, Portugal had brought an action for annulment of Council Decision 94/578/EC concerning the conclusion of the Cooperation Agreement between what was then the European Community and the Republic of India on Partnership and Development.[39] The contested decision was based on the development cooperation and CCP legal bases. Portugal challenged the EU's competence and the correctness of the legal basis of the Agreement on several grounds, which, according to Portugal, all found their origin in the fact that EU development cooperation policy and national development cooperation policy are complementary (see Chapter 5). With the first complaint, Portugal argued that the EU was not allowed to develop a distinct development policy, including agreements with third states, on the basis of the development cooperation legal basis in the Treaty, then Article 130y EC, alone. The fact that the Treaty stated that the EU's development cooperation policy was complementary to that of the Member States brought about that the EU's policy was subordinate to the national policies and could merely coordinate them, according to Portugal.

---

[36] For a discussion of the use of the centre of gravity test as a means to establish the legal basis for the conclusion of international agreements involving development cooperation, the CCP, or the CFSP, see: G. De Baere, T. Van den Sanden, 'Interinstitutional Gravity and Pirates of the Parliament on Stranger Tides: the Continued Constitutional Significance of the Choice of Legal Basis in Post-Lisbon External Action', 2016 EU Const Law Review, 85–113.

[37] Case C-268/94, *Portugal/Council*, EU:C:1996:461.

[38] S. Peers, 'Case C-268/94, Portugal v. Council, (development policy), [1996] ECR I-6177 (Full Court)', 35 Common Market Law Review, 1998, 541.

[39] Council Decision 94/578/EC of 18 July 1994 concerning the conclusion of the Cooperation Agreement between the European Community and the Republic of India on Partnership and Development, OJ 1994 L223/23.

Any distinct EU development cooperation policy and hence cooperation agreements would have to be based on Article 235 EC. Second, the inclusion of the specific clauses on human rights, which were considered to be an essential element of the agreement, energy, tourism, culture, intellectual property, and drug abuse control not only required the agreement to be based on Article 235 EC, but also necessitated the conclusion of a mixed agreement because they affected sectors within the competence of the Member States, Portugal argued.

The Court started its reasoning by clarifying the central issue to be answered: the extent to which an agreement which is concluded between the EU and a third country on the basis of Article 130y EC, could lay down provisions on specific matters, without necessitating the addition of other legal bases or the participation of the Member States.[40] In order to answer this, the Court used a two-pronged test. First, in order to qualify as a development cooperation agreement, the agreement must pursue the development cooperation objectives, at the time laid down in Article 130u EC Treaty. These objectives are broad enough that measures required for their pursuit can concern a variety of specific matters, particularly when an agreement establishes the framework of cooperation, the Court considered. The Court emphasised that requiring a development cooperation agreement to be based on additional legal bases each time it touches on a specific matter would render the development cooperation competence and procedures 'devoid of substance'. A development cooperation agreement can therefore contain clauses concerning various specific matters without altering the characterisation of the agreement. Second, the characterisation of the agreement has to be determined having regard to its essential object and not in terms of individual clauses, provided that these did not impose such extensive obligations concerning the specific matters referred to that those obligations in fact constitute objectives distinct from those of development cooperation.[41] The Court found on the merits that the cooperation provided for by the agreement took particular account of the needs of a developing country and thus contributed to furthering the development cooperation objectives.[42] As the provisions of the agreement were limited to determining the areas for cooperation and to specifying certain of its aspects, they were limited to establishing the framework of cooperation and did not prescribe in concrete terms the manner in which cooperation in each specific area envisaged was to be implemented.

The *Small Arms and Light Weapons* case is not only important for the specific delimitation between development cooperation policy and the CFSP (see

---

40 Case C-268/94, *Portugal/Council*, EU:C:1996:461, para. 35.

41 Case C-268/94, para. 37–39.

42 Case C-268/94, para. 44.

below); it is also important for the definition of the objectives of EU development cooperation. In this case, the Court further clarified that the objectives of development cooperation policy should not be limited to measures directly related to the campaign against poverty. Nevertheless, if a measure was to fall within development cooperation policy, it had to contribute to the pursuit of that policy's economic and social development objectives.[43] With this the Court clarified that the aims of development cooperation go beyond poverty reduction or eradication to also cover broader economic and social development objectives.[44] The traces of this reasoning can already be found in *Portugal/Council*, where the Court assessed whether the provisions on drug abuse control could be covered by the development cooperation agreement by determining that drug-related activities can constitute 'serious impediments to economic and social development'.[45]

The *Philippines PCA* case gave the Court the opportunity to clarify the scope of development cooperation policy in the post-Lisbon era – 20 years after *Portugal/Council* was rendered. This case concerned the scope of development cooperation in relation to the Framework Agreement on Partnership and Cooperation between the EU and its Member States and the Republic of the Philippines ('Philippines PCA' or 'PPCA'). The Commission proposal for the Council decision on the signing of this agreement was based on Article 207 TFEU on the CCP, and Article 209 TFEU on development cooperation.[46] The Council, however, added the legal bases on readmission of third-country nationals (Article 79(3) TFEU), transport (Articles 91 and 100 TFEU), and the environment (Article 191(4) TFEU) to Articles 207 and 209 TFEU, reason for which the Commission asked the Court to annul this decision. Interestingly, the Advocate General describes EU development cooperation as a 'multi-faceted' policy, referring to the European Consensus and the requirement of policy coherence for development.[47] Further, with reference to the *Portugal/Council* test which he thereby confirms post-Lisbon, he concludes that the PCA remains within the framework of the development cooperation policy objectives, as both the agreement itself and the specific provisions on

---

[43] Case C-91/05, *Commission v Council*, EU:C:2008:288, para. 67.

[44] See also: R. Schütze, 'EU Development Policy: Constitutional and legislative foundations', 706.

[45] Case C-268/94, para. 60.

[46] Proposal for a Council Decision on the signing of the Framework Agreement on Partnership and Cooperation between the European Union and its Member States, of the one part, and the Republic of the Philippines, of the other part (COM(2010) 460 final).

[47] Opinion of AG Mengozzi in C-377/12, Commission v Council, EU:C:2014:1903, points 25–30; 40–42.

transport, the environment, and the readmission of third-country nationals contribute to the objectives of development cooperation policy, without constituting distinct objectives.

The Court followed this line and indeed recalled and confirmed its two-pronged test developed in *Portugal/Council* to determine the appropriate scope of development cooperation agreements.[48] The Court first indicated that the title of the agreement was irrelevant: contrary to the India Cooperation Agreement, the word 'development' does not appear in the title of the PPCA. Instead, the Court held that the intention of the contracting parties to promote sustainable social and economic development, the eradication of poverty, and the achievement of the MDGs is affirmed in the preamble, the general principles set out in Article 1, and in various other provisions. Moreover, it was apparent from the whole of the PPCA that the cooperation and partnership laid down in the agreement took account especially of the needs of a developing country and therefore contributed to furthering pursuit of the objectives referred to in Articles 21(2)(d) TEU and 208(1) TFEU on development cooperation, the Court indicated.[49] With regard to the question whether the development cooperation competence was sufficiently broad to also cover the specific provisions, the Court made use of the *Portugal/Council* test: first, the Court concluded that the provisions relating to readmission, transport, and the environment, consistently with the European Consensus, contributed to the pursuit of the objectives of development cooperation.[50] In this respect the Court recalled that migration, transport, and the environment are integrated into development policy as defined in the European Consensus, as well as that they are also included in the Development Cooperation Instrument I (DCI I) as areas of development cooperation that may receive EU assistance.[51] Specifically, the PPCA itself, and in particular its Articles 26, 34, and 38, linked the cooperation that it aims to establish in these areas to the objectives of development cooperation. Second, the provisions of the PPCA relating to readmission of nationals of the contracting parties, to transport, and to the environment did not contain obligations so extensive that they could be considered to constitute objectives distinct from those of development cooperation, according to the Court.[52] The Council should therefore not have added Articles 79(3), 91, 100, and 191(4) TFEU as legal bases for the contested decision, and

---

[48] Case C-377/12, paras. 38–39, recalling Case C-268/94, paras. 37–39.
[49] Case C-377/12, paras. 45–47.
[50] Case C-377/12, paras. 49–55.
[51] Regulation 1905/2006 of 18 December 2006 establishing a financing instrument for development cooperation, OJ 2006 L378/41.
[52] Case C-377/12, paras. 56–59.

the Court annulled the decision insofar as it contained these supererogatory legal bases.

The consequence of the judgment in *Philippines PCA* would therefore be that the pre-Lisbon case law remains largely relevant for the construction of the post-Lisbon scope of development cooperation.[53] In this, the Court has confirmed the potentially broad scope of development cooperation policy by confirming the policy's broad objectives.[54] In reaching its conclusion, the Court's interpretation of the primary objective of poverty eradication, as well as the link with the common external action objectives in Article 21 TEU, is particularly interesting.

The Court referred to the wide definition of 'poverty eradication' as formulated by the basic non-legally binding policy documents on Union development cooperation, as well as secondary EU law, using them as an interpretative tool to support the wide scope of EU development cooperation policy.[55] The Council had argued that the nature of partnership and cooperation agreements had evolved remarkably as they had come to establish a comprehensive relationship covering many different areas of cooperation, in line with the extension of EU competences and that the Court's analysis in *Portugal v Council* could therefore not be transposed to the *Philippines PCA* case.[56] The Court disagreed and on the contrary held that the evolution outlined by the Council corresponded to an increase in the objectives of development cooperation and in the matters concerned by it, which reflected the EU vision for development set out in the European Consensus, and that this in fact confirmed rather than distinguished *Portugal/Council.* The Court therefore took account of the developments that took place in the concept of EU development cooperation policy in policy documents and secondary legislation since the *Portugal/ Council* case, which corresponded to an increase in the objectives of development cooperation and in the matters concerned by it.[57] In line therewith, the

---

[53] M. Broberg, R. Holdgaard, 'Demarcating the Union's Development Cooperation Policy after Lisbon: *Commission v. Council (Philippines PCFA)*', 2 Common Market Law Review, 2015, 562; G. De Baere, T. Van den Sanden, 96.

[54] This would be in line with the argument that a posteriori judicial control over the principle of conferral in general often leads to a broad interpretation of objectives and means to attain these objectives: K. Lenaerts, 'De Europese Unie: doel of middel?' RW, 1998–1999, 695.

[55] B. Van Vooren as regards the Small Arms and Light Weapons case: B. Van Vooren, 'The Small Arms Judgment in an Age of Constitutional Turnmoil', 2 *Foreign Affairs Review*, 2009, 235; M. Cremona, 'A reticent court? Policy objectives and the Court of Justice', 19.

[56] Case C-377/12, para. 41.

[57] M. Broberg, R. Holdgaard, 'EU development cooperation post-Lisbon: main constitutional challenges', 353.

Court referred to the broad notion of development cooperation and poverty eradication as a multifaceted concept as upheld by the European Consensus and the DCI I.[58] As such, the Court relied on a non-legally binding instrument, as well as a legislative instrument of secondary law, in order to determine the objective and appropriate legal basis of a measure.[59] The Court did the same in order to define the scope of the development cooperation competence in the *Philippines Borders Management*[60] and the *Small Arms and Light Weapons* cases.[61] This would indicate that the Court's reliance on policy documents in order to support the choice and scope of a legal basis is particularly prominent in cases concerning development cooperation.[62] It needs to be underlined that the Court indeed used the instruments to support its choice of legal basis rather than that it defined the limits of primary law competences by using secondary hard and soft law, which arguably would be in conflict with the hierarchy of norms.[63] In any event, even if the development cooperation competence were to be limited solely to the explicitly formulated primary objective of 'poverty eradication', the Court's broad interpretation of poverty eradication as the principal objective of development cooperation policy provides for an extensive scope of development cooperation measures.[64]

---

58 Case C-377/12, para. 42.

59 M. Cremona, 'A reticent court? Policy objectives and the Court of Justice', 19; M. Broberg, R. Holdgaard, 'Demarcating the Union's Development Cooperation Policy after Lisbon', 562–563.

60 The Court referred to both the European Consensus and the DCI to link development cooperation and capacity building in border management and fight against terrorism: Case C-403/05, *Parliament/Commission,* EU:C:2007:624, para. 57–58. For an extensive analysis of this case, see: T. Van den Sanden, 'Laying the foundation for a broad scope of EU development cooperation policy and its delimitation with other EU external competence: Philippines Border Management', in G. Butler, R.A. Wessel (ed.), *EU External Relations Law: The Cases in Context,* Oxford: Hart Publishing, forthcoming.

61 The Court relied extensively on the European Union strategy to combat illicit accumulation and trafficking of small arms and light weapons adopted by the European Council on 15 and 16 December 2005 (Council document No 5319/06 PESC 31 of 13 January 2006) as well as on the European Consensus: Case C-91/05, paras. 66, 69, 90–91.

62 P. Eeckhout, *EU external relations law*, 138; M. Cremona, 'Structural principles and their role in EU external relations law', in M. Cremona, Structural principles in EU external relations law, Hart, 2018, 10.

63 M. Broberg, R. Holdgaard, 'EU development cooperation post-Lisbon: main constitutional challenges', 353–354.

64 G. De Baere, T. Van den Sanden, 96. See also R. Schütze, 'EU Development Policy: Constitutional and legislative foundations', 707, who concludes that much will depend on how broadly the Court interprets the scope of 'poverty eradication'.

In determining the scope and objectives of EU development cooperation, the Court nevertheless further referred to Article 21(2)(d) TEU – the objective of fostering the sustainable economic, social, and environmental development of developing countries with the primary aim of eradicating poverty – as an example of one of the objectives in Article 21(2) TEU that development cooperation can primarily pursue. Still, the Court emphasised that EU development cooperation is not limited to measures directly aimed at the eradication of poverty, but can also pursue the objectives laid down in Article 21(2) TEU, confirming in that respect *Small Arms and Light Weapons*.[65] The Court therefore would not see the common EU external action objectives in Article 21 TEU as only incidental to the specific objectives mentioned in the specific provisions on each policy area.[66] The Court held that this follows from the fact that Article 208(1) TFEU provides for Union development cooperation policy to be conducted within the framework of the principles and objectives of the Union's external action (as laid down in Article 21 TEU), while Article 209(2) TFEU provides that the Union may conclude any agreement helping to achieve the objectives referred to in Article 21 TEU and Article 208 TFEU.[67] With this statement the Court therefore strengthens the notion of policy coherence for development, by explicitly referring to the Treaty articles on this subject.

The Court further confirmed the scope of the objectives of EU development cooperation, and hence, its scope in two cases regarding the delimitation between development cooperation and the CFSP (see further below): *PCA Kazakhstan* case[68] and *CEPA Armenia* case.[69] In *CEPA Armenia* in particular, the Court does a detailed analysis of all criteria to determine the appropriate legal basis. In relation to the objectives, the Court referred to their broad notion, as formulated in earlier case law, confirming that the objectives are not limited to measures directly aimed at the eradication of poverty but that it must be possible for the measures required for their pursuit to concern a variety of specific areas.[70] The Court also confirmed further the link between the objectives of development cooperation and the common external action objectives: in line with *Philippines PCA*, the Court referred to the integration into development cooperation of the common external action objectives laid down in Article 21(2) TEU, while, at the same time, also explicitly referring to the specific objective laid down in Article 21(2)(c) TEU.[71] Interestingly, the Court also

---

65 Case C-377/12, paras. 37 and 47.

66 G. De Baere, T. Van den Sanden, 94.

67 Ibid., para. 36.

68 Case C-244/17, *Commission/Council*, EU:C:2018:662.

69 Case C-180/20, *Commission/Council*, EU:C:2021:658.

70 Case C-180/20, para. 50–51.

71 Case C-180/20, para. 49.

seemed to integrate the test on the limit of the scope of EU development cooperation, which it before mainly tested in relation to the content criterion, also in relation to the objectives as well. In this regard, the Court held that, although some of the specific aims of *CEPA Armenia* may be linked to the CFSP, the enumeration of those specific aims is not accompanied by any programme of action or concrete terms governing cooperation in that field. This further confirmed that the CFSP did not constitute one of the distinct components of *CEPA Armenia*, outside the scope of those aspects connected with trade and development cooperation.[72] As will be further developed below, although the Court's assessment in *CEPA Armenia* further develops and details its assessments in *Portugal/Council* and *PCA Philippines*, the substance of the test on the scope of EU development cooperation policy would remain the same.

With the assessment in the *Portugal/Council*, the *Philippines PCA*, and *CEPA Armenia* cases that the objectives of development cooperation policy are broad enough that the measures to pursue them can cover a variety of specific matters, the Court confirmed the wide nature of the objectives of development cooperation policy. Together with the recognition of a corresponding broad policy notion, this allows for an expansive development cooperation competence, involving elements of other EU competences. As was shown in the previous chapter, this corresponds to what constitutes 'EU development cooperation policy' following its basic documents: a multifaceted field. The EU defends the idea that only a comprehensive vision on development can help to meet the needs of the developing countries. A restrictive legal scope would in any event hinder the possibility of developing such a policy.[73] However, because of the nature of the development cooperation policy objectives, a too broad interpretation of these objectives might lead to the situation where this policy potentially covers nearly any area of Union external action.[74] In this regard, Advocate General Mengozzi called in *Philippines PCA* for 'a certain vigilance'.[75] With this, the principle of conferral comes at the forefront. Determining the limits of development cooperation policy solely on the basis of its objectives is therefore a precarious exercise.[76] However, settled

---

72 Case C-180/20, para. 52.

73 See also: S. Peers, 'Fragmentation or evasion in the Community's development policy? The impact of Portugal v. Council', in A. Dashwood and C. Hillion (eds), *The General Law of EC External Relations*, Sweet & Maxwell, 2000, 112.

74 Cf the Opinion of AG Mengozzi, Case C-377/12, point 29. See also: J. Silga, 'Assessing the consistency of EU development cooperation with readmission in the EU-Philippines Agreement Case – a balancing exercise', 3 European Law Review, 2015, 444.

75 Opinion of AG Mengozzi, Case C-377/12, point 43.

76 G. De Baere, T. Van den Sanden, 96.

case law on the choice of the appropriate legal basis determines that the choice of legal basis must rest on objective factors amenable to judicial review, not only including the aim but also the content and increasingly also the context of the measure. The next section will argue that this second component finds a particular application in the area of development cooperation policy, which is essential to determine the competence's limits.

2.2.2 Striking the balance: the implementation criterion

A too broadly defined development cooperation policy is objectionable because of the risk of violating the principle of conferral. It is the Advocate General in the *Philippines PCA* case rather than the Court who expressed the biggest concerns in this regard.[77] A reasoning to determine the scope of development cooperation solely on the basis of its objectives would therefore be problematic. Nevertheless, the test formulated in *Portugal/Council* and confirmed in *Philippines PCA* is two-pronged. Not only do the provisions have to contribute to the pursuit of the development cooperation objectives; they must not contain obligations so extensive that they may be considered to constitute objectives distinct from those of development cooperation that are neither secondary nor indirect.[78] In order to determine whether this second aspect of the test is fulfilled, the Court uses a content-based criterion.[79]

In the *Portugal/Council* case the Court held that the provisions on specific matters merely established the framework of cooperation between the contracting parties: they were limited to determining the areas for cooperation and to specifying certain of its aspects and various actions to which special importance was attached. By contrast, they did not prescribe in concrete terms the manner in which cooperation in each specific area envisaged was to be implemented.[80] The Court added that 'the mere inclusion of provisions for cooperation in a specific field does not therefore necessarily imply a general power such as to lay down the basis of a competence to undertake any kind of cooperation action in that field'.[81] After *Portugal/Council* it was believed that this criterion developed by the Court essentially involved the question

[77] 'I find it, by contrast, more difficult to regard the legal basis for development cooperation alone as sufficient when so many and varied areas are covered by the same agreement. I call, in that regard, for a certain vigilance, precisely because the determination of the appropriate legal basis "has constitutional significance" for the European Union': Opinion of Advocate General Mengozzi in C-377/12, point 43.

[78] Case C-268/94, para. 39.

[79] G. De Baere, T. Van den Sanden, 97.

[80] Case C-268/94, para. 45.

[81] Case C-268/94, para. 47.

whether the EU had to commit to a concrete obligation in a specific field.[82] It was argued that when an agreement brings about clear rights and obligations in specific fields[83] or when the future negotiation of specific agreements is mandatory rather than permissive,[84] additional legal bases need to be added. The agreement with India was a framework agreement without further clear obligations. How the Court would decide in a case concerning a more far-going agreement, bringing about more clearly formulated obligations and commitments, remained unanswered.

The Court had this opportunity in the *Philippines PCA* case, where it further developed the second criterion. There, the Court considered that the provisions on environment and transport covered declarations of the contracting parties on the aims of their cooperation and the subjects to which that cooperation will have to relate, but that they 'do not determine in concrete terms the manner in which the cooperation will be implemented'.[85] With regard to the provisions on readmission of third country nationals, the Court recognised that Article 26(3) PCA contained specific obligations. Following this provision, the Philippines, as well as the EU, *shall* admit back any of its nationals present in the other party's territory, who do not fulfil, or no longer fulfil, the conditions of entry or residence on the territory of the other party. They *will* provide their nationals with required documents for such purposes. Moreover, following Article 26(4) PCA the EU and the Philippines *agree to conclude* as soon as possible an agreement for the admission/readmission of their nationals. However, the Court still concluded that these provisions did not contain obligations so extensive that they may be considered to constitute objectives distinct from those of development cooperation. According to the Court, this followed from the fact that the readmission of persons residing without authorisation was included in Article 26 as one of the matters upon which cooperation on migration and development would have to focus:

> without it being covered at this stage by detailed provisions enabling its implementation, such as those contained in a readmission agreement. It cannot therefore be considered that Article 26 of the Framework Agreement prescribes in concrete terms the manner in which cooperation concerning readmission of nationals of the

[82] S. Peers, 'EC Frameworks of International Relations: Cooperation, Partnership and Association' in A. Dashwood and C. Hillion (eds), *The General Law of EC External Relations*, Sweet & Maxwell, 2000, 172.

[83] N. Burrows, 'Development cooperation defined', 6 European Law Review, 1997, 598.

[84] S. Peers, 'EC frameworks of international relations', 173.

[85] Case C-377/12, para. 56.

contracting parties is to be implemented, a conclusion which is reinforced by the commitment, in Article 26(4), to conclude a readmission agreement very soon.[86]

Hence, the Court considered that although it recognises that the provisions on readmission did contain specific obligations and that they were to some extent concrete as to how the readmission was to be carried out, they still needed to be implemented further by concluding a readmission agreement. The provisions in the PCA itself therefore did not cover in a detailed manner the cooperation in the area of readmission so as to enable its immediate and concrete implementation: a readmission agreement with detailed provisions on the readmission of nationals was necessary in order to further implement the commitments.

The second aspect of the test therefore focuses rather on the content of the provisions than on the objectives. Consequently, the Court tackles the risk that development cooperation policy potentially covers nearly any other area of EU external action by merely applying an objectives-based approach to development cooperation policy in combination with a wide interpretation of its objectives.[87] The Court's interpretation of the criterion developed, when comparing *Portugal/Council* and *Philippines PCA*: while in *Portugal/Council* the question was more whether the provisions on other policy areas were declaratory or concrete, the decisive criterion in *Philippines PCA* is whether they require specific further implementation. Of course, the 'implementation' criterion was already present in *Portugal/Council*,[88] but in *Philippines PCA* it was conclusive. The Court's recognition that the provisions on readmission were more than merely declaratory but nevertheless still within the scope of development cooperation because they required further implementation would indicate a subtle but significant broadening of the scope of development cooperation.[89] With its reasoning on the provisions on readmission, the Court shows that development cooperation can be used for relatively deep forms of cooperation, as the implementation criterion is a narrower test and can therefore lead to more concrete cooperation in specific fields under the scope of development cooperation policy.[90] Interestingly, in its formulation of the criterion in *PCA Kazakhstan* and *CEPA Armenia*, the Court seemed to go back to the test as

---

[86] Case C-377/12, para. 57–58.

[87] G. De Baere, T. Van den Sanden, 97. See also: A. Ott, 'The legal bases for international agreements post-Lisbon; Of pirates and The Philippines', 4 *Maastricht Journal of European and Comparative Law*, 2014, 744.

[88] Case C-268/94, para. 47, 67.

[89] G. De Baere, T. Van den Sanden, 101.

[90] M. Broberg, R. Holdgaard, 'Demarcating the Union's development cooperation policy after Lisbon', 564.

formulated in the *Portugal/Council* case. In *PCA Kazakhstan*, it limited itself to indicating that the provisions on CFSP were limited to declarations on the aims of the parties' cooperation and the subjects of that cooperation, while they did not determine in concrete terms the manner in which the cooperation is implemented.[91] In *CEPA Armenia*, the Court added that while a few provisions of CEPA Armenia covered subjects capable of falling within the CFSP, those provisions were limited to declarations 'of a programmatic nature', which merely described the relationship between the CEPA Armenia's parties' common future intentions, without establishing a 'programme of action or determining the concrete terms governing their cooperation'.[92] With the test formulated in *CEPA Armenia*, the Court formulated another variation of its test, which seems to combine both the declaratory nature of the objectives and the fact that they still needed specific further implementation. Nevertheless, the different expressions and formulations of the test, depending on the specificities of the case, would all relate to the substance and core of the Court's assessment. That is whether the provisions on other matters fall within the scope of EU development cooperation as the centre of gravity or whether, by contrast, the provisions impose such extensive obligations in the specific areas that they cover, that those obligations in fact constitute objectives distinct from those of development cooperation.[93]

The fact that the Court accepts that clear legal obligations in the area of readmission can fall under the scope of development cooperation, although the issue of readmission has its own treaty-making competence and a specific decision-making procedure which differs from development cooperation, is legally not entirely unproblematic according to some authors.[94] However, the initial test developed by the Court in *Portugal/Council* may, perhaps counterintuitively, also restrict the scope of development cooperation policy. In particular, the requirement that the provisions with respect to the other areas of cooperation must not entail extensive obligations and must be restricted to identifying the aims and subjects of the cooperation, could lead to the situation where development cooperation agreements can only provide the most general of frameworks for cooperation in specific areas. That may in turn hamper the effective development of this area,[95] and appears to contradict the broad notion

---

[91] Case C-244/17, para. 45.

[92] Case C-180/20, para. 46.

[93] Case C-263/14, para. 47, Case C-377/12, para. 39; Case C-244/17, *Commission/Council*, EU:C:2018:662 para. 46, Case C-180/20, para. 45.

[94] M. Broberg, R. Holdgaard, 'EU development cooperation post-Lisbon: main constitutional challenges', 354.

[95] See also: Eeckhout, *EU external relations law*, 136; S. Peers, 'Fragmentation or evasion in the Community's development policy? The impact of Portugal v. Council', 112.

of development cooperation policy espoused by the EU. The Court itself has expressed its concern both in *Portugal/Council* and in *Philippines PCA* that it should be ensured that the development cooperation competence is not rendered 'devoid of substance'.[96]

Therefore, the expression of the test in *Philippines PCA* is necessary in order to retain the space that the development cooperation competence occupies in the general system of EU external relations law and it ensures that this competence is not limited to the most general of cooperation forms. The latter entails the risk that the development cooperation objectives are reduced to an overall principle or value of EU external action, rather than respecting the fact that development cooperation policy is a competence of EU external action on its own. Moreover, development cooperation may not be reduced to the mere grant of financial assistance to developing countries.[97] The test in *Philippines PCA* arguably even creates the opportunity to take more integrated measures, enabling a more comprehensive and coherent approach.[98] This is in line with the policy objectives the EU sets itself and the view that only a comprehensive approach will help meet the needs of the developing countries. While the test makes more integrated measures possible, it is clear that a detailed agreement in a specific field, on the other hand, such as the readmission agreement in *Philippines PCA*, will have to be adopted under another legal basis.[99] This is demonstrated by the agreements concluded with Indonesia: the agreement is split between a PCA that excludes readmission[100] and a separate agreement that concerns readmission and that is based on the readmission legal basis of Article 79(3) TFEU.[101] Concerns in light of the principle of conferral therefore need to be rebutted.

With its two-step test, the Court strikes a balance between the attainment of the development cooperation objectives by allowing the competence's

---

[96] Case C-268/94, para. 38; Case C-377/12, para. 38.

[97] Opinion of Advocate General Mengozzi in C-377/12, point 22.

[98] G. De Baere, T. Van den Sanden, 101.

[99] Opinion of Advocate General Mengozzi, Case C-377/12, point 77.

[100] Council Decision of 14 April 2014 on the conclusion of the Framework Agreement on Comprehensive Partnership and Cooperation between the European Community and its Member States, of the one part, and the Republic of Indonesia, of the other part, with the exception of matters related to readmission, OJ 2014 L125/44. However, the addition in the Council Decision of the legal bases on transport and environment, to the legal bases of development cooperation and the CCP is not in line with the *Philippines PCA* case which was rendered two months later.

[101] Council Decision of 14 April 2014 on the conclusion of the Framework Agreement on Comprehensive Partnership and Cooperation between the European Community and its Member States, of the one part, and the Republic of Indonesia, of the other part, as regards matters related to readmission, OJ 2014 L125/46.

broad scope, in line with the policy concept as formulated by the EU on the one hand and respect for the principle of conferral on the other hand. The judgments in both *Portugal/Council* and *Philippines PCA* demonstrate the importance and precariousness of the balancing act between, on the one hand, interpreting development cooperation wide enough so as to avoid making its legal basis futile and devoid of substance[102] by requiring additional legal bases for every element touching on another EU competence, and, on the other hand, interpreting it so widely that development cooperation policy invades other areas of EU external action.[103] The Court succeeds in finding that balance by giving equal weight to the aim and content criterion of the test on choice of legal basis. With the objectives-based criterion of the test it confirms the broad notion of EU development cooperation policy and its objectives. By formulating the second element of the test as a content-based criterion, on the other hand, it limits the potentially too encompassing scope of development cooperation policy, causing concerns under both the principle of conferral and the institutional balance. The Court therefore perfectly balances the aim and content aspect of the choice of legal basis theory in relation to development cooperation policy, which leads *in casu* to a balanced scope of development cooperation policy. In *CEPA Armenia* the Court also took the context criterion into account, which emerged in case law as an additional criterion (see further below). The Court confirmed that in each specific case all objectively identifiable factors pertaining to one or to the other of those criteria should be taken into account, although in *CEPA Armenia* the Court considered that there would be no specific contextual link that would change its findings regarding the objective and content.[104]

In order to further assess the scope of the EU's competence in development cooperation policy, the next sections will go into the delimitation of the area with the areas of environment and the CCP and subsequently the CFSP.

---

[102] Or 'nugatory' as the Court states in relation to the CCP: Opinion 1/78, paras. 43–45 (see below).

[103] See also: S. Peers, 'Fragmentation or evasion in the Community's development policy? The impact of Portugal v. Council', 112.

[104] Case C-180/20, para. 33, 54–55.

3. Delimitation with environment, common commercial policy, and common foreign and security policy

1. DELIMITATION WITH OTHER TFEU LEGAL BASES: ENVIRONMENT

1.1 Rules on the Choice of the Appropriate Legal Basis

The consequence of the abovementioned case law on the scope of development cooperation policy is that provisions on other areas such as on environment, transport, migration, energy, intellectual property, tourism, culture, and the control of drug abuse and presumably also on other areas can, within certain limits, fall under the scope of development cooperation policy. The following sections focus on the delimitation between development cooperation policy on the one hand and environment on the other hand. These areas have been chosen because of their particular intertwinement (see also Chapter 1). Development cooperation and environmental protection are strongly intertwined issues, as developing countries are disproportionately impacted by climate change and natural disasters, while lacking the resources to deal with the negative effects. They are also often particularly dependent on natural resources, aggravating their vulnerability to degradation and depletion of the environment. On the other hand, development and growth contribute to prosperity but they also cause environmental challenges.[1] In the context of the sustainability agenda[2] and the MDGs and subsequently the SDGs,[3] poverty eradication is seen as an essential requirement for and one of the overarching objectives of sustainable

1 A decent life for all, 4.

2 World Commission on Environment and Development, Our Common Future, www.un-documents.net, 1987; UN General Assembly, *Report of the United Nations Conference on Environment and Development,* Rio de Janeiro, 3–14 June 1992.

3 Outcome document of the special event to follow up efforts made towards achieving the Millennium Development Goals, A/68/L.4, 1 October 2013; Synthesis Report of the Secretary-General on the post-2015 Agenda, The road to dignity by 2030: Ending poverty, transforming all lives and protecting the planet, 4 December 2014.

development.[4] At the EU level, the link is emphasised in all documents guiding the EU's vision on development. By confirming the possibility for agreements in the area of development cooperation to contain provisions on environment, the judgment in *Philippines PCA* appears to be in line with the Union's evolving policy approach to development cooperation policy and the integration of environmental protection issues in that area.[5]

Legally, the development cooperation policy and environment competence have in common that they are both shared competences. The environmental competence is, however, a regular shared competence pursuant to Article 4(2) TFEU, while the development cooperation policy competence belongs to the category of parallel, irregular shared or non-pre-emptive competences on the basis of Article 4(4) TFEU, Article 209(2) TFEU, and Article 211 TFEU. This difference is crucial, as the environmental competence, contrary to the development cooperation policy competence, can become exclusive on the basis of implied exclusivity formulated in Article 3(2) TFEU, while this is not the case for the development cooperation policy competence because of its irregular shared nature (see below Section 2 of Chapter 5). The environmental legal basis is provided by Articles 191 and 192 TFEU. Article 191(4) TFEU holds that 'within their respective spheres of competence' the EU and the Member States can cooperate with third countries and international organisations 'without prejudice to Member States' competence to negotiate in international bodies and to conclude international agreements'. This language is therefore similar to Article 209(2) TFEU on development cooperation policy. However, this article does not make the environmental competence an irregular shared competence. The legal basis used for international agreements in the area of environment is Article 192(1) TFEU: in *Opinion 2/00*[6] and the *Mox Plant*[7] case the Court determined that Article 192(1) TFEU is the appropriate legal basis for concluding international agreements on substantive cooperation on environmental protection. Action based on this legal basis can become exclusive through the application of the *ERTA* principle.[8] As will be analysed in detail below in Section 2 of Chapter 5, the development cooperation policy competence is without doubt an irregular shared competence. This follows not only from Article 209(2) TFEU and Article 211 TFEU, which contain language similar to Article 191(4) TFEU, but even more so from the explicit singling out of the development cooperation policy competence in a separate paragraph 4 of Article 4 TFEU, which determines that the exercise of Union competence

---

4 UN General Assembly, The future we want, A/RES/66/288, 27 July 2012, 2.
5 G. De Baere, T. Van den Sanden, 100.
6 Opinion 2/00, para. 44.
7 Case C-459/03, *Mox Plant*, EU:C:2006:345, para. 90–91.
8 Opinion 2/00, para. 45–46.

in the area of development cooperation policy and humanitarian aid cannot result in Member States being prevented from exercising theirs. The Court has moreover confirmed the irregular shared nature of development cooperation policy in case law (see further Chapter 5).[9]

Following the case law in *Portugal/Council* and *Philippines PCA*, provisions on environmental protection can, to a certain extent, be included in a development cooperation policy agreement, without the need to add the legal basis on environment. However, as soon as they reach the threshold of the second aspect of the test, an additional legal basis is needed. In the *Portugal/Council* and *Philippines PCA* cases, the Court applied a so-called 'centre of gravity' test in order to determine whether the use of the additional legal bases alongside the legal bases on development cooperation and the CCP was justified. The test formulated by the Court is the expression of the centre of gravity test: the determination of the essential object refers to the identification of the main aim, while the requirement that the specific provisions may not contain obligations so extensive that they in fact constitute distinct objectives expresses their incidental or secondary nature, which causes them to fall under the main objective of development cooperation policy.[10]

A few observations can be made with regard to the application of the centre of gravity test in these cases. The Court started its reasoning in *Philippines PCA* with the statement that it had to be 'determined whether, among the provisions of the Framework Agreement, those relating to readmission of nationals of the contracting parties, to transport and to the environment also fall within development cooperation policy or whether they go beyond the framework of that policy and therefore require the contested decision to be founded on additional legal bases'.[11] On that basis, one could argue that it was to a certain extent the starting point of the Court's reasoning that development cooperation policy was the main purpose or component of the PPCA, rather than that the Court starts in detail with a clear prior examination of the aim and content of the measure.[12] Furthermore, the test formulated by the Court would

---

9 See, however: G. De Baere, 'Mercury rising: the European Union and the international negotiations for a globally binding instrument on mercury', 5 European Law Review, 2012, 642–643.

10 The latter is even more emphasised in the *Philippines PCA* than in *Portugal/Council*, where the Court adds that the specific provisions on environment, transport, and readmission *in casu* do not contain obligations so extensive that they may be considered to constitute objectives distinct from those of development cooperation that are neither secondary nor indirect in relation to the latter objectives: Case C-377/12, para. 48, 59.

11 Case C-377/12, para. 35.

12 See in a similar sense on the *Small Arms Light Weapons* judgment: B. Van Vooren, 'The Small Arms Judgment in an Age of Constitutional Turmoil', 235–236.

relate to a particular form of the centre of gravity test, named 'the absorption doctrine' by Maresceau.[13] The Court introduced this test in *Opinion 1/78*, where it held that 'an agreement must be assessed having regard to its essential objective rather than in terms of individual clauses of an altogether subsidiary or ancillary nature'.[14] The fact that the agreement in that case also covered subjects such as technological assistance, research programmes, labour conditions in the industry, or consultations relating to certain national tax policies could not modify its qualification as a CCP agreement. In this sense, the main objective 'absorbed' the other provisions relating to distinct objectives. A similar reasoning was followed in the judgment in *Portugal/Council* and *Philippines PCA*. While the agreements with India and the Philippines were based on the development cooperation and the CCP legal bases, they also covered provisions on human rights, energy, intellectual property, tourism, drug abuse control, environment, transport, and readmission.[15] Hence, the development cooperation legal basis 'absorbed' the other substantive provisions, which are of an 'altogether subsidiary or ancillary nature', except for the trade aspect (see below Section 2 for the analysis on the development cooperation policy – CCP delimitation).

A crucial provision to understand the relationship between environment and development cooperation would be Article 11 TFEU, which states that 'Environmental protection requirements must be integrated into the definition and implementation of the Union's policies and activities, in particular with a view to promoting sustainable development'. Article 11 TFEU therefore requires environmental protection measures to be integrated or 'mainstreamed' into the definition and implementation of the Union's policies, in particular with a view to promoting sustainable development. Development cooperation and environmental protection therefore both contain an integration requirement: environmental, as well as development concerns have to be taken into account when conducting other policies. They can therefore both be described as fields containing 'horizontal objectives': objectives that not only have to be pursued when conducting the objectives' own policy but also when acting in any other domain of EU competence.[16] As is the case for the integration requirement in development cooperation policy, the rationale behind the

---

The same can be said of recent cases determining the scope of the CCP: Case C-414/11, *Daiichi Sankyo*, EU:C:2013:520; Case C-137/12, *Commission/Council (Conditional Access)*, EU:C:2013:675.

[13] M. Maresceau, 156–157.

[14] Opinion 1/78, *International Agreement on Natural Rubber*, EU:C:1979:224, para. 56.

[15] Case C-268/94, para. 39.

[16] K. Lenaerts, 'De Europese Unie: doel of middel?', 698.

environmental integration requirement is also countering the risk that actions in other policy fields harm progress in the area of environmental protection.[17] When comparing both integration requirements, a few differences become apparent, however. First, while the integration requirement in the area of development cooperation policy can be found in the Treaty provisions on this area in Article 208(1) TFEU, the environmental integration requirement in Article 11 TFEU falls under the title 'Provisions having general application'. Second, the wording of the requirement in the field of environmental protection ('must', 'requirements') is stronger than the one for development cooperation policy ('shall', 'take account', 'objectives', 'likely to affect developing countries').[18] Article 11 TFEU is formulated in mandatory terms: it implies an obligation for the Union to not only mainstream environmental protection and sustainable development into its policies, but also to ensure consistency between environmental policy and its other policies.[19] The environmental integration principle in Article 11 TFEU is therefore an expression of positive coherence, creating synergies, and complementarity, because of the duty that it lays down to mainstream environmental concerns into other areas (see Chapter 1 on the different dimensions of coherence). However, at the same time, the integration requirement might create tensions leading to delimitation issues because of the correlation of multiple objectives or aspects in one measure.[20]

The Court has referred to the environmental integration requirement, at that time included in Article 130r(2) EC Treaty, to conclude that

> Articles 130r and 130s are intended to confer powers on the Community to undertake specific action on environmental matters. However, those articles leave intact the powers held by the Community under other provisions of the Treaty, even if the measures to be taken under the latter provisions pursue at the same time any of the objectives of environmental protection. Moreover, that interpretation is confirmed by the second sentence of Article 130r(2), pursuant to which 'environmental protection requirements shall be a component of the Community's other policies'. That provision, which reflects the principle whereby all Community measures must satisfy the requirements of environmental protection, implies that a Community

17 G. Duran, E. Morgera, *Environmental integration in the EU's external relations: beyond multilateral dimensions*, Hart, 2012, 28.

18 N. Schrijver, 'When will the new emperor wear its clothes? The efforts of the European Union towards a common development cooperation policy', in M. Bulterman, L. Hancher, A. McDonnell, H. Sevenster (eds), *Views of European law from the mountain: Liber Amicorum for Piet Jan Slot*, Kluwer, 2009, 385.

19 M. Cremona, 'Coherence and EU external environmental policy', 36.

20 Ibid., 39.

measure cannot be part of Community action on environmental matters merely because it takes account of those requirements.[21]

It therefore seems that because of the strongly formulated environmental integration requirement, the Court accepts more easily the inclusion of environmental aspects in measures, without necessitating the addition of the environmental legal basis. Merely taking account of environmental concerns does not suffice to bring a measure under the environmental competence, as this is exactly what the environmental integration requirement demands: taking account of environmental concerns when conducting other policies.

The *Philippines PCA* test would be in line with this, as it ensures the possible integration of environmental concerns in development cooperation policy. The second aspect of the test nevertheless safeguards respect for the principle of conferral and protects the proper existence of the environmental competence: as soon as the provisions on environment contain obligations so extensive that they can be considered to be distinct objectives, and hence can no longer be seen as secondary or indirect, they need their own legal basis. Also, the first step in the Court's test is an important element in the delimitation exercise between environment and development cooperation policy, as the environmental provisions must in the first place pursue the objectives of EU development cooperation policy in order to fall in the scope of that policy. A confirmation of this approach and illustration can be found in the *PFOS* case (Chapter 5 will discuss this case further from the angle of the principle of sincere cooperation).[22] An important element in the Union's position on PFOS was the effect that the control on PFOS would have on developing countries.[23] However, this did not lead to the inclusion of the development cooperation policy legal basis: the measure concerned a 'pure' environmental measure, as it did not pursue the objectives of EU development cooperation policy. However, the EU did take into account the concerns of developing countries and the development cooperation policy objectives. This is therefore an example of policy coherence in the opposite direction than examined above: an environmental measure takes account of the objectives of development cooperation policy, without the need to incorporate the development cooperation policy legal basis.[24] The next section will confirm this: the EU has concluded several international agreements with developing countries that qualify as 'pure' environmental agreements and that are based on the environment legal

[21] Case C-62/88, *Greece/Council*, EU:C:1990:153, para. 19–20; Case C-405/92, *Mondiet*, EU:C:1993:906, para. 26–27; G. Duran, E. Morgera, 29.

[22] Case C-246/07, *Commission v Sweden*, EU:C:2010:203.

[23] Case, C-246/07, para. 39.

[24] See also: M. Cremona, 'Coherence and EU external environmental policy', 44.

basis alone. They do not fall under the development cooperation policy competence, as they do not fulfil the first element of the test (see further below).

1.2 Consistent Application?

This section will evaluate whether and how the rules on the scope of EU development cooperation policy and its delimitation with environment, as described above, are reflected in practice. First, it looks at the international agreements concluded between the EU and developing countries which contain an environmental aspect and identifies different categories or types of such agreements. Second, it looks at secondary legislation in the area of development cooperation policy to see how environment is integrated. As such, it addresses the implementation of the development cooperation competence both by concluding international agreements (Article 209(2) TFEU) and by adopting measures necessary for the implementation of development cooperation (Article 209(1) TFEU).

1.2.1 International agreements

The Treaty articles on development cooperation policy grant in Article 209(2) TFEU the EU the explicit competence to conclude international agreements in this area. This competence would naturally flow from the area's essential purpose, which is to establish relationships with developing countries. External competences, such as development cooperation policy, are therefore described by *Dashwood* as 'dedicated external relations provisions', as they essentially aim to set up a relationship with third actors.[25] Article 209(2) TFEU clarifies that the EU has the competence to conclude agreements 'helping to achieve the objectives referred to in Article 21 of the Treaty on European Union and in Article 208 of this Treaty'. This article would therefore explicitly emphasise that development cooperation policy agreements can pursue the area's clearly identified primary objective, poverty eradication, as well as the general EU external action objectives formulated in Article 21 TEU. As outlined above, the Court aimed to find a balance with its test formulated in the *Portugal/Council*[26] and *Philippines PCA*[27] cases between coherent action, ensuring the integration of various objectives in development cooperation policy, and the delimitation of these various competence areas. This section will analyse the EU's practice in this regard.[28] The question is how the choice of legal basis is

---

[25] A. Dashwood, 'The attribution of external relations competence', 121.

[26] Case C-268/94, *Portugal/Council*, EU:C:1996:461.

[27] C-377/12, *Commission/Council*, EU:C:2014:1903.

[28] For other analyses and categorisations of international agreements concluded by the Union, see: S. Peers, 'EC Frameworks of International Relations: Cooperation,

made in practice when an international agreement touches upon developmental and environmental issues. When does a development cooperation policy agreement in practice absorb the environmental provisions in this agreement or when does it bring about the addition of the environmental legal basis?

While the title of an agreement may sometimes give indications about the particular form of cooperation that it covers,[29] the name of agreement is not a decisive criterion to clarify the content of the agreement, nor its legal basis. Agreements concluded with developing countries have been given several types of names: trade and cooperation agreement,[30] framework cooperation agreement,[31] partnership and cooperation agreement,[32] or cooperation agreement on partnership and development.[33] This is further demonstrated by the two cases on the scope of development cooperation policy discussed above: while the Cooperation Agreement between the European Community and the Republic of India on Partnership and Development in *Portugal/Council* contains an express reference to 'development', the Framework Agreement on Partnership and Cooperation between the European Union and the Republic of the Philippines in *Philippines PCA* does not hold such an explicit reference.

When examining the EU's agreements in the area of development cooperation policy, a lot of confusion remains.[34] Nevertheless, it is possible to identify a few clear patterns that apply to the categorisation and corresponding choice

---

Partnership and Association' in A. Dashwood and C. Hillion (eds), *The General Law of EC External Relations,* Sweet & Maxwell, 2000, 160–176; M. Maresceau, 'Bilateral agreements concluded by the European Community', *Académie de Droit International – Recueil des Cours*, 2006, 125–452; S. Adam, 'The legal basis of international agreements of the European Union in the post-Lisbon era', in I. Govaere, P. Van Elsuwege, E. Lannon, S. Adam (eds), *The European Union in the world: essays in honour of Marc Maresceau*, Nijhoff, 2014, 63–86.

29 M. Maresceau, 311.

30 For example: Euro-Mediterranean Interim Association Agreement on trade and cooperation between the European Community, of the one part, and the Palestine Liberation Organization (PLO) for the benefit of the Palestinian Authority of the West Bank and the Gaza Strip, of the other part, OJ 1997 L187/3.

31 For example: Framework Cooperation Agreement between the European Economic Community and the Republics of Costa Rica, El Salvador, Guatemala, Honduras, Nicaragua and Panama, OJ 1999 L63/39.

32 For example: Partnership and Cooperation Agreement between the European Communities and their Member States, of the one part, and Georgia, of the other part, OJ 1999 L205/3.

33 For example: Cooperation Agreement between the European Community and the Democratic Socialist Republic of Sri Lanka on partnership and development, OJ 1995 L85/33.

34 Opinion of AG Mengozzi in C-377/12.

of legal basis of development cooperation agreements with an environmental aspect.

First, practice reflects the necessary fulfilment of the first criterion of the *Portugal/Council* and *Philippines PCA* test, the pursuance of the objectives of EU development cooperation policy, for an agreement to be adopted on the development cooperation policy legal basis. As indicated above, the fulfilment of this criterion is indispensable for an agreement to fall under development cooperation policy and proves to be essential in the delimitation between development cooperation policy and environmental policy. Some 'pure' environmental agreements are concluded with developing countries, which are based solely on the environmental legal basis, as they are not specifically aimed at pursuing the development cooperation policy objectives of economic and social development. They rather concern environmental agreements that are concluded by the EU with developing countries. Following the test formulated by the Court, this does not make them development cooperation policy agreements. Interestingly, most of these agreements would be multilateral agreements. Examples of such agreements are the Basel Convention on the control of transboundary movements of hazardous wastes and their disposal,[35] the Convention on biological diversity,[36] the Convention on access to information, public participation in decision making and access to justice in environmental matters,[37] the Stockholm Convention on Persistent Organic Pollutants,[38] or the Cartagena Protocol on biosafety to the convention on biological diversity.[39] The same can be said to be true for agreements on transport and readmission (the other areas at issue in the *Philippines PCA*): agreements that are purely about transport, although they have been concluded with a developing country, are based solely on the transport legal basis.[40] Specific

---

[35] OJ 1993 L39/3.

[36] OJ 1993 L309/3.

[37] OJ 2005 L124/4.

[38] OJ 2006 L209/2.

[39] OJ 2002 L201/50.

[40] See e.g. Council Decision of 5 April 2001 on the conclusion by the European Community of the Convention for the Unification of Certain Rules for International Carriage by Air (the Montreal Convention), OJ 2001 L194/38 or agreements on air services such as the Agreement between the European Union and the Republic of Cape Verde on certain aspects of air services (Council Decision of 13 December 2010 on the signing, on behalf of the Union, and provisional application of the Agreement between the European Union and the Republic of Cape Verde on certain aspects of air services, OJ 2011 L96/1). For more on the inclusion of trade in transport services in horizontal trade agreements, see: S. Adam, 'The legal basis of international agreements of the European Union in the post-Lisbon era', in I. Govaere, P. Van Elsuwege, E. Lannon, S. Adam (eds), *The European Union in the world: essays in honour of Marc Maresceau*, Nijhoff, 2014, 172–173.

readmission agreements are consequently based on Article 79 TFEU.[41] Apart from these 'pure' environmental agreements, the 'United Nations Convention to Combat Desertification in Countries Experiencing Serious Drought and/or Desertification, Particularly in Africa'[42] is based on both the environmental as well as the development cooperation policy legal basis. The '2006 International Tropical Timber Agreement'[43] is based on the environment and CCP legal basis.

Second, several development cooperation policy agreements include environmental provisions. The European Council politically mandated the integration of environmental concerns in EU bilateral and interregional agreements.[44] As will be further discussed below in Section 2, development cooperation policy agreements almost always include the CCP legal basis, next to the explicit development cooperation policy legal basis, or the flexibility clause for agreements concluded before the Treaty of Maastricht. They respond to the first requirement of the test 'pursuing the development cooperation policy objectives': they pursue the development cooperation objectives as their main aim and also include specific titles, provisions, and references on sustainable development, development cooperation, aid, or poverty eradication. They often also refer to international development cooperation policy initiatives, such as the MDGs. Especially in agreements concluded with LDCs or low middle-income countries, the development cooperation policy aspects are emphasised.[45] In agreements concluded with upper middle-income

---

41 E.g.: Council Decision of 7 October 2010 on the conclusion of the Agreement between the European Community and the Islamic Republic of Pakistan on the readmission of persons residing without authorization OJ 2010 L287/50; Council Decision of 3 March 2005 concerning the conclusion of the Agreement between the European Community and the Democratic Socialist Republic of Sri Lanka on the readmission of persons residing without authorisation OJ 2005 L124/41. The practice with regard to the inclusion or exclusion of current Article 79 TFEU as a legal basis in cooperation agreements is, however, not coherent (see overviews of agreements, most notably the Framework Agreement on Partnership and Cooperation between the European Union and its Member States, of the one part, and Mongolia, of the other part which is based on Articles 79, 207 and 209 TFEU or the Partnership and Cooperation Agreement between the European Union and its Member States, of the one part, and the Republic of Iraq, of the other part which is based on Articles 79(3), 91, 100, 192(1), 194, 207 and 209 TFEU (see also: Opinion of AG Mengozzi in C-377/12)).

42 OJ 1998 L83/3.

43 OJ 2007 L262/8.

44 Brussels Council conclusions 2006.

45 For example: Cooperation Agreement on Partnership and Development between the European Union and its Member States, of the one part, and the Islamic Republic of Afghanistan, of the other part, OJ 2017 L67/3.

countries, this would be less the case.[46] The references to the objectives of development cooperation policy contain references to the primary aim of development cooperation policy, poverty eradication, as well as more general references to the economic and social development objectives. For example, in the Cooperation Agreement between the European Community and the Lao People's Democratic Republic,[47] Article 3 on development cooperation refers to the achievement of 'sustainable economic development and the social progress of its people'. This would be in accordance with the broader formulation of development cooperation policy objectives as economic and social development objectives, as formulated in *Small Arms and Lights Weapons*.

It seems to be standard practice that development cooperation agreements include provisions on environmental protection. The development cooperation policy agreements have been categorised in generations of agreements.[48] While the 'first-generation' agreements contained only provisions on trade, the 'second-generation' agreements extended to limited areas of cooperation as well. The 'third-generation' agreements cover a variety of areas of cooperation, aimed at a comprehensive framework of cooperation.[49] The difference between second- and third-generation agreements is, for example, apparent in the agreements with Pakistan.[50] In 1986, the EU concluded a second-generation agreement with the country, which focused on commercial and economic cooperation, as well as development cooperation.[51] In 2004,

---

46 For example: Political Dialogue and Cooperation Agreement between the European Community and its Member States, of the one part, and the Andean Community and its member countries, the Republics of Bolivia, Colombia, Ecuador, Peru and the Bolivarian Republic of Venezuela, of the other part, JOIN/2016/04 final; Framework Agreement for trade and economic cooperation between the European Economic Community and the Argentine Republic, OJ 1990 L295/67.

47 This is one of the 'second-generation' agreements, as indicated by Peers: S. Peers, 'EC Frameworks of International Relations: Cooperation, Partnership and Association' in A. Dashwood and C. Hillion (eds), *The General Law of EC External Relations*, Sweet & Maxwell, 2000, 163. Council Decision of 10 November 1997 concerning the conclusion of the Cooperation Agreement between the European Community and the Lao People's Democratic Republic, OJ 1997 L334/14.

48 S. Peers, 'EC Frameworks of International Relations: Cooperation, Partnership and Association', 163.

49 M. Maresceau, 177.

50 The same is true for the relationship with Mongolia: the Framework Agreement on Partnership and Cooperation between the European Union and its Member States, of the one part, and Mongolia, of the other part concluded in 2017 is a much broader agreement than the Agreement on trade and economic cooperation between the European Economic Community and Mongolia OJ 1993 L41/46.

51 Agreement for commercial, economic and development cooperation between the European Economic Community and the Islamic Republic of Pakistan, OJ 1986 L108/2.

the EU and Pakistan concluded a Cooperation Agreement on Partnership and Development which sets out a broader framework for cooperation between the two countries. Apart from trade, economic cooperation, and development cooperation, it sets the framework for sectoral cooperation in *inter alia* the areas of industry and services, agriculture, livestock and fisheries, tourism, energy, science and technology, information, culture and communication, or drug abuse control and money laundering.[52] As regards the inclusion of environment in development cooperation policy, the third generation is more comprehensive in this respect as well: while environment was included in the second-generation agreement as one of the objectives of economic cooperation between the parties,[53] environment is one of the areas of sectoral cooperation in the third-generation agreement.[54] In this regard, the *Portugal/Council* case was not only important to define the scope of the new Treaty title on development cooperation policy. As it concerned the legality of the EU–India agreement, a prototype of the so-called 'third-generation agreements', the case was also decisive for the future of these agreements.[55]

In more trade-oriented agreements, the aspect of environmental protection might be limited to underlining the importance of environmental protection in general.[56] Most agreements, however, include a specific article or even title on environmental protection. They are drafted in a similar way: some of them formulate the explicit link between the need to protect the environment and the ability to attain sustainable development.[57] Some agreements also refer to

---

[52] Cooperation agreement between the European Community and the Islamic Republic of Pakistan, relating to the partnership and to development, OJ 2004 L378/23.

[53] Article 3 Agreement for commercial, economic and development cooperation between the European Economic Community and the Islamic Republic of Pakistan, OJ 1986 L108/2.

[54] Article 5 Cooperation agreement between the European Community and the Islamic Republic of Pakistan, relating to the partnership and to development, OJ 2004 L378/23.

[55] Opinion of AG La Pergola in Case C-268/94, point 5.

[56] For example: Interim Agreement with a view to an Economic Partnership Agreement between, the European Community and its Member States, of the one part, and the SADC EPA States, of the other part, OJ 2009 L319/3; Framework Agreement for trade and economic cooperation between the European Economic Community and the Argentine Republic, OJ 1990 L295/67.

[57] For example: Political Dialogue and Cooperation Agreement between the European Union and its Member States, of the one part, and the Republic of Cuba, of the other part, OJ 2016 L337I/1; Framework Agreement on Partnership and Cooperation between the European Union and its Member States, of the one part, and Mongolia, of the other part, OJ 2017 L326/52; Framework Agreement on Comprehensive Partnership and cooperation between the European Community and its Member States, of the one part, and the Republic of Indonesia, of the other part, OJ 2014 L125/17.

the environmental integration requirement in this respect.[58] The articles and titles on environmental protection further set out the more specific areas of cooperation or objectives of cooperation in the field of environmental protection and some even specify the means to further this cooperation, such as the development of environmental impact studies, the development of legislation on environmental protection, or joint research.[59] It is, however, clear that these provisions on cooperation in the area of environmental protection and the commitments made in this regard all remain quite general in scope, which makes further implementation necessary.[60] It is therefore in line with the case law of the Court that these agreements do not include the environmental legal basis. It can be assumed, in parallel with the readmission agreements or agreements on visas, that specific implementation measures will require the addition of the environment legal basis.

Third, there are some agreements concluded with developing countries that have been based on a multitude of legal bases, described by Peers as 'transversal partnership agreements'.[61] It is argued that the EU concluded these agreements on a variety of legal bases as a reaction to *Opinion 1/94*.[62] These agreements are very similar in structure and content. They formulate the same objectives, i.e., to provide an appropriate framework for cooperation and contain a similar article on economic cooperation which refers to the sustainable development of the country in question as the ultimate goal. The majority

---

58 For example: Cooperation Agreement between the European Community and the Kingdom of Cambodia, OJ 1999 L269/18; Framework Agreement on Partnership and Cooperation between the European Union and its Member States, of the one part, and Mongolia, of the other part, OJ 2017 L326/52.

59 For example: Framework Cooperation Agreement between the European Economic Community and the Republics of Costa Rica, El Salvador, Guatemala, Honduras, Nicaragua and Panama, OJ 1999 L63/39; Framework Agreement for Cooperation between the European Economic Community and the Federative Republic of Brazil, OJ 1995 L262/54.

60 See also: S. Peers, 'Fragmentation or evasion in the Community's development policy? The impact of Portugal v. Council', 108.

61 S. Peers, 'EC Frameworks of International Relations: Cooperation, Partnership and Association', 164.

62 Ibid., 164–165. In Opinion 1/94 the Court seemed to argue that international agreements should include as many legal bases as competences were covered by the agreement. As a result of Opinion 1/94, the Council Decision 94/800/EC concerning the conclusion on behalf of the European Community, as regards matters within its competence, of the agreements reached in the Uruguay Round multilateral negotiations, OJ 1994 L336/1, included 11 legal bases: R. Gosalbo-Bono, F. Naert, 'The reluctant (Lisbon) Treaty and its implementation in the practice of the Council', in P. Eeckhout and M. López-Escadero, *The European Union's external action in times of crisis*, Hart, 2016.

of these agreements include, however, no further specific titles, provisions, or references to sustainable development, development aid, or poverty eradication: they are rather formulated as a form of cooperation between equals than as part of development cooperation policy. Another aspect that these agreements have in common is the type of country or the region they are part of: while included in the OECD-DAC list of recipients of Official Development Aid (ODA), they are all post-Soviet countries and the majority are currently part of the neighbourhood.[63] Arguably, the fact that these agreements are not based on the development cooperation and CCP legal basis, like the agreements above, follows from the fact that the fulfilment of the first criterion of the test, i.e., pursuing the objectives of development cooperation policy, is lacking in these agreements.[64] It has also been argued that positioning these agreements not as development cooperation agreements but rather as a form of cooperation between equals is also a matter of politics.[65]

The agreements with Mexico and with Iraq are also worth mentioning. The Economic Partnership, Political Co-ordination and Co-operation Agreement concluded with Mexico[66] has received attention in literature before for standing out as a special case.[67] It seems that qualifying the agreement is difficult but it is clear that this does not concern a classic development cooperation policy agreement.[68] The Partnership and Cooperation Agreement between the European Union and its Member States, of the one part, and the Republic of

63 Examples of these agreements: Partnership and Cooperation Agreement establishing a partnership between the European Communities and their Member States, of the one part, and the Republic of Tajikistan, of the other part, OJ 2009 L350/3; Partnership and Cooperation Agreement between the European Communities and their Member States, of the one part, and Georgia, of the other part, OJ 1999 L205/3; Partnership and Cooperation Agreement between the European Communities and their Member States, of the one part, and the Republic of Azerbaijan, of the other part, OJ 1999 L246/3.

64 By contrast, the protocols to these agreements that take account of the accession of the Republic of Bulgaria and Romania to the European Union are, on the other hand, based on the development cooperation policy legal basis. For example: Protocol to the Partnership and Cooperation Agreement between the European Communities and their Member States, of the one part, and the Republic of Armenia, of the other part, to take account of the accession of the Republic of Bulgaria and Romania to the European Union, OJ 2007 L202/26.

65 S. Peers: The type of agreement which the EU concludes with a third state is determined by politics, not law: S. Peers, 'EC frameworks of international relations: co-operation, partnership and association', 160; M. Maresceau, 313.

66 OJ 2000 L276/45.

67 M. Maresceau, 173.

68 M. Maresceau, 184.

Iraq, of the other part,[69] is even more exceptional, particularly as regards the development cooperation–environment nexus: the agreement is also based on the environment legal basis. Comparing this agreement with the other abovementioned agreements, it is, however, not clear why the addition of the environmental legal basis was necessary, as the provisions on environmental protection are quite similar to the ones in the agreements above.

1.2.2 Measures

Apart from the explicit competence to conclude international agreements in the field of development cooperation policy, Article 209(1) TFEU also provides a legal basis for the formulation of legislation in this field. In particular, Article 209(1) TFEU grants the competence to the Parliament and the Council to adopt the measures necessary for the implementation of development cooperation policy, which 'may relate to multiannual cooperation programmes with developing countries or programmes with a thematic approach'.

After the entry into force of the Treaty of Maastricht, the EU adopted various Regulations in the area of development cooperation policy, scattering the secondary legal framework over several different measures. In the 1990s and early 2000s, the EU also adopted a few regulations in the area of development cooperation policy and environmental protection. These included Regulation 722/97 on the adoption of environmental measures in developing countries,[70] Regulation 2493/2000 on the promotion of the full integration of the environmental dimension in the development process of developing countries,[71] and Regulation 2394/2000 promoting the conservation and sustainable management of tropical forests and other forests in developing countries.[72] These regulations were based on the dual development cooperation policy and environment legal basis and they provide financial development cooperation policy support to attain the environmental and sustainable development cooperation policy goals formulated in the regulations.

---

[69] OJ 2012 L204/20.

[70] Regulation 722/97 of 22 April 1997 on environmental measures in developing countries in the context of sustainable development, OJ 1997 L108/1.

[71] Regulation 2493/2000 of the European Parliament and of the Council of 7 November 2000 on measures to promote the full integration of the environmental dimension in the development process of developing countries, OJ 2000 L288/1.

[72] Regulation 2494/2000 of the European Parliament and of the Council of 7 November 2000 on measures to promote the conservation and sustainable management of tropical forests and other forests in developing countries, OJ 2000 L288/6.

The Development Cooperation Instrument, both the 2006[73] and the 2014 Regulation,[74] included the possibility for development cooperation to cover programmes on environmental protection. Pursuant to Article 2(1)(b)(i) Regulation 233/2014, fostering sustainable economic, social, and environmental development was one of the Regulation's objectives, consistently with the primary objective of poverty eradication. Climate change and environment were further areas of cooperation under the geographic programmes,[75] while environment was strongly embedded in the thematic cooperation with the thematic programme Global Public Goods and Challenges.[76] Further, Article 2(6) Regulation 236/2014[77] on the common implementing rules moreover clarified that environmental screening, possibly including conducting environmental impact assessments, needs to be undertaken at project level. Under the NDICI–Global Europe, environmental protection is a specific objective as one of the global challenges to be addressed at global level. Environmental protection and the fight against climate change are mainstreamed in the programmes and actions under the Instrument.[78] More specifically, environment and climate change are one of the areas of cooperation under the geographic programmes, as well as under the thematic programmes.[79] The Instrument's EFSD+ also pursues environmental development and promotes socio-economic and environmental resilience in partner countries with a particular focus on the eradication of poverty.[80] Appropriate environmental screening at the level of actions is also still foreseen,[81] while the Instrument foresees stronger provisions on commitments related to environmental protection.[82]

---

[73] Regulation 1905/2006 of the European Parliament and of the Council of 18 December 2006 establishing a financing instrument or development cooperation, OJ 2006 L378/41.

[74] Regulation 233/2014 of the European Parliament and of the Council of 11 March 2014 establishing a financing instrument for development cooperation for the period 2014–2020, OJ 2014 L77/44.

[75] Article 5(3)(b)(vi) Regulation 233/2014.

[76] Article 7 Regulation 233/2014.

[77] Regulation 236/2014 of the European Parliament and of the Council of 11 March 2014 laying down common rules and procedures for the implementation of the Union's instruments for financing external action, OJ 2014 L77/95.

[78] Article 8(8) Regulation 2021/947 of the European Parliament and of the Council of 9 June 2021 establishing the Neighbourhood, Development and International Cooperation Instrument – Global Europe, amending and repealing Decision No 466/2014/EU and repealing Regulation (EU) 2017/1601 and Council Regulation (EC, Euratom) No 480/2009, OJ 2021 L209/1.

[79] Article 11(1)(d)(viii) Regulation 2021/947.

[80] Article 31(2) Regulation 2021/947.

[81] Article 25(5) Regulation 2021/947.

[82] Article 13(2)(c), 19(2)(b), 29(b), 35(2) and 41(8) Regulation 2021/947.

The *Portugal/Council* and the *Philippines PCA* cases concerned the validity and scope of international agreements concluded in the area of development cooperation policy. In these cases, the Court did not address the question of the legality of development cooperation policy legislation, nor criteria to assess their validity. Nonetheless, the Court's findings in these cases can be arguably transposed to assess the legality of development cooperation policy measures as well. According to Peers, development cooperation policy legislation must be valid if it primarily contributes to the objectives of development cooperation policy, without involving external obligations for the EU beyond overseeing appropriate control over spending. He describes the first criterion as addressing impediments to economic and social development or aiming for economic and social development, while the second criterion requires that no obligations are imposed beyond administering funding in accordance with specified criteria.[83] According to Broberg and Holdgaard, the consequence of the streamlining of the development cooperation policy objectives with poverty reduction and eradication as the primary objective is that this objective 'will be accorded particular weight'. Therefore, according to these authors, in the pursuance of the traditional economic and social development objectives, there should be a stronger and more specific focus on poverty reduction and eradication in the Union's policy formulation. In concrete terms this would bring about that specific development initiatives must always (also) pursue the objective of poverty reduction or eradication. On the other hand, measures in the field of development cooperation policy which do not have as their primary objective poverty reduction or eradication – or at least do not contribute to this – no longer fall within the scope of EU development cooperation policy.[84] The Court's reasoning in *Portugal/Council* and *Philippines PCA* related to the scope of EU development cooperation on the basis of its objectives, the formulation in Article 208 TFEU and its link with Article 21 TEU is indeed not limited to international agreements in the area but also necessarily applies to secondary legislation in the area. Moreover, as argued above, the broad meaning of the notion of poverty eradication allows for a broad scope in any event. The cooperation under the financing instruments as indicated above is indeed directed towards the overarching objective of poverty eradication.

The legal delimitation between the areas of development cooperation policy and environment is therefore in accordance with policy perspectives that emphasise the need to integrate environmental issues into development

---

83 S. Peers, 'Fragmentation or evasion in the Community's development policy? The impact of Portugal v. Council', 103.

84 M. Broberg, R. Holdgaard, 'EU development cooperation post-Lisbon: main constitutional challenges', 352.

cooperation policy. The Court's test defining the legal scope of development cooperation policy ensures the possible integration of environmental concerns in development cooperation policy by allowing development cooperation instruments to cover environmental protection issues and provisions. However, the test as formulated by the Court also ensures that the environmental competence is protected as a proper competence on its own by preventing that every environmental measure taken vis-à-vis a developing country would be absorbed by the development cooperation policy legal basis. The test ensures that only environmental measures that pursue development cooperation policy aims fall under the development cooperation policy competences. Moreover, the second aspect of the test in particular safeguards respect for the principle of conferral: as soon as the provisions on environment contain obligations so extensive that they can be considered to be distinct objectives, and hence can no longer be seen as secondary or indirect, they need their own legal basis. The analysis on the application of the delimitation rules to the conclusion of international agreements and the adoption of measures on the development cooperation–environment nexus further confirms this. A first category of international agreements concerns 'pure' environmental agreements. As they do not fulfil the first aspect of the test on the scope of development cooperation policy, pursuing the development cooperation policy objectives, they are generally based on the environmental competence only.[85] Second, almost all development cooperation policy agreements include environmental provisions or titles on environmental protection. As will be further analysed below in light of the development cooperation policy–CCP delimitation, the development cooperation policy agreements are usually based on the development cooperation policy and CCP legal basis. The environmental provisions are therefore absorbed by the development cooperation policy competence. This happens in accordance with the test formulated in the case law: the provisions on environmental protection in the development cooperation policy agreements are of a rather general scope, which makes subsequent implementation necessary. Unilateral development cooperation policy measures incorporate environmental protection and climate change issues because they either directly support these issues or they mainstream these issues, in accordance with both the policy objectives and with the legal delimitation rules.

[85] An exception is the United Nations Convention to Combat Desertification in Countries Experiencing Serious Drought and/or Desertification, Particularly in Africa, OJ 1998 L83/3.

2. DELIMITATION WITH THE COMMON COMMERCIAL POLICY

2.1 Rules on the Choice of the Appropriate Legal Basis

As discussed above, environmental matters can, to a certain extent, be covered by the development cooperation policy competence when they pursue the objectives of EU development cooperation policy. In determining the scope of development cooperation, the Court applies a centre of gravity test. The consequence is that specific provisions on other areas, such as on environment, fall under the scope of development cooperation policy unless they constitute obligations so extensive that they are to be considered as distinct objectives. In the latter case, the specific provisions are no longer subordinate to the development cooperation policy objective, which requires the addition of the environment legal basis.

It seems, however, that matters are different with respect to trade provisions in development cooperation policy agreements. While the development cooperation legal basis can absorb provisions in the international agreement on other substantive areas of cooperation, provisions with respect to trade seem to require the CCP legal basis.[86] The development cooperation policy competence's absorbing capacity therefore seems to end when the CCP is involved.

In *Portugal/Council*, Portugal had argued that then Article 113 TEC on the CCP was 'redundant as a legal basis for the conclusion of the Agreement', as then Article 130y on development cooperation policy constituted 'a sufficient basis for the provisions in the Agreement concerning commercial policy, since the principal objective of the Agreement is development cooperation and the Community possesses specific powers of action in the sphere of the common commercial policy'. The Court declined to go into the point, noting that the deletion of Article 113 EC would make no difference to the decision-making procedure and hence to the content of the act.[87] In the *Philippines PCA* case, the scope of the development cooperation policy legal basis was disputed, while the presence of the CCP legal basis was not the subject of the dispute. When examining Title III 'Trade and Investment' of the Framework Agreement with the Philippines, however, the provisions in this title do not seem to go beyond the test formulated to assess whether additional legal bases are necessary: i.e., the provisions on trade and investment do not seem to go beyond declarations on the aims and subjects of the cooperation and therefore do not contain obligations so extensive that they form distinct objectives. The same is true for

---

86 Maresceau, 176–177.

87 Case C-268/94, paras. 78–79.

the *PCA Kazakhstan* and *CEPA Armenia* case: in search for the appropriate legal basis, the Court assesses the centre of gravity with reference to the test on the scope of EU development cooperation but accepts the presence of the CCP legal basis as a given.[88] Another explanation for the presence of the CCP legal basis must therefore be sought: the relationship between the CCP and development cooperation can be explained by the specific nature of the CCP competence on the one hand and by historical reasons on the other hand.[89]

Like development cooperation policy, the CCP has a very broad scope. This is not only the case for its horizontal scope. Vertically speaking, the CCP's is, unlike development cooperation, which is a parallel competence,[90] an *a priori* exclusive competence.[91] The CCP's broad scope affects the development cooperation policy–CCP delimitation: the CCP is able to invade development cooperation, whereas development cooperation in turn is capable to do so in relation to other areas of cooperation, which is demonstrated by the *Philippines PCA* and the *Portugal/Council* cases. The dominance of the CCP over the development cooperation policy competence would speak from the fact that CCP provisions in international agreements need the addition of the CCP legal basis and that CCP measures have been used to attain development cooperation objectives (see the analysis in Section 2 below).

The Court already confirmed the CCP's broad horizontal and vertical scope in *Opinion 1/75*,[92] and more particularly in *Opinion 1/78*. There, the Court held that a broad interpretation of the CCP should be maintained, as a restrictive interpretation would risk disturbing intra-Community trade.[93] The Court aimed to adapt the CCP to the fact that international trade was increasingly based on regulation rather than pure liberalisation, holding that a more restricted CCP 'would be destined to become nugatory in the course of time'.[94] In that respect, the Court laid the basis for a wide CCP that goes beyond traditional aspects of trade: it needs to be possible for the CCP to include 'more elaborate means' to further the development of trade as well.[95] As a result of *Opinion 1/78*, com-

---

88 Case C-244/17, para. 46; Case C-180/20, para. 53.

89 G. De Baere, T. Van den Sanden, 102.

90 See Article 4(4) TFEU. For a detailed analysis: see Chapter 5.

91 See Art. 3(1) TFEU.

92 Opinion 1/75, EU:C:1975:145, 1362–1363. See further G. De Baere and I. Van Damme, 'Co-Adaptation in the International Legal Order: The EU and the WTO', in J. Crawford and S. Nouwen (eds), *Select Proceedings of the European Society of International Law*, Hart, 2012, 311–325; G. De Baere and P. Koutrakos, 'The interactions between the legislature and the judiciary in EU external relations', in P. Syrpis (ed.), *The Judiciary, the Legislature and the EU Internal Market*, CUP, 2012, 245–246.

93 Opinion 1/78, para. 45.

94 Opinion 1/78, paras. 43–45.

95 Opinion 1/78, para. 44.

modity agreements drafted in the framework of the UN Conference on Trade and Development (UNCTAD) that regulate trade but that also have a clear development cooperation aim are based on the CCP competence. In case *Regione autonoma Friuli-Venezia Giulia*, building on previous case law,[96] the Court established its well-known test to assess whether a measure falls within the scope of the CCP: EU action falls within the CCP 'if it relates specifically to international trade in that it is essentially intended to promote, facilitate or govern trade and has direct and immediate effects on trade'.[97]

The Treaty provisions on the CCP progressively evolved over time to include the Court's case law and to respond to economic and political evolving views on the EU's CCP.[98] The Treaty of Lisbon further added fundamental changes to the Treaty provisions on the CCP, which led to a further broadening of the scope of the area. The inclusion of the fields of services, trade-related aspects of intellectual property rights, and foreign direct investment are the most important innovations in that respect.[99] The Treaty articles on the CCP formulate its objectives in a broad but also uncommon manner. Article 206 TFEU lays down the objective traditionally assigned to the CCP, the liberalization of international trade, which is a very broad objective.[100] Article 206 TFEU further recalls its origins in the General Agreement on Tariffs and Trade (GATT), which requires a customs union to establish a common external tariff. The creation of a customs union, linked to the aim of building the common market, constitutes the foundation of the CCP.[101] Apart from Article 206

---

96 Opinion 1/94, para. 57; Opinion 2/00, para. 40; Case C-281/01, para. 40–41.

97 Case C-347/03 *Regione autonoma Friuli-Venezia Giulia and ERSA*, EU:C:2005:285, para. 75. See Case C-137/12, para. 57, and the case law cited there.

98 C. Kaddous, 'The Transformation of the EU Common Commercial Policy' in P. Eeckhout, M. López-Escudero, *The European Union's External Action in Times of Crisis*, Hart, 2016, 434. For an overview of the evolving Treaty framework on the CCP, see: G. De Baere, P. Koutrakos, 244–255.

99 See in relation to intellectual property rights: Y. Tanghe, 'The borders of EU competences with regard to the international regulation of intellectual property rights: constructing a dam to resist a river bursting its banks', *Utrecht Journal of International and European Law* 2016, 27–43

100 A. Dimopoulos, 'The effects of the Lisbon Treaty on the principles and objectives of the Common Commercial Policy' 2 European Foreign Affairs Review, 2010, 159–161; S. Gstöhl, 'The European Union's trade policy', 11 Ritsumeikan International Affairs, 2013, 8; C. Vedder, 'Linkage of the Common Commercial Policy to the general objectives for the Union's external action' in M. Bungenberg, C. Herrmann, *Common Commercial Policy after Lisbon. European Yearbook of International Economic Law*, 2013, 118.

101 S. Gstöhl, 2.

TFEU, Article 207 TFEU does not refer to an objective as such, but rather to issues which the CCP can cover.[102]

Building on the earlier case law, post-Lisbon case law further confirms the CCP's scope and its delimitation with other competences. In *Daiichi Sankyo*, on the CCP's scope in relation to commercial aspects of intellectual property,[103] the Court held that a Union act needed to have more than mere implications for international trade to be covered by the CCP. The Court confirmed its case law on the scope of the CCP by holding that a Union act falls within the CCP 'if it relates specifically to international trade in that it is essentially intended to promote, facilitate or govern trade and has direct and immediate effects on trade' and, hence, only rules on intellectual property with a specific link to international trade fall within the CCP.[104] In the *Conditional Access Convention* case, the Court recalled its findings in *Daiichi Sankyo* on the scope of the CCP to conclude that the primary objective of the Council Decision on the signing on behalf of the European Union of the European Convention on the legal protection of services based on, or consisting of, conditional access[105] had a specific connection with international trade and was therefore covered by the common commercial policy.[106] In *Opinion 3/15* on the Marrakech Treaty to Facilitate Access to Published Works for Persons who are Blind, Visually Impaired or Otherwise Print Disabled,[107] on the other hand, the Court determined that the conclusion of the Marrakech Treaty did not fall within the scope of the CCP, as the measures merely indirectly affected international trade.[108] Also in *Opinion 2/15*, the Court determined that the sustainable development chapter displays a specific link with and has direct and immediate effects on trade.[109]

---

[102] G. De Baere, T. Van den Sanden, 97.

[103] Earlier the Court had held in Opinion 1/94 that only the parts of the TRIPs agreement fell within the scope of the CCP. The other parts fell outside the scope of the CCP because they did not specifically relate to international trade, but would bring about harmonisation of intellectual property rights within the EU: Opinion 1/94, EU:C:1994:384.

[104] Case C-414/11, *Daiichi Sankyo Co. Ltd,* EU:C:2013:520, para. 1–56.

[105] Council Decision 2011/853/EU of 29 November 2011 on the signing, on behalf of the Union, of the European Convention on the legal protection of services based on, or consisting of, conditional access, OJ 2011 L 336/1.

[106] Case C-137/12, *Commission/Council*, EU:C:2013:675, para. 58–65; 76.

[107] Council Decision 2014/221/EU of 14 April 2014 on the signing, on behalf of the European Union, of the Marrakesh Treaty to Facilitate Access to Published Works for Persons who are Blind, Visually Impaired, or otherwise Print Disabled, OJ 2014 L115/1.

[108] Opinion 3/15, para. 101, following Opinion 2/00 (Cartagena Protocol on Biosafety), of 6 December 2001, EU:C:2001:664, para. 40.

[109] Opinion 2/15, para. 152–155.

The *Daiichi Sankyo* and *Conditional Access Services* cases put the content-based reasoning, focusing on the content and the context of measures, to determine the appropriate legal basis more at the forefront.[110] Both judgments use the standard test that the measure 'essentially intends to promote, facilitate or govern trade and has direct and immediate effects on trade',[111] but they add the criterion of the 'specific link with international trade': only those acts with a specific link to international trade are capable of falling within the CCP.[112] While in the *Conditional Access Convention* case, the Court established such a link referring to the content,[113] in *Daiichi Sankyo* the Court also referred to the context.[114] Combined with the initial test formulated in *Opinion 2/00*,[115] which arguably focuses more on the aim, the test to determine the scope of the CCP therefore includes both the aim and content aspect. In *Opinion 3/15*[116] and in *Opinion 2/15*,[117] the Court confirmed this, by referring to the 'specific link with international trade' criterion to determine the scope of the CCP, while assessing further both the aim and the content.

The CCP's broad scope follows from the area's broad and unusually formulated objectives in Article 206 and 207 TFEU and the broad scope of the test established by the Court. The Court's case law brings about that both measures that pursue the CCP's aim and measures that do not exclusively pursue commercial aims but that are of a commercial nature fall within the scope of the CCP. The post-Lisbon Treaty provisions and the addition of the specific link with international trade criterion to the Court's test have arguably further broadened the scope of the CCP in that regard.[118] This also affects the delimitation between the CCP and other areas of EU external action.

Trade measures are said to be the clearest example of instruments that are used to attain other aims: since its creation, the EU has used trade to achieve non-trade objectives.[119] The specific Treaty provisions on the CCP make an

---

[110] G. De Baere, T. Van den Sanden, 98–99; L. Ankersmit, 'The scope of the Common Commercial policy after Lisbon: the Daiichi Sankyo and Conditional Access Services Grand Chamber Judgments', 2 Legal Issues of Economic Integration, 2014, 206–207.

[111] Opinion 2/00, para. 40; C-347/03, para. 75; C-411/06, para. 71.

[112] C-414/11, para. 52, C-137/12, para. 58.

[113] C-137/12, para. 58–65.

[114] C-411/06, para. 52–60.

[115] Opinion 2/00, para. 40.

[116] Opinion 3/15, para. 78.

[117] Opinion 2/15, para. 37.

[118] See also: J. Larik, 'No mixed feelings: The post-Lisbon Common Commercial Policy in Daiichi Sankyo and Commission v. Council (Conditional Access Convention)', 52 *Common Market Law Review*, 2015, 792.

[119] M. Cremona, 'Coherence and EU environmental policy', 47.

explicit link with the common external action objectives. Article 207 TFEU demands that 'the common commercial policy shall be conducted in the context of the principles and objectives of the Union's external action', therefore referring to the common objectives of external action formulated in Article 21 TEU. With this explicit reference to the common external action objectives, the CCP is brought within the general framework of EU external action. The Court confirmed this in *Opinion 2/15*, where it determined that an obligation applies on the EU to integrate the common external action objectives and principles into the CCP, on the basis of Article 207(1) TFEU, Article 21(3) TEU and Article 205 TFEU.[120] Often the alignment between the CCP objectives and the general external action objectives has been used to explain the established practice following which trade agreements and measures are used to attain other objectives of EU (external) action. Arguments in this regard focus on the renewed possibility and duty under Article 21 TEU and Article 207 TFEU to take into account non-commercial policy objectives when implementing the CCP.[121] The requirement to consider non-trade objectives when implementing the CCP is beneficial to attain coherent external action. Extending this integration too far would, however, lead to the conclusion that nearly every action can be pursued under the scope of the CCP.[122] This would violate the principle of conferral. Trade measures have not only been used to attain development cooperation policy objectives, but also to attain other aims, such as environmental protection or even CFSP objectives.[123] The topical cases to highlight the use of CCP measures to pursue CFSP objectives are the *Werner* and *Leifer* cases on dual-use goods. There, the Court clarified that a national measure on dual-use goods does not fall outside the scope of the CCP on the ground that it has foreign policy and security objectives.[124] The adoption of CCP measures in order to pursue environmental objectives is most notably present in the *Energy Star Agreement* and *Rotterdam Convention* cases.[125]

Opinion 2/15 on the FTA between the EU and Singapore is mostly known for its repercussions for the issue of mixed agreements, but it is also important for the scope of the CCP and its delimitation with other areas and the link

---

120 Opinion 2/15, para. 143.

121 A. Dimopoulos, 161–165; C. Vedder, 137–143.

122 G. De Baere, T. Van den Sanden, 98; J. Larik, 'Trade and sustainable development: Opinion 2/15 and the EU's foreign policy objectives', Europe and the World: A Law Review Blog, 2017.

123 M. Cremona, 'Coherence through law: What difference will the Treaty of Lisbon make?', 20.

124 Case C-83/94, *Leifer*, EU:C:1995:329, para 11; Case C-70/94, *Werner*, EU:C:1995:328, para 10. See: I. Govaere, 'Annotation Case C-70/94, Werner v. Germany and Case C-83/94, Leifer and Others' 4 Common Market Law Review, 1997, 1019–1037.

125 Case C-281/01, EU:C:2002:761; Case C-94/03, EU:C:2006:2.

between the CCP and sustainable development in particular. In that regard, the Court referred to the duty for the EU to integrate the common external action objectives, including the sustainable development aim laid down in Article 21(2)(f) TEU, in its CCP. It further referred to Articles 9 and 11 TFEU on the duty to mainstream social protection and environmental protection respectively to conclude that 'the objective of sustainable development henceforth forms an integral part of the common commercial policy'.[126] The Court considered that the specific sustainable development chapter in the Singapore FTA responded to the test on the CCP's scope: it had a specific link with international trade and it had direct and immediate effects on that trade.[127] Interestingly, the Court determined that a breach of the provisions on environmental protection and the social protection of workers authorised the parties, under customary international law, to terminate or suspend trade relations, as Chapter 13 'plays an essential role in the envisaged agreement',[128] reminiscent of the human rights clauses in FTAs.[129] This makes the respect for the environmental and social protection provisions in FTAs enforceable, although questions remain on how that would be implemented in practice.[130] The Court seemed to be aware of the CCP's all-encompassing nature by trying to mitigate its dominating effect: it determined that the CCP competence could not be exercised to regulate the levels of environmental and social protection in the third countries' territory, as this was governed by the division of competences between the Union and the Member States. The Court added that the CCP did not prevail over other provisions of the TFEU.[131] The Court moreover emphasised that *Opinion 2/15* concerned making the trade liberalisation between the EU and Singapore subject to the condition that parties complied with international obligations in the field of environmental and social protection, but that it did not in any way involve the harmonisation of the environmental and social protection of the parties.[132] From a coherence and enforcement perspective, the compelling integration of sustainable development requirements in the trade relation

---

[126] Opinion 2/15 para. 142–147.

[127] Opinion 2/15, para. 155–162.

[128] Opinion 2/15, para. 161.

[129] L. Bartels, 'Human Rights and Sustainable Development Obligations in EU Free Trade Agreements', Cambridge Legal Studies Research Paper Series, 24/2012; L. Bartels, 'The EU's Human Rights Obligations in Relation to Policies with Extraterritorial Effects', EJIL, 2014, 1071–1091.

[130] On this issue: L. Ankersmit, 'Opinion 2/15: Adding some spice to the trade & environment debate', European Law Blog, June 2017; G. Marin Duran, 'Sustainable development chapters in EU free trade agreements: emerging compliance issues', Common Market Law Review, 2020, 1031–1068.

[131] Opinion 2/15, para. 164.

[132] Opinion 2/15, para. 164–166.

between the EU and a third country is significant. The Court's statement about the limits of this competence demonstrates that the Court is sensitive for the potentially too dominant scope of the CCP competence. By clarifying that the competence does not go that far as to be able to regulate the environmental and social protection itself, the Court's statement recalls the *Philippines PCA* test:[133] the development cooperation policy competence is able to formulate the framework for cooperation, but the implementation of the cooperation in the specific areas takes place on the basis of the specific competences in these areas.

The relationship between the development cooperation policy and CCP competence can be further explained by *Opinion 3/15*. This case demonstrates that the scope of the CCP is also to an important extent determined on the basis of the nature of the measures taken, regardless of the objectives pursued. This criterion is able to further expand the CCP's scope and it explains to an important extent the domination of the CCP competence over the development cooperation policy competence. In *Opinion 3/15*, the Court confirmed the test that it established in *Daiichi Sankyo*[134] on the inclusion of commercial aspects of intellectual property in the CCP's scope. It decided, however, that the conclusion of the Marrakech Treaty fell outside this test, as the purpose of the Treaty was to improve the position of beneficiary persons by facilitating their access to published works, which is a non-commercial objective of the Treaty.[135] The Court clarified why the conclusion of the Marrakech Treaty should be distinguished from *Opinion 1/78*,[136] the *Werner* case,[137] and the *Energy Star Agreement*[138] and *Rotterdam Convention*[139] cases, which do fall under the CCP's scope although they respectively (also) pursue development cooperation policy, CFSP, and environmental protection aims. The Court explained that although the measures taken in the latter cases did not pursue exclusively commercial aims, they were, however, based on the adoption of measures of a commercial nature. Merely indirectly affecting international trade, however, which is the case in the Marrakech Treaty, is insufficient to fall within the scope of the CCP.[140] Hence, in *Opinion 3/15*, the Court reached the conclusion

133 C-377/12, *Commission/Council*, EU:C:2014:1903.
134 Case C-414/11, *Daiichi Sankyo*, EU:C:2013:520.
135 Opinion 3/15, para. 89–90.
136 Opinion 1/78, EU:C:1979:224.
137 Case C-70/94, *Werner*, EU:C:1995:328.
138 Case C-281/01, *Commission/Council*, EU:C:2002:761.
139 Case C-94/03, *Commission/Council*, EU:C:2006:2.
140 Opinion 3/15, para. 99–100.

that the Marrakech Treaty did not fall within the CCP, as a non-commercial objective was pursued by measures of a non-commercial nature.[141]

The scope of the CCP is therefore to an important extent also based on the nature of the measures: commercial measures fall under the scope of the CCP, although they primarily pursue other objectives. CCP measures can therefore pursue other objectives, as long as the content is of a commercial nature. *Eeckhout* formulates it as: 'trade measures are trade measures, whatever the objectives pursued, even if their objective is wholly unrelated to commercial or economic considerations.'[142] The establishment of the CCP's scope on the basis of the commercial nature of the measures widens further the CCP's scope and explains to an important extent why measures that pursue development cooperation policy objectives are taken on the basis of the CCP[143] or why trade chapters in development cooperation policy agreements necessitate the addition of the CCP legal basis. Both trends will be further analysed in the next subsection.

The *GSP* case further demonstrates this. The Generalised Scheme of Preferences (GSP) was created on the basis of UNCTAD recommendations in 1971 and is, in a revised form, still in place today. It established reduced tariffs to enter the EU market for goods originating from developing countries, promoting the export from developing countries to the EU. It therefore pursues an important development cooperation policy aim: through the additional export revenue, created by the reduced tariffs, the GSP stimulates growth in the countries' income and supports economic growth and job creation. As such, it assists developing countries in their efforts to reduce poverty, promote good governance, and sustainable development.[144] *Case 45/86* concerned the correct legal basis of Regulations 3599/85 and 3600/85 establishing the GSP for the year 1986. The Court decided the case on the basis of the nature of the measure: it assessed that the tariff preferences granted by the GSP were changes in tariff rates within the meaning of then Article 113 EEC. The Court rebutted the Council's argument that the aims pursued by the GSP Regulations went beyond the CCP's scope by referring to the 'new concept of international trade relations' of which the EU's CCP should be part. The Court determined that the inclusion of development cooperation aims played an important role in this new concept of trade relations. A clear link with development cooperation policy therefore does not bring about that a measure is excluded from the

---

[141] Opinion 3/15, para. 90, 99.

[142] P. Eeckhout, *EU external relations law*, 39.

[143] M. Cremona, 'Structural principles and their role in EU external relations law', 9.

[144] Report from the European Commission to the European Parliament and the Council, Report on the Generalised Scheme of Preferences covering the period 2014–2015, COM(2016) 29 final.

CCP's scope. The Court reiterated its statement made in *Opinion 1/78* in which it held that if the CCP would not be able to include instruments going beyond those intended to have an effect only on the traditional aspects of external trade, the CCP would become 'nugatory', as it would no longer be possible to 'carry on any worthwhile CCP'.[145]

While this is true, it is remarkable that these developments and new concepts in international policy formulation only benefit the CCP competence to the detriment of the development cooperation policy competence, an area in which new policy concepts emerged as well. In that regard the Court's reasoning on the use of then Article 235 EEC, the flexibility clause, is significant. The Court concluded in the *GSP* case that it was not justified to add then Article 235 EEC as a legal basis, as the measure could have legitimately been based on the CCP legal basis alone.[146] It is indeed true that the flexibility clause is used when no other legal basis provides for the necessary competence.[147] The Court's statement nevertheless implies that the Court did consider the CCP legal basis to be sufficient to cover the scope of the measures taken, despite their clear development cooperation policy aim. This is remarkable, considering the fact that the international agreements with developing countries at the time were based on the CCP legal basis and the flexibility clause because of the lack of an express development cooperation policy legal basis (see the analysis of international agreements concluded with developing countries in Section 2.2 below). This further demonstrates that the commercial nature of the measures is an essential criterion to qualify them under the scope of the CCP.

Another element to explain the domination of the CCP over the development cooperation policy objective could be found in more pragmatic and historical reasons. From a historical perspective, the CCP predates development cooperation as an express EU competence. As a result, early international agreements and measures at the interplay of development cooperation policy and the CCP have been based on the CCP alone or on the CCP legal basis and the flexibility clause. The fact that the CCP legal basis was therefore consistently present in development cooperation agreements and measures could explain the ongoing presence of the CCP legal basis. This issue will be discussed in detail in the next subsection, which discusses the patterns in the application of the development cooperation policy–CCP delimitation.

---

145 Case 45/86, Commission v Council, EU:C:1987:163, para. 17–20.
146 Case 45/86, para. 21.
147 Case 45/86, para. 13.

2.2 Consistent Application?

Similar to Section 1 on the application of the delimitation between development cooperation policy and environment, this section will evaluate whether and how the rules on the scope of EU development cooperation policy and its delimitation with the CCP, as described above, are reflected in practice. It will become apparent that the definition of the CCP's scope affects the CCP–development cooperation policy relationship, as the CCP is able to dominate the development cooperation policy competence. The analysis of the application of the development cooperation policy–CCP delimitation in this subsection will lead to two conclusions in this regard: (i) development cooperation policy agreements that cover a trade chapter necessitate the addition of the CCP legal basis; and (ii) trade measures have been adopted to attain development cooperation policy objectives. In that sense, the test formulated to define the scope of development cooperation policy, as developed in *Portugal/ Council* and *Philippines PCA*, apparently does not apply to the CCP.

2.2.1 International agreements

The question here is how the choice of legal basis is made in practice when an international agreement touches upon development and trade issues. When is an agreement concluded with a developing country based on the trade legal basis, when is it based on the development cooperation policy legal basis, or when is it based on a dual CCP–development cooperation policy legal basis? Three main categories of agreements can be identified that are relevant for the trade–development cooperation policy nexus: (i) development cooperation policy agreements that contain trade provisions; (ii) economic partnership agreements (EPAs); and (iii) FTAs with more advanced developing countries and other trade agreements that are concluded vis-à-vis developing countries and that are concluded as pure CCP agreements.

The historical context is of particular importance in the assessment of the first subcategory to discuss: the development cooperation policy agreements that also contain a trade chapter. Important to consider is the fact that the CCP predates development cooperation policy as an express EU competence: while the latter was only inserted by the Treaty of Maastricht, the former constitutes one of the EU's first two express external competences. Moreover, the relationship between the EU and the developing countries has from the start been based on a trade and aid rationale (see above).[148] Hence, from the very

[148] T. Van den Sanden, 'The EU perspective on the post-2015 development framework and the legal scope of EU development cooperation', *Studia Diplomatica* 2014, 87.

beginning, trade constituted an essential element in the EU's relationship with developing countries. As the CCP competence had its own explicit legal basis, it quickly dominated over the development cooperation policy competence. The early cases on the delimitation between the CCP and development cooperation policy in the pre-Maastricht Treaty era, namely *Opinion 1/78*[149] and the *GSP* case,[150] therefore maintained a negative reasoning towards the development cooperation policy competence: they focused on what development cooperation policy was not, compared with the CCP.[151] Consequently, during this time, development cooperation policy was constructed as a policy 'subordinate to or subsumed in' the CCP.[152] It should also be kept in mind that in the 1960s and 1970s, the CCP too was a new competence which had to be further developed as well and which had to respond to new evolutions in international economics and trade.[153]

As already pointed out in the previous section on the development cooperation policy–environment delimitation, the agreements concluded with the developing countries can be classified in different generations of agreements. The 'first-generation' agreements contained only provisions on trade.[154] The 'second-generation' agreements extended to limited areas of economic cooperation as well,[155] while the 'third-generation' agreements cover a variety of areas of cooperation, aimed at a comprehensive framework of cooperation.[156] The agreements of the first type were based on the CCP legal basis alone, while the broadening of the agreements to economic cooperation led to adding the flexibility clause as a legal basis. Before Maastricht, the 'third-generation' agreements were based on the CCP and the flexibility clause, as an express

---

[149] Opinion 1/78, EU:C:1979:224.

[150] Case 45/86, Commission/Council, EU:C:1987:163.

[151] S. Peers, 'Case C-268/94, Portugal v. Council, (development policy)', 541.

[152] M. Broberg, R. Holdgaard, 'EU external action in the field of development cooperation policy. The impact of the Lisbon Treaty', Swedish Institute for European Policy Studies, 2014, 15.

[153] Opinion 1/78, para. 44.

[154] Examples are the agreements concluded with Argentina OJ 1971 L249/19, Uruguay OJ 1973 L333, India OJ 1974 L82, Brazil OJ 1974 L102/23, Sri Lanka OJ 1975 L247/2, Mexico OJ 1975 L247/11, Pakistan OJ 1976 L168/1, Bangladesh OJ 1976 L319/1, China OJ 1978 L123.

[155] Agreements concluded with: Yemen OJ 1985 L23/2, the Gulf Cooperation Council OJ 1989 L54/3, China OJ 1985 L250/1, India OJ 1981 L 328/5, Pakistan OJ 1986 L108/2, ASEAN OJ 1982 L144/1, Central American States OJ 1986 L172/1, Andean States OJ 1998 L127, Brazil and Argentina OJ 1990 L295.

[156] M. Maresceau, 160–165, S. Peers, 'EC frameworks of international relations: Co-operation, partnership and association', 160–165. See Section 1.2.1 above, comparing the second- and third-generation agreement for Pakistan and Mongolia.

development cooperation legal basis in the Treaties was still lacking.[157] After the Maastricht Treaty, they were based on the CCP and development cooperation legal bases.[158] The CCP legal basis was therefore consistently present in the agreements that the EU concluded with developing countries. This could explain why the provisions in international agreements including a trade chapter bring about the addition of their own legal basis. Maresceau refers in this regard to the 'classical pattern' following which development cooperation policy agreements are traditionally based on both the development cooperation policy and CCP legal bases.[159] The most recent agreements include cooperation in additional areas: on small arms and light weapons, weapons of mass destruction, migration matters and legal cooperation, combating terrorism and transnational crimes, data protection, and promoting cooperation between NGOs.[160] Hence, within the category of third-generation agreements, the agreements concluded or revised in recent years are even more advanced, as they cover an increasing number of areas of cooperation. Another interesting evolution is that the EU concludes with certain developing countries both a cooperation agreement and an FTA (see below).

The trade titles in the cooperation agreements are not that extensive in scope. They contain trade and economic or commercial cooperation titles, aimed at stimulating trade and economic cooperation. Some of the agreements contain an MFN clause,[161] while others grant preferential treatment. Apart from this, the chapters define the aims and subject of the cooperation and, as such, therefore do not seem to go beyond the test formulated in *Portugal/Council* and *Philippines PCA* to assess whether additional legal bases are necessary, as they do not contain obligations so extensive that they form distinct objectives. Still, the CCP legal basis is always present in the agreements. An exception is the Political Dialogue and Cooperation Agreement between the European Community and its Member States, of the one part, and the Republics of Costa Rica, El Salvador, Guatemala, Honduras, Nicaragua and Panama, of the other part.[162] Otherwise, development cooperation policy agreements are, as men-

157 For example: the Trade and Economic Cooperation Agreement between the European Economic Community and the People's Republic of China, OJ 1985 L250/1.

158 For example: Cooperation Agreement between the European Community and the Republic of Yemen, OJ 1998 L72/17.

159 M. Maresceau, 176–177.

160 See for example: Framework Agreement on Partnership and Cooperation between the European Union and its Member States, of the one part, and Mongolia, of the other part, OJ 2017 L326/7.

161 These countries can, however, still have preferential market access under the GSP (see below).

162 Council Decision 2014/211/EU of 14 April 2014 on the conclusion on behalf of the European Union of the Political Dialogue and Cooperation Agreement between

tioned by Maresceau,[163] indeed as 'a standard rule' based on the development cooperation policy and CCP legal basis.[164] It therefore seems that as soon as a development cooperation agreement contains provisions related to the CCP – which it always does – the CCP legal basis needs to be added. Therefore, while the development cooperation policy competence is sufficient to cover aspects of the agreement that relate to other specific areas of action, the trade provisions bring about the addition of the CCP legal basis.[165] While the specific and broad scope of the CCP can explain its dominance over several areas, it seems that with regard to the development cooperation policy competence in particular, the fact that the CCP was consistently a (co-) legal basis for development cooperation policy agreements also explains to an important extent why that is still the case.

A second interesting category of agreements to highlight in the development–trade nexus are the Economic Partnership Agreements (EPAs). The EPAs are the trade agreements that the EU concludes with regional blocks of ACP countries (see above for the difference between ACP and non-ACP developing

the European Community and its Member States, of the one part, and the Republics of Costa Rica, El Salvador, Guatemala, Honduras, Nicaragua and Panama, of the other part, with the exception of Article 49(3) thereof, OJ 2014 L111/4. Despite lacking a CCP legal basis, the agreement contains an Article 13 on 'Trade cooperation'.

163 M. Maresceau, 170.

164 For example from the different generations of agreements: Political Dialogue and Cooperation Agreement between the European Union and its Member States, of the one part, and the Republic of Cuba, of the other part, OJ 2016 L337I/1; Cooperation Agreement on Partnership and Development between the European Union and its Member States, of the one part, and the Islamic Republic of Afghanistan, of the other part, OJ 2017 L67/3; Cooperation Agreement between the European Community and the Republic of Yemen, OJ 1998 L72/18; Cooperation Agreement between the European Community and the Kingdom of Nepal, OJ 1996 L137/15.

The difference between the generations of agreements is also apparent when comparing the agreements with Vietnam: Cooperation Agreement between the European Community and the Socialist Republic of Vietnam, OJ 1996 L136/29; Framework Agreement on Comprehensive Partnership and Cooperation between the European Union and its Member States, of the one part, and the Socialist Republic of Viet Nam, of the other part, OJ 2016 L329/6.

Also the 'transversal partnership agreements' (see above) always also include the CCP legal basis: Partnership and Cooperation Agreement establishing a partnership between the European Communities and their Member States, of the one part, and the Republic of Tajikistan, of the other part, OJ 2009 L350/3; Partnership and Cooperation Agreement between the European Communities and their Member States, of the one part, and Georgia, of the other part, OJ 1999 L205/3.

165 M. Maresceau, 170, 176–177.

countries). They find their origin in the Cotonou Agreement:[166] the previous Lomé Convention established agreements that were preferential vis-à-vis the ACPs. Due to their WTO incompatibility, the Cotonou Agreement aimed to establish reciprocal WTO-compatible trade agreements.[167] The Cotonou reciprocal rights and obligations[168] are found to be WTO-compatible as the EPAs create free trade areas, which abolish tariffs between the members.[169] While creating these free trade areas, the link between trade cooperation and regional integration is firmly established as a core principle in Article 2 of the Agreement:[170] the EPAs are to be concluded with seven regional ACP blocs, five of which are African trade bloc and one within the Caribbean and the Pacific. The EU will become a party to each of these regional free trade areas. The LDCs will nevertheless still enjoy preferential treatment under the EBA system (see Section 2.2.2 below). The EPAs pursue a development cooperation aim, as they aim to contribute, through trade and investment, to sustainable development and poverty reduction. Despite the fact that the EPAs are of a reciprocal nature; they aim to take the development cooperation policy dimension into account by recognising the developing country status of the partner country. The agreements refer to development cooperation policy objectives as the ultimate aim of the EPA.[171] In that regard, they go beyond traditional FTAs, as they take into account particular socio-economic circumstances, include cooperation and assistance to help ACP countries implement the agreements, they exclude sensitive products from liberalisation and provide for long liberalisation periods, flexible rules of origin, and special safeguards and measures for agriculture, food security, and infant industry

---

[166] Council Decision of 19 December 2002 concerning the conclusion of the Partnership Agreement between the African Caribbean and Pacific Group of States, of the one part, and the European Community and its Member States, of the other part, signed in Cotonou on 23 June 2000, OJ 2003 L65/27.

[167] Green Paper on relations between the European Union and the ACP countries on the eve of the 21st century: Challenges and options for a new partnership, COM(96) 570 final, 20 November 1996, p. 20.

[168] Article 36 Cotonou Agreement.

[169] M. Broberg, 'From colonial power to human rights promoter: on the legal regulation of the European Union's relations with the developing countries', 7.

[170] Article 35(2); article 37(8) Cotonou Agreement; S. Bartelt, 15–16.

[171] Article 1(a) Economic Partnership Agreement between the CARIFORUM States, of the one part, and the European Community and its Member States, of the other part, OJ 2008 L289.

protection.[172] The EPAs are also, as a rule,[173] based on the CCP and the development cooperation policy legal basis.[174]

The EU–ACP Partnership Agreements[175] were concluded on the legal basis for concluding association agreements, current Article 217 TFEU. The single association legal basis is in that case sufficient to cover the various aspects of the cooperation. Article 217 TFEU determines that 'The Union may conclude with one or more third countries or international organisations agreements establishing an association involving reciprocal rights and obligations, common action and special procedure'. Apart from the EU–ACP Partnership Agreements, the EU has also concluded association agreements with other individual or specific groups of developing countries. More than indicating

---

[172] European Commission Fact Sheet, http://trade.ec.europa.eu/doclib/docs/2017/february/tradoc_155300.pdf.

[173] The Interim Partnership Agreement with the Pacific States constitutes an important exception, as it is based solely on the CCP legal basis: Interim Partnership Agreement between the European Community, of the one part, and the Pacific States, of the other part, OJ 2009 L272/2. In the EPA with CARIFORUM, the legal bases on free movement of capital and transport are added to the CCP and development cooperation policy legal bases: Economic Partnership Agreement between the CARIFORUM States, of the one part, and the European Community and its Member States, of the other part, OJ 2008 L289/3.

[174] Economic Partnership Agreement between the European Union and its Member States, of the one part, and the SADC EPA States, of the other part, OJ 2016 L250/3; Proposal for a Council Decision on the conclusion of the Economic Partnership Agreement between the East African Community Partner States, of the one part, and the European Union and its Member States, of the other part, COM/2016/064 final; Stepping stone Economic Partnership Agreement between Ghana, of the one part, and the European Community and its Member States, of the other part, OJ 2016 L278/3, Stepping Stone Economic Partnership Agreement between Côte d'Ivoire, of the one part, and the European Community and its Member States, of the other part, OJ 2009 L59/3; Interim Agreement establishing a framework for an Economic Partnership Agreement between the Eastern and Southern Africa States, on the one part, and the European Community and its Member States, on the other part, OJ 2012 L111/2; Interim Agreement with a view to an Economic Partnership Agreement between the European Community and its Member States, of the one part, and the Central Africa Party, of the other part, OJ 2009 L57/2.

[175] Agreement amending for the second time the Partnership Agreement between the members of the African, Caribbean and Pacific Group of States, of the one part, and the European Community and its Member States, of the other part, signed in Cotonou on 23 June 2000, as first amended in Luxembourg on 25 June 2005, OJ 2010 L287/3; Fourth ACP-EEC convention signed at Lomé on 15 December 1989, OJ 1991 L229/3; Convention of Association between the European Economic Community and the African and Malagasy States associated with that Community, signed at Yaounde on 29 July 1969, Full text on: https://publications.europa.eu/en/publication-detail/-/publication/ff8c0117-3514-4119-8da0-a617ce3321fb/language-en.

the comprehensiveness of the cooperation, this type of association agreement would often primarily be based on political and strategic reasons, rather than legal reasons:[176] they are the expression of a special relation with or a particular strategy towards a certain country or group of countries. Certain countries belong to the neighbourhood region or are candidate countries,[177] while others are graduating developing countries.[178]

The final category of international agreements to discuss consists of the agreements concluded with developing countries that are based on the CCP legal basis alone. This category covers 'pure' CCP agreements on the one hand (although some of them have an important development cooperation policy dimension) and FTAs concluded with developing countries. Several international agreements concluded with developing countries can be described as 'pure' CCP agreements because they focus on boosting trade and economic development in a certain field or sector. Maresceau therefore describes them as 'sectoral agreements'.[179] However, several of these agreements have a clear development cooperation policy dimension or their ultimate goal is economic development with the aim to eradicate poverty. This is particularly true for the Agreement on the Common Fund for Commodities.[180] Other agreements are indeed sectoral agreements, but they concern sectors that are of essential importance for certain developing countries, such as the coffee, cocoa, or sugar sector. It is therefore clear that these agreements have been based solely on the trade legal basis, following the nature of the measures. It could

---

176 M. Maresceau, 313.

177 For example: Agreement creating an association between the European Economic Community and Turkey, OJ 1964 L217/3687; Euro-Mediterranean Agreement establishing an Association between the European Communities and their Member States, of the one part, and the Arab Republic of Egypt, of the other part, OJ 2004 L304/38; Stabilisation and Association Agreement between the European Communities and their Member States, of the one part, and the former Yugoslav Republic of Macedonia, of the other part, OJ 2015 L164/548.

178 Agreement establishing an Association between the European Union and its Member States, on the one hand, and Central America on the other, OJ 2012 L346/3; Agreement establishing an association between the European Community and its Member States, of the one part, and the Republic of Chile, of the other part, OJ 2002 L352/3. In November 2017, the EU launched negotiations to conclude a revised Association Agreement with Chile, which aims to deepen cooperation in areas such as climate change, peace and security, sectoral cooperation, and trade matters: Council of the EU, 13 November 2017, Directives for the negotiation of a modernised association agreement with Chile, 13553/17. The conclusion of an Association Agreement with Chile is also relevant in light of Chile's graduation from the OECD DAC list, as it has exceeded the high-income country threshold.

179 M. Maresceau, 166.

180 OJ 1990 L182/2.

be argued, however, that on the basis of their objectives, some of them could have been based on a development cooperation policy legal basis as well. This is particularly the case for agreements concerning commodities and food security.[181] Another interesting type of agreement in this respect are the FLEGT agreements: while they are also trade agreements, they have important environmental and development cooperation goals.[182]

Finally, the EU has concluded, or is in the process of concluding, FTAs with developing countries. The EU concluded a Trade Agreement with Colombia and Peru,[183] to which Ecuador acceded as well.[184] It is a comprehensive FTA, in line with the EU's newest generation of FTAs. It covers trade in goods and services, competition, intellectual property, sustainable development, sanitary and phytosanitary measures. The conclusion of this type of agreement is important for more advanced developing countries, also from an economic perspective. As an increasing number of measures is focusing on the LDCs and lower middle-income countries, it is important for upper middle-income countries to retain favourable market access in order to ultimately further develop and, in any event, retain their economic status.[185] Colombia, Peru, and Ecuador indeed fall in the category of upper middle-income countries. Interestingly, the EU also concluded a trade agreement with Vietnam, which is a lower middle-income country. The EU's evolving relationship with Vietnam is also an interesting illustration of the interplay of different types of agreement. The Cooperation Agreement between the European Community and the Socialist Republic of Vietnam entered into force in 1996.[186] As a third-generation agreement, it covered development cooperation, trade, commercial and economic cooperation, investments, intellectual property rights, science and technology, environmental cooperation, regional cooperation, and drug abuse

---

[181] International Coffee Agreement, OJ 2008 L186/13; International Cocoa Agreement, OJ 2011 L259/8; Geneva Agreement on Trade in Bananas, OJ 2010 L141/3.

[182] For example the agreement concluded with Indonesia: Voluntary Partnership Agreement between the European Union and the Republic of Indonesia on forest law enforcement, governance and trade in timber products to the European Union, OJ 2014 L150/250.

[183] Trade Agreement between the European Union and its Member States, of the one part, and Colombia and Peru, of the other part, OJ 2012 L354/3.

[184] Council Decision 2016/2369 on the signing, on behalf of the Union, and provisional application of the Protocol of Accession to the Trade Agreement between the European Union and its Member States, of the one part, and Colombia and Peru, of the other part, to take account of the accession of Ecuador, OJ 2016 L356/1.

[185] C. Steven, J. Kean, L. Bartels, S. Woolcock, 'European Union Trade Agreement with Colombia and Peru', European Parliament Study, 2012, 23.

[186] OJ 1996 L136/29.

control. In 2016, the Framework Agreement on Comprehensive Partnership and Cooperation between the European Union and its Member States, of the one part, and the Socialist Republic of Viet Nam, of the other part entered into force.[187] It establishes indeed a comprehensive framework for cooperation between the two parties and, as such, it goes beyond the 1996 agreement by establishing more in-depth and comprehensive cooperation.[188] The aims and forms of the development cooperation policy are specified, while the cooperation covers a comprehensive range of areas such as countering the proliferation of weapons of mass destruction, combating the trade in small arms and light weapons, cooperation on legal matters, cooperation in combating money laundering and terrorism financing and organized crime, data protection, migration, industrial policy, and urban planning. Next to this Framework Agreement on Comprehensive Partnership and Cooperation, the EU concluded in 2020 an FTA and signed an Investment Protection Agreement with Vietnam.[189] Both cooperation agreements are based on the dual CCP–development cooperation policy legal basis, while the FTA and the Investment Protection Agreement are based on the CCP legal basis alone. The PCA and the FTA are formally linked to each other: the FTA contains a reference to the PCA as the instrument that governs the overall relationship between the two countries. Article 17.22 clarifies that the FTA is part of the overall relationship between the parties as provided for in the Partnership and Cooperation Agreement and that it forms part of this common framework. Institutionally, the two agreements are further linked via the bodies set up by the agreements[190] and via the fulfilment of obligations provision.[191] The PCA therefore provides for the overall comprehensive framework for cooperation, while the FTA further develops the trade aspect. Interestingly, the PCA is also still based on the development

187 OJ 2016 L329/8.

188 As set out above, other examples of evolving cooperation agreements are those with Mongolia and Pakistan: Agreement for commercial, economic and development cooperation between the European Economic Community and the Islamic Republic of Pakistan, OJ 1986 L108/2; Cooperation agreement between the European Community and the Islamic Republic of Pakistan, relating to the partnership and to development, OJ 2004 L378/23. Framework Agreement on Partnership and Cooperation between the European Union and its Member States, of the one part, and Mongolia, of the other part, OJ 2012 L134/4: Agreement on trade and economic cooperation between the European Economic Community and Mongolia, OJ 1993 L41/46.

189 Free Trade Agreement between the European Union and the Socialist Republic of Viet Nam, OJ 2019 L177/1; Investment Protection Agreement between the European Union and its Member States, of the one part, and the Socialist Republic of Viet Nam, of the other part, OJ 2019, L175/1.

190 Article 17.1(5) Free Trade Agreement.

191 Article 17.18 Free Trade Agreement.

cooperation policy and the CCP legal basis, which confirms the findings above regarding the choice of legal basis for cooperation agreements with developing countries.

2.2.2 Measures

Apart from the international agreements discussed in the previous subsection, it is useful to discuss unilateral trade measures that find themselves at the interplay between trade and development cooperation policy. They are based on the CCP legal basis alone, while they also have clear development cooperation policy aims.[192] Their CCP qualification is therefore based on the trade or commercial policy nature of the measures, regardless of the aims pursued.

The Generalised Scheme of Preferences (GSP) is a central measure to discuss in this respect. The GSP is governed by Regulation 978/2012 and is based on Article 207 TFEU alone.[193] As already discussed, the Court determined in the *GSP* case that the CCP legal basis alone is indeed sufficient as a basis for the GSP system. The Court decided the case on the basis of the nature of the measure: it assessed that the tariff preferences granted by the GSP were changes in tariff rates within the meaning of then Article 113 EEC. The Court determined that development cooperation aims played an important role in the new concept of trade relations and that, hence, a clear link with development cooperation policy did not bring about that a measure was excluded from the CCP's scope.[194] This reasoning brought the GSP entirely under the CCP's scope, despite the fact that the scheme ultimately pursues development cooperation policy aims: the tariff reductions for goods originating from developing countries entering the EU market promote the export from developing countries to the EU. They therefore pursue an important development cooperation policy aim, as through the additional export revenue, created by the reduced tariffs, the GSP stimulates growth in the countries' income and supports economic growth and job creation. As such, it assists developing countries in their efforts to reduce poverty, promote good governance, and sustainable development.[195] The preamble to the GSP Regulation even determines that the

---

[192] Cremona refers in that regard to the 'instrumentalisation' of the CCP, in the sense of measures that affect trade, to attain different policy objectives: M. Cremona, 'Structural principles and their role in EU external relations law', in M. Cremona, *Structural principles in EU external relations law*, Hart, 2018, 9.

[193] Regulation 978/2012 of 25 October 2012 applying a scheme of generalised tariff preferences and repealing Council Regulation 732/2008, OJ 2012 L303/1.

[194] Case 45/86, para. 17–20.

[195] Report from the European Commission to the European Parliament and the Council, Report on the Generalised Scheme of Preferences covering the period 2014–2015, COM(2016) 29 final.

tariff preferences should focus on helping developing countries having greater development, trade, and financial needs.[196]

The GSP covers three separate schemes, depending on the partner country's level of development. The fact that the schemes are based on the needs and level of development of the partner countries also demonstrates the development cooperation policy dimension of the system. First, the general scheme applies to low middle-income countries: the LDCs are excluded, as well as the high-income countries and middle-income countries that have been qualified as such in three consecutive years.[197] This illustrates the importance for upper middle-income countries to close FTAs or to receive benefits under a different scheme. Second, a special incentive scheme for sustainable development and good governance, or the GSP+ scheme, applies to economically vulnerable low middle-income countries. In order to be eligible, the partner country needs to have ratified and applied several international agreements in the area of labour rights, core human rights, environmental protection, and good governance.[198] With the GSP+ scheme, the EU further confirms the link between trade and sustainable development. The third specific scheme under the GSP establishes the most beneficial measures towards developing country partners. The Everything But Arms (EBA) initiative focuses on LDCs by granting them full duty-free and quota-free access to the EU market for all their exports with the exception of arms and armaments.

A second type of measure to discuss is development cooperation assistance that aims to support developing countries' trade, ultimately with the aim to attain development cooperation policy objectives related to poverty eradication: Aid for Trade is the overarching term that is used to characterise these measures. It covers both direct trade-related assistance, supporting the formulation and implementation of trade policies, and a wider aid for trade rationale, supporting the partner country's capacity to trade. The Aid for Trade initiative was launched by the WTO in 2005, alongside the Doha round. The EU implemented the initiative with its 2007 Aid for Trade Strategy, which refers to the WTO's building blocks: (i) trade policy and regulations; (ii) trade development; (iii) trade-related infrastructure; (iv) building productive capacity; (v) trade-related adjustment; and (vi) other trade-related needs.[199] The Strategy

---

196 Preamble (7) to Regulation 978/2012 of 25 October 2012 applying a scheme of generalised tariff preferences and repealing Council Regulation 732/2008, OJ 2012 L303/1.

197 Article 4 Regulation 978/2012.

198 Article 9 Regulation 978/2012.

199 Conclusions of the Council and of the Representatives of the Governments of the Member States meeting within the Council, EU Strategy on Aid for Trade: Enhancing EU support for trade-related needs in developing countries – 29 October 2007, 3.

was updated in 2017 in order to respond to the new policy environment in light of the SDGs and to increase coherence with other initiatives in the area of development cooperation policy.[200]

As follows from the analysis in this section, the areas of development cooperation policy and trade are strongly intertwined in the EU's overall policy vis-à-vis developing countries, while both areas' broad legal scope raises the question about the legal delimitation between the two areas. The delimitation is distinct from development cooperation policy's delimitation with other TFEU competences, such as the environmental competence. While the development cooperation competence is predominant vis-à-vis environment, it seems that the CCP invades the development cooperation policy competence. The CCP's domination follows from two characteristics of the development cooperation policy–CCP delimitation: (i) development cooperation policy agreements that cover a trade chapter necessitate the addition of the CCP legal basis; and (ii) trade measures have been adopted to attain development cooperation policy objectives. Indeed, examination of the international agreements reveals that the CCP legal basis is consistently present in the different types of agreement concluded with developing countries. The GSP is also a clear expression of the CCP's domination over the development cooperation policy competence: this unilateral measure is based on the CCP legal basis, while it clearly also pursues development cooperation policy aims. Its CCP qualification is therefore based on the commercial policy nature of the measures, regardless of the aims pursued. Finally, comparable to the assessment of the delimitation with environment, the EU provides development cooperation assistance under its development cooperation policy instrument to support developing countries' trade. As such, they are entirely part of the development cooperation policy competence. The next section on the delimitation between development cooperation policy and the CFSP is yet another nexus that demonstrates the balancing act between conferral and coherence.

3. DELIMITATION WITH THE COMMON FOREIGN AND SECURITY POLICY

The delimitation between development cooperation policy and the CFSP is specific, which is mainly due to the CFSP's distinct character. Pursuant to Article 24 TEU, the CFSP is subject to specific rules and procedures, which

[200] Communication from the Commission to the European Parliament, the Council, the European Economic and Social Committee and the Committee of the Regions, Achieving Prosperity through Trade and Investment: Updating the 2007 Joint EU Strategy on Aid for Trade, COM(2017) 667 final.

relate to the institutions' competences, the voting rules, and the type of measures.[201] The delimitation between the CFSP and other areas of Union external action is, moreover, governed by a specific provision in the Treaties, which is currently laid down in Article 40 TEU. Before assessing the current status of the delimitation between development cooperation policy and the CFSP, it is useful to briefly look into the status quo before the Treaty of Lisbon.

3.1 Pre-Lisbon Demarcation: Certainty in Light of Conferral, Questions in Light of Coherence

The Treaty provision which governed the delimitation between the CFSP and the non-CFSP in the pre-Lisbon era was former Article 47 TEU, which prohibited the former CFSP pillar from affecting then Community law or the so-called first pillar. As such, Article 47 TEU aimed to protect the ordinary external action, following the need to protect the *acquis communautaire* in accordance with Article 2 and 3 TEU from encroachment by the intergovernmental CFSP pillar.[202] Former Article 47 TEU therefore further reinforced the division between the CFSP and the non-CFSP with its principled stance on protecting the non-CFSP in its delimitation with the CFSP. In order to fully understand the impact of Article 47 TEU on the delimitation between the CFSP and the non-CFSP, case law needed to further interpret this article and its exact consequences on the division of competences. In the pre-Lisbon era, several cases were rendered on the delimitation between the former first and third pillars. The *Airport Transit Visas*,[203] *Environmental Penalties*,[204] and *Ship-Source Pollution*[205] cases clarified that former Article 47 TEU demanded that third-pillar measures could not encroach upon the competences conferred on the then Community.[206]

The *Small Arms and Light Weapons* case is the only case which interpreted and applied Article 47 TEU in the context of the delimitation between the ordinary EU external action competences and the CFSP, or the former first and

---

[201] For an extensive analysis of the CFSP, its institutions, competence, and procedures, see: G. Butler, *Constitutional Law of the EU's Common Foreign and Security Policy*, Hart Publishing, 2019, 348 p.

[202] Case C-91/05, para. 59.

[203] Case C-170/96, *Commission/Council*, EU:C:1998:219, para. 16.

[204] Case C-176/03, *Commission/Council*, EU:C:2005:542, para. 39.

[205] Case C-440/05, *Commission/Council*, EU:C:2007:625, para. 53.

[206] For a detailed analysis of the case law on the delimitation between the first and the third pillar: A. Dashwood, 'Article 47 TEU and the relationship between first and second pillar competences', in A. Dashwood, M. Maresceau (eds), *Law and Practice of EU External Relations: Salient Features of a Changing Landscape*, CUP, 2008, 70–103.

second pillars, building on the previous case law on the delimitation with the former third pillar. The case concerned the delimitation between the CFSP and development cooperation policy.[207] The Commission had launched an action for annulment against Council Decision 2004/833/CFSP[208] and a plea of illegality against Joint Action 2002/589/CFSP,[209] on which the Council Decision was based. Both instruments concerned the EU's contribution to the Economic Community of West African States (ECOWAS) actions to fight small arms and light weapons. The Commission argued that the Council had wrongly adopted its Decision under the CFSP: the Commission held that the issue of combating the accumulation of small arms and light weapons was covered by the Cotonou Agreement, which brought the Decision under the scope of EU development cooperation policy.

The Court's reasoning is built on the formulation of former Article 47 TEU, which was to protect ordinary external action from the CFSP. In accordance with this article, the Court clarified at the start of its reasoning that it was the Court's task to ensure that CFSP acts that were capable of having legal effects did not encroach upon the powers as conferred in the context of the non-CFSP.[210] The relevant criterion was the question whether provisions of the contested decision affected non-CFSP competences, which followed from the assessment that they could have been adopted on the basis of ordinary EU external action provisions.[211] Central was the question whether the provisions of a measure adopted under the CFSP, on the basis of both their aim and content, had as their main purpose the implementation of an ordinary external action policy and whether, therefore, they could properly have been adopted on that basis. If this was the case, these provisions infringed Article 47 TEU.[212] The Court therefore examined whether the Decision violated former Article 47 TEU, in the sense that it could have been adopted on the basis of ordinary EU

[207] For an extensive analysis of the *Small Arms and Light Weapons* case, including the background of the case, see: J. Heliskoski, 'Small arms and light weapons within the Union's pillar structure: an analysis of Article 47 of the EU Treaty' 6 European Law Review, 2008, 898–912.

[208] Council Decision 2004/833/CFSP of 2 December 2004 implementing Joint Action 2002/589/CFSP with a view to a European Union contribution to ECOWAS in the framework of the Moratorium on Small Arms and Light Weapons, OJ 2004 L359/65.

[209] Council Joint Action 2002/589/CFSP of 12 July 2002 on the European Union's contribution to combating the destabilising accumulation and spread of small arms and light weapons and repealing Joint Action 1999/34/CFSP, OJ 2002 L191/1.

[210] Case C-91/0, para. 56.

[211] Case C-91/05, para. 58.

[212] Case C-91/05, para. 60, referring to Case C-176/03, para. 51–53; Case C-440/05, para. 69–74.

external action competences, *in casu* on the basis of development cooperation policy.[213] To assess whether this was the case, the Court first aimed to demarcate the CFSP and development cooperation policy. As discussed in the section on the scope of EU development cooperation, in doing so, the Court contributed to the broad interpretation of development cooperation policy and its objectives. Referring to *Portugal/Council*, the Court confirmed that the objectives of development cooperation policy were broad, in the sense that it must be possible for development cooperation policy measures to concern various specific matters. The Court emphasised the close link between development cooperation policy and the CFSP by confirming the widely used statement that there can be no sustainable development and poverty eradication without peace and security. The Court then further broadened the scope of the development cooperation policy objectives by holding that these objectives should not be limited to measures directly related to the fight against poverty but that it is necessary, for a measure to fall within the area's scope, that it contributes to the pursuit of the policy's economic and social development objectives.[214] An important element in the Court's reasoning was the assessment that measures aimed at preventing fragility in developing countries, including measures to fight the proliferation of small arms and light weapons, could contribute to the elimination or reduction of obstacles to the economic and social development of these countries. To support this statement, the Court relied heavily on policy documents and soft law adopted in the area of development cooperation policy, which demonstrates the importance of this type of instrument to clarify the scope of EU development cooperation policy (see also above).[215]

Nevertheless, the Court continued its reasoning by confirming the application of the centre of gravity test to the demarcation of the CFSP from the non-CFSP: a measure aimed at fighting the proliferation of small arms and light weapons could only be adopted on the basis of development cooperation policy if the measure, on the basis of both its aim and content, fell under the area's scope. This was not the case if the measure had as its main purpose the implementation of the CFSP, even if it contributed to the economic and social development of the developing country.[216] The centre of gravity test could therefore play in the CFSP's advantage. The Court, however, did not follow the traditional case law on the possibility of using a dual legal basis for measures which pursue a twofold aim or have a twofold component, without one being subordinate to the other. The general rule is that in such a case the

---

213 Case C-91/05, para. 63.

214 Case C-91/05, para. 64–67, referring to Portugal/Council, para. 44, 60, 63, 73.

215 Case C-91/05, para. 68–70.

216 Case C-91/05, para. 71–72.

measure can exceptionally be based on the various corresponding legal bases. However, the Court clarified that this did not apply to the delimitation between the CFSP and the non-CFSP: former Article 47 TEU prevented, as a principle, a measure to be based on a dual CFSP and development cooperation legal basis.[217] The Court argued that as former Article 47 TEU prevented the EU from adopting a CFSP measure which could be properly adopted on the basis of ordinary EU external action, the Union could not adopt a measure on the basis of the CFSP if that measure also fell within an ordinary EU external action competence.

To determine the correct legal basis of the Decision at issue, the Court therefore proceeded by examining whether the decision fell within EU development cooperation policy, on the basis of both its aim and content. It concluded that the aim of the decision was to implement the contested joint action, whose objectives could be achieved by both development cooperation policy measures and CFSP measures. Furthermore, in that light, the development cooperation policy objective of reducing and eliminating obstacles to the development of the countries concerned was not purely incidental to the CFSP objective of preserving peace and strengthening international security.[218] The Court therefore concluded that the Decision equally pursued both development cooperation policy aims and CFSP objectives, without one being incidental to the other. The Court again referred extensively to policy documents and soft law instruments to support its statement that the objectives of the action could be achieved by both CFSP and development cooperation policy measures.[219] Although in its analysis of the content of the measure, the Court linked the content again to the objectives,[220] the examination of the decision's content did not alter the assessment that the decision covered a CFSP and a development cooperation policy component, without one being incidental. As the measure also fell within development cooperation policy, while it had been adopted on a CFSP legal basis, the Decision violated former Article 47 TEU.[221]

A first conclusion that emerges from an analysis of the *Small Arms and Light Weapons* case is the finding that the pre-Lisbon Treaty articles and the case law gave priority to the then first pillar or the ordinary external action competences. In the pre-Lisbon framework, it is quite evident that the Court did not have significant room to reach another decision: the pre-Lisbon Treaty included a clear preference for ordinary external action in former Article 47 TEU, as well as in Articles 2 and 3 TEU, to protect the *acquis communautaire*

---

[217] Case C-91/05, para. 75–76.
[218] Case C-91/05, para. 88, 92, 96.
[219] Case C-91/05, para. 89–91.
[220] Case C-91/05, para. 104–105.
[221] Case C-91/05, para. 109.

and the corresponding ordinary external action. The Court's principled stance in *Small Arms and Light Weapons* was therefore in accordance with and a consequence of the former Treaty framework, which protected the former first pillar.

After the *Small Arms and Light Weapons* case, the 'possible scenarios'[222] for measures relating to both the CFSP and the non-CFSP were the following. First, if a main aim or component could be identified, the application of the centre of gravity test required that measures would be based on that single legal basis. This implied that if the measure mainly pursued a non-CFSP objective, it had to be based on the corresponding ordinary external action legal basis, although it could cover incidental CFSP elements. Vice versa, if the measure mainly pursued CFSP objectives and only incidentally ordinary external action, the measure should be based on a CFSP legal basis, although, as will be explained below, the centre of gravity seemed to benefit ordinary external action. Second, if a measure equally related to the CFSP and the non-CFSP, without one element being incidental, priority was given to the TFEU legal basis: if the measure could be based on a non-CFSP competence, it should have been based on that competence.[223] The priority granted to ordinary external action and the protection of the *acquis communautaire* in the pre-Lisbon era therefore followed from both the Court's principled stance on the impossibility to combine a CFSP and a non-CFSP legal basis and its subsequent conclusion that no measure could be adopted under the CFSP if it was capable to be adopted under the ordinary external action competences.[224]

In its decision on the choice of the correct legal basis, the Court followed to a certain extent the traditional rules on the choice of legal basis. It used the aim and content as the basis to determine the correct legal basis, while it also used a centre of gravity test when the measure pursued a twofold aim or covered a twofold component.[225] In this regard, the Court also consequently applied the centre of gravity test vis-à-vis the CFSP: if the measure had as its main aim and component the implementation of the CFSP, it was a CFSP measure.[226] The Court, however, took a principled position on the impossibility to use

---

[222] C. Hillion, R. Wessel, 'Competence distribution in EU external relations after ECOWAS: clarification or continued fuzziness?', 2 Common Market Law Review, 2009, 574.

[223] G. De Baere, T. Van den Sanden, 104.

[224] A. Dashwood, 'The continuing bipolarity of EU external action', in I. Govaere, P. Van Elsuwege, E. Lannon, S. Adam (eds), *The European Union in the world: essays in honour of Marc Maresceau*, Nijhoff, 2014, 11.

[225] C-91/05, 73, referring to C-211/01, *Commission/Council*, EU:C:2003:452, para. 39; C-338/01, *Commission/Council*, EU:C:2004:253, para. 55; C-94/03, para. 35; C-176/03, para. 51–53; C-440/05, para. 71–73.

[226] C-91/05, para. 71–72.

a dual CFSP and non-CFSP legal basis when a measure equally related to the CFSP and a non-CFSP competence. The Court interpreted 'affecting' in the sense of former Article 47 TEU by determining that a CFSP measure having legal effects affected ordinary EU external action whenever it could have been adopted on the basis of ordinary external action.[227] Former Article 47 TEU therefore prevented the EU from taking CFSP action if that action could also be taken under the ordinary external action competences.[228] With the conclusion that a measure could not be adopted under the CFSP if it was capable of being adopted on the basis of a TFEU competence, the Court followed the Advocate General's reasoning that if a measure *can* be adopted on the basis of ordinary external action, it *should* be adopted on that basis.[229]

The Court's determination of the correct legal basis in the *Small Arms and Light Weapons* case has been criticised in this light for being too rigid.[230] Also here, like in *Philippines PCA*, it could indeed be argued that the Court's starting point was the assessment of the possibility to establish the measure on the basis of development cooperation policy to subsequently conclude that, on the basis of aim and content, the measure could have been based on development cooperation policy.[231] The central criterion to establish whether a violation of former Article 47 TEU took place was therefore the assessment if the measure could have been based on development cooperation policy. Hence, one could argue that the centre of gravity test was not consequently applied vis-à-vis the CFSP and the non-CFSP, as it clearly applied in favour of ordinary external action.

In the *Small Arms and Light Weapons* case, the Court ruled out the possibility to establish a measure on a dual CFSP and non-CFSP legal basis. It did not, however, base this conclusion on the argument of the procedural incompatibility of both legal bases, as it previously did in its traditional case law on

---

227 C-91/05, para. 60.

228 G. De Baere, *Constitutional principles of EU external relations*, 289, referring to the Opinion of Advocate General Mengozzi in C-91/05, point 116.

229 Opinion of Advocate General Mengozzi in C-91/05, point 116.

230 B. Van Vooren, 'The Small Arms judgment in an age of constitutional turmoil', 231; A. Dashwood, 'The continuing bipolarity of EU external action', 12; G. De Baere, *Constitutional principles of EU external relations*, 291. Also, AG Mengozzi considered that the aim of improving the social and economic development of the countries concerned 'appeared rather remote, indirect and secondary' to the CFSP aim of preserving regional security. As a consequence, according to him, the Decision did not violate former Article 47 TEU: Opinion of Advocate General Mengozzi in C-91/05, points 204–206; 213; 221.

231 Case C-91/05, para. 71–72 compared to para. 78.

the choice of the correct legal basis in the area of the ordinary competences.[232] Instead, it held that, as a principle, former Article 47 TEU prevented measures from being adopted on a dual CFSP and non-CFSP legal basis.[233] The combination of a CFSP and a non-CFSP legal basis was therefore in principle not permitted.[234] This assessment had severe consequences on the possibility to adopt integrated, and therefore coherent, measures that relate both to the CFSP and to the non-CFSP development cooperation policy in particular. As was analysed in Chapter 1, several challenges in developing countries require the adoption of an integrated approach, addressing several issues in an inclusive manner, including solutions that relate to both CFSP and non-CFSP action. By applying a centre of gravity test, it was still possible for the institutions to adopt integrated measures, addressing both the CFSP and development cooperation policy, as long as one element was incidental to the other. However, integrated measures or cross-pillar measures that equally address the CFSP and development cooperation policy were principally excluded on the basis of the Court's case law. This entailed that a strategy addressing both CFSP and development cooperation policy issues could not be adopted in a single instrument, which might have been necessary in light of coherence.[235] The consequence was that such a strategy needed to be adopted on the basis of two separate acts, one CFSP measure and one development cooperation policy instrument.[236]

The impossibility to use a dual CFSP and non-CFSP legal basis, as it followed from *Small Arms and Light Weapons*, complicated the attainment of coherent EU external action, as it prevented the adoption of all-encompassing legal instruments.[237] The pre-Lisbon delimitation was nevertheless quite straightforward from the perspective of the principle of conferral: the non-CFSP had priority, unless the instrument was undoubtedly a CFSP measure. In that light, the Court's principled case law was indeed effective in protecting ordinary external action from the CFSP, as required by the Treaty framework at that time. The pre-Lisbon delimitation between development cooperation policy

---

[232] Case C-300/89, *Commission/Council*, EU:C:1991:244. See: G. De Baere, 'From "Don't mention the Titanium Dioxide judgment" to "I mentioned it once, but I think I got away with it all right". Reflections on the choice of legal basis in EU external relations after the Legal Basis for Restrictive Measures judgment', Cambridge Yearbook of European Legal Studies, 2013, 537–562.

[233] Case C-91/05, para. 76–77.

[234] G. De Baere, *Constitutional principles of EU external relations*, 287.

[235] Ibid., 292.

[236] C. Hillion, R. Wessel, 'Competence distribution in EU external relations after ECOWAS: clarification or continued fuzziness?', 574–575.

[237] P. Eeckhout, *EU External Relations Law*, 180.

and the CFSP was therefore characterised by a certain degree of clarity, which was, however, detrimental to coherent action.[238]

3.2 Quest for Coherence with an Integrated, yet Still Distinct, CFSP

3.2.1 New Treaty framework

Despite the formal depillarisation installed by the Treaty of Lisbon, the CFSP is still very much a specific area of EU external action: Article 24 (1) TEU explicitly recognises that 'the common foreign and security policy is subject to specific rules and procedures'. This is demonstrated by the fact that the area still follows its own decision-making procedures in order to adopt distinct instruments by certain actors. The distinct character of the CFSP competence is further demonstrated by Article 2(4) TFEU in which the CFSP is singled out in the categorisation of competences. Practically speaking, the distinct character of the CFSP is further indicated by its location in a separate chapter in a separate treaty: the specific provisions on the CFSP are laid down in Chapter 2 of Title V of the TEU, while the provisions governing the ordinary external action are formulated in Part Five of the TFEU. Hence, despite the formal depillarisation achieved in the Treaty of Lisbon, de facto different pillars are still standing between the CFSP and the non-CFSP. Van Vooren describes the structure as follows: 'rather than merging the first and second pillar, the Lisbon Treaty connects them under the umbrella of the Union'.[239] There is therefore still a need to define the limits of each competence area.[240] The former third pillar, by contrast, was integrated into the overall EU framework. In particular, the continued distinct character of the CFSP, its specific institutional and procedural set-up make the question about the choice of the correct legal basis in the delimitation between development cooperation policy and the CFSP still highly relevant and controversial.[241]

While the CFSP remains a distinct area of action, the Treaty of Lisbon made the CFSP at the same time subject to general EU principles.[242] The Treaty of Lisbon has created a single Union order of which the CFSP is part. In line therewith, the common principles, values, procedures, and institutional frame-

---

238 C. Hillion, R. Wessel, 'Competence distribution in EU external relations after ECOWAS: Clarification or continued fuzziness?', 574–575; 581.

239 B. Van Vooren, 'The Small Arms judgment in an age of constitutional turmoil', 239.

240 Advocate General Bot in C-130/10, *Parliament/Council*, EU:C:2012:50, point 9.

241 A. Dashwood, 'The continuing bipolarity of EU external action', 11.

242 C. Eckes, 'The CFSP and other EU policies: a difference in nature?', 4 European Foreign Affairs Review, 2015, 550.

work apply to the CFSP as well.[243] Post-Lisbon case law further confirms that the CFSP is increasingly subject to these common principles.[244] Post-Lisbon, the CFSP therefore finds itself in the contradictory situation in which it is still recognised as a distinct area of EU external action, while it is at the same time increasingly subject to integration in the overall Treaty framework and hence arguably approximation with the non-CFSP.[245] This could raise additional questions about the CFSP's character and its delimitation with the non-CFSP, while it would also be able to further increase the amount of disputes concerning the correct legal basis.[246]

There are in particular two major innovations brought about by the Treaty of Lisbon that further influence to an important extent the delimitation between the CFSP and the non-CFSP: the common external action objectives formulated in Article 21(2) TEU and the mutual non-affectation clause laid down in Article 40 TEU.

The provision governing the delimitation between the CFSP and the non-CFSP in the current Treaty framework is Article 40 TEU, which replaced former Article 47 TEU. The wording of the Treaty provision that governs the delimitation between the CFSP and the non-CFSP has changed fundamentally: Article 40 TEU now contains a mutual non-affectation clause, which requires that the CFSP not only cannot affect the former first pillar TFEU competences but, vice versa, the latter can also not affect the former. The ordinary (external) Union action and acquis is protected from CFSP affectation, but the CFSP's integrity is equally protected against using TFEU instruments and procedures for CFSP actions.[247] The Lisbon framework therefore ensures that the CFSP's scope is equally protected, no longer allowing priority to be given to ordinary external action: the mutual non-affectation clause laid down in Article 40 TEU gives the CFSP and the non-CFSP the same constitutional weight.[248] In that respect, the provision again corresponds with Article 1 TEU and Article

---

[243] Articles 1–2 TEU.

[244] Case C-439/13 P, *Eulex Kosovo*, EU:C:2015:753; Case C-455/14 P, *H/Council*, EU:C:2016:569; Case C-72/15, *Rosneft*, EU:C:2017:236.

[245] P. Koutrakos, 'Judicial review in the EU's Common Foreign and Security Policy', International and Comparative Law Quarterly 2017, 4.

[246] C. Eckes, 'The CFSP and other EU policies: a difference in nature?', 550.

[247] B. Van Vooren, 'The Small Arms judgment in an age of constitutional turmoil', 231; C. Hillion, 'A powerless Court? The European Court of Justice and the Common Foreign and Security Policy', in M. Cremona, A. Thies, *The European Court of Justice and external relations law: constitutional challenges*, Hart, 2014, 58.

[248] C. Hillion, R. Wessel, 'Competence distribution in EU external relations after ECOWAS: clarification or continued fuzziness?', 583.

1(2) TFEU, which state that both the TEU and the TFEU have the same legal value.[249]

A second major innovation in the Treaty of Lisbon that affects the delimitation between development cooperation policy and the CFSP is the transfer of the CFSP's specific objectives to Article 21(2) TEU, which contains the common EU external action objectives. The CFSP has lost its specific objectives, which were previously laid down in former Article 11 TEU. This article identified (i) the strengthening of the security of the Union, (ii) the perseverance of peace and strengthening of international security, (iii) the promotion of international cooperation, and (iv) the development and consolidation of democracy and the rule of law and respect for human rights and fundamental freedoms as the objectives of the Union's CFSP. Currently, Article 24(1) TEU holds that the CFSP covers all areas of foreign policy and all questions relating to the Union's security, including the progressive framing of a common defence policy.[250] Article 24(2) TEU underscores that the conduct, definition, and implementation of the CFSP take place within the framework of the principles and objectives of the Union's external action, which is confirmed by Article 23 TEU, which in turn refers back to the common external action objectives.

Article 21(2) TEU and Article 40 TEU, the central provisions in the delimitation between the CFSP and the non-CFSP, demonstrate the ambiguous character of the Treaty framework. The latter in turn affects the scope of the CFSP and its delimitation with other areas. The new Treaty framework at first sight arguably establishes a more proper balance between the principles of delimitation and coherence: Article 40 TEU grants the CFSP the same weight as the non-CFSP, while Article 21(2) TEU strongly reinforces coherence in a compulsory manner.[251] However, despite the fact that Article 40 TEU grants equal weight to the CFSP and the non-CFSP, its aim is still to govern the delimitation of competences. The overall external action objectives laid down in Article 21(2) TEU, on the other hand, aim to strengthen the overall coherence of EU external action by guiding all EU external action towards the achievement of the common objectives, regardless of the applicable specific competence. In

[249] This mirrors how former Article 47 TEU was based on former Articles 2 and 3 TEU.

[250] This should be understood in light of the Treaty framework and Article 40 TEU in particular: the CFSP covers 'all areas of foreign policy' to the extent that does not invade on other areas of Union external action: G. De Baere, *Constitutional principles of EU external relations*, 102.

[251] C. Hillion, R. Wessel, 'Competence distribution in EU external relations after ECOWAS: Clarification or continued fuzziness?', 581.

that sense, they no longer function as competence conferring provisions.[252] The common objectives therefore require both the CFSP and the non-CFSP to be steered towards the achievement of the same common objectives, while Article 40 TEU still requires that the CFSP and the non-CFSP be separated. As Advocate General Bot puts it: 'the Treaties have not abolished or merged the different Union policies and the corresponding legal bases through which these horizontal objectives are to be achieved, and each measure remains distinct and subject to its own legal basis and decision-making rules'.[253] This contradiction in the Treaty framework between Article 21(2) TEU and Article 40 TEU demonstrates the 'fuzziness', as Hillion and Wessel call it, between the principles of the allocation of competences on the one hand and the aim to attain coherence on the other hand that is inherent in the EU.[254]

The principles laid down in Article 21(2) TEU on the one hand and in Article 40 TEU on the other hand, combined with the loss of specific CFSP objectives, raise the question on how to delimitate the CFSP from the non-CFSP. It is clear that the *Small Arms and Light Weapons* case law, which granted priority to TFEU external action, can no longer be applied in the post-Lisbon framework: the equal constitutional weight that the CFSP and the non-CFSP have acquired prevents such a hierarchical relationship.[255] What is unclear, however, is how the CFSP and development cooperation policy should be delimitated from each other. The disappearance of the specific CFSP objectives raises in particular the question whether a centre of gravity test, which mainly uses an objectives-based approach to determine that centre of gravity, as applied in *Small Arms and Light Weapons*, is still a valid methodology to determine the correct legal basis between development cooperation policy and the CFSP post-Lisbon.[256] It is clear that the application of a revised centre of gravity test

---

[252] B. Van Vooren, 'The Small Arms judgment in an age of constitutional turmoil', 240–241.

[253] Advocate General Bot in C-658/11, point 23.

[254] C. Hillion, R. Wessel, 'Competence distribution in EU external relations after ECOWAS: Clarification or continued fuzziness?', 552.

[255] Ibid., 583; B. Van Vooren, 'The Small Arms judgment in an age of constitutional turmoil', 243.

[256] G. De Baere, 'From "Don't mention the Titanium Dioxide Judgment" to "I mentioned it once, but I think I got away with it all right"', 554; G. De Baere, T. Van den Sanden, 103–108; C. Hillion, R. Wessel, 'Competence distribution in EU external relations ater ECOWAS: Clarification or continued fuzziness?', 583; B. Van Vooren, 'The Small Arms judgment in an age of constitutional turmoil', 242; P. Van Elsuwege, 'EU external action after the collapse of the pillar structure: In search of a new balance between delimitation and consistency', 4 Common Market Law Review, 2010, 1004; C. Hillion, 'A powerless Court? The European Court of Justice and the Common Foreign and Security Policy', 60.

which goes beyond an objectives-based analysis is the only viable solution to delimitate the CFSP and the non-CFSP from each other. The next section will analyse how this revised test is indeed emerging in the Court's post-Lisbon case law. For the specific delimitation between development cooperation and the CFSP, the case law on the scope of EU development cooperation will prove to be crucial as well.

3.2.2 Delimitation between the CFSP and the non-CFSP: confirmation of a balanced centre of gravity test

Case law is further shaping the delimitation between development cooperation and the CFSP as governed by the framework set by the Treaty of Lisbon. Of particular importance in this regard are the *Legal Basis for Restrictive Measures*,[257] the *Tanzania Agreement*,[258] the *PCA Kazakhstan*,[259] and the *CEPA Armenia*[260] cases. They demonstrate that the Court uses a centre of gravity test to delineate the CFSP from the TFEU competences and applying the *Portugal/Council* and *PCA Philippines* test in particular. As such, the rules on the choice of legal basis are unified. However, the Treaty provisions governing the distinct nature of the CFSP provoke continued difficulties with delimiting the CFSP and the TFEU competences. They relate to the criteria that need to be used to determine that centre of gravity, as well as to the role of the common external action objectives laid down in Article 21(2) TEU and the mutual non-affectation clause established in Article 40 TEU.

In light of the principles established in the case law, it is opportune to first discuss the *Legal Basis for Restrictive Measures* and *Tanzania Agreement* cases together. In the *Legal Basis for Restrictive Measures* case,[261] the Parliament had asked the Court to annul Regulation 1286/2009 imposing restrictive measures directed against persons and entities associated with Usama bin Laden, Al-Qaida, and the Taliban.[262] As a response to the *Kadi*

[257] Case C-130/10, *Parliament/Council*, EU:C:2012:472.
[258] Case C-263/14, *Parliament/Council*, EU:C:2016:435.
[259] Case C-244/17, *Commission/Council*, EU:C:2018:662.
[260] Case C-180/20, *Commission/Council*, EU:C:2021:658.
[261] See for an extensive discussion: G. De Baere, 'From "Don't mention the Titanium Dioxide Judgment" to "I mentioned it once, but I think I got away with it all right". Reflections on the choice of legal basis in EU external relations after the Legal Basis for Restrictive Measures judgment', Cambridge Yearbook of European Legal Studies, 2013, 537–562.
[262] Regulation 1286/2009 amending Regulation (EC) No 881/2002 imposing certain specific restrictive measures directed against certain persons and entities associated with Usama bin Laden, the Al-Qaida network and the Taliban, OJ 2009 L346/42.

judgment,[263] this regulation amends Regulation 881/2002[264] in order to ensure that the listing procedure to impose restrictive measures takes place in accordance with fundamental rights standards, particularly the right to be heard. The Parliament argued that the regulation was wrongly based on Article 215 TFEU, on the EU's external action in the context of which the Parliament is merely informed, as the correct legal basis should have been Article 75 TFEU on the AFSJ, which involves the Parliament on the basis of co-decision. The *Tanzania Agreement* case concerned the correct legal basis of the agreement at issue, which related to the transfer to Tanzania of persons arrested and detained by EUNAVFOR. Following several resolutions adopted in 2008 by the UN Security Council about piracy in the Gulf of Aden and Horn of Africa region, the EU adopted a joint action in support of these resolutions.[265] The joint action established operation ATALANTA (EU NAVFOR), the Union's first Common Security and Defence Policy (CSDP) naval mission. It provides *inter alia* for the transfer of persons arrested and detained by EU NAVFOR to a third country which exercises jurisdiction in order to prosecute them in accordance with international human rights standards. In view of attaining this aim, the EU concludes several international agreements with third countries in the region. This case concerns the Council Decision on the signature and conclusion of the Agreement with Tanzania,[266] which was based on Article 37 TEU and Article 218(6), second subparagraph TFEU concerning the conclusion of international agreements that relate exclusively to the CFSP. The Parliament requested the annulment of the Decision, based on the argument that (i) the Decision was adopted on the wrong legal basis, as the agreement had a twofold purpose, covering AFSJ issues as well, and therefore did not classify as an agreement relating exclusively to the CFSP and (ii) the Parliament was not immediately

---

263 Joined Cases C-584/10 P, C-593/10 P and C-595/10 P, *European Commission and Others/Yassin Abdullah Kadi*, EU:C:2013:518.

264 Regulation 881/2002 imposing certain specific restrictive measures directed against certain persons and entities associated with Usama bin Laden, the Al-Qaida network and the Taliban, and repealing Council Regulation (EC) No 467/2001 prohibiting the export of certain goods and services to Afghanistan, strengthening the flight ban and extending the freeze of funds and other financial resources in respect of the Taliban of Afghanistan, OJ 2002 L139/9.

265 Joint Action 2008/851/CFSP of 10 November 2008 on a European Union military operation to contribute to the deterrence, prevention and repression of acts of piracy and armed robbery off the Somali coast, OJ 2008 L301/33.

266 Council Decision 2014/198/CFSP of 10 March 2014 on the signature and conclusion of the Agreement between the European Union and the United Republic of Tanzania on the conditions of transfer of suspected pirates and associated seized property from the European Union-led naval force to the United Republic of Tanzania, OJ 2014 L10//1.

and fully informed at all stages of the procedure, as required by Article 218(10) TFEU.

The Court determined the relevant rules on the choice of legal basis in a 'preliminary observations' section in the *Legal Basis for Restrictive Measures* case, emphasising the importance and broader relevance of its statement. As regards the rules applicable to the choice of legal basis, the Court returned to the traditional principles on the choice of the correct legal basis, as they were developed in the framework of the choice of legal basis issues between the ordinary TFEU competences.[267] The first step in the long-standing case law is that the choice of legal basis must rest on objective factors amenable to judicial review, including the aim and content of the measure. If a measure pursues a twofold purpose or has a twofold component, and if one of those is identifiable as the main or predominant purpose or component, the measure must be founded on a single legal basis: the legal basis that corresponds with the main or predominant purpose or component. Exceptionally, when it is established that the measure pursues several objectives that are inseparably linked, without one being secondary and indirect to the other, the measure must be founded on the various corresponding legal bases. Pre-Lisbon, the Court determined in the *Small Arms and Light Weapons* case[268] that the use of a dual legal basis was in principle impossible when confronted with a CFSP and a non-CFSP legal basis. In the *Legal Basis for Restrictive Measures* case, the Court continued its reasoning by referring to the traditional case law developed to determine the correct legal basis in the ordinary competences of the Union, as laid down in the *Titanium Dioxide* case.[269] As such, it held that such a dual legal basis is impossible when the procedures laid down for the relevant legal bases are incompatible with each other. The Court therefore explicitly confirmed this case law in the post-Lisbon period and to the delimitation between the CFSP and the non-CFSP.[270] The Court further specified that *in casu* measures based on Article 75 TFEU are adopted following the ordinary legislative procedure, with full participation of the European Parliament and qualified majority voting in the Council. Article 215(2) TFEU, by contrast, entails a mere informing of the European Parliament, while the CFSP decision which necessarily precedes the decision adopted on the basis of Article 215(2) TFEU brings about unanimous voting in the Council.

---

[267] Case C-130/10, *Parliament/Council*, EU:C:2012:472, para. 42–46; Case C-263/14, *Parliament/Council*, EU:C:2016:435, para. 43–44.

[268] Case C-91/05. *Commission/Council*, ECLI:EU:C:2008:288.

[269] C-300/89, *Commission v Council*, EU:C:1991:244. G. De Baere, 'From "Don't mention the Titanium Dioxide judgment" to "I mentioned it once, but I think I got away with it all right".'

[270] Case C-130/10, para. 46.

The Court's pre-Lisbon and post-Lisbon case law on the delimitation between the CFSP and the non-CFSP is therefore fundamentally different. While a dual CFSP and non-CFSP legal basis was in principle excluded on the basis of former Article 47 TEU in the pre-Lisbon era, the Court establishes the impossibility to combine CFSP and non-CFSP legal bases in the *Legal Basis for Restrictive Measures* case on their procedural incompatibility, building on old case law stemming from the choice of legal basis in ordinary EU competences. By applying the general line of case law on the choice of the correct legal basis, the delimitation between the CFSP and the non-CFSP is normalised. In the *Small Arms and Light Weapons* case,[271] the Court could have based its reasoning on the procedural incompatibility of the procedures as well, as the *Titanium Dioxide* case[272] had already laid down this principle in the choice of legal basis case law.[273] The possible legal bases in the *Small Arms and Light Weapons* case indeed suffered from procedural incompatibility: a former CFSP joint action is adopted solely by the Council acting unanimously, while development cooperation measures are adopted in accordance with the co-decision procedure. The Court, however, took a principled position on the impossibility to combine a CFSP and a non-CFSP legal basis, in accordance with the principled stance laid down in Article 47 TEU.

In the *Legal Basis for Restrictive Measures* case the Court, by contrast, does not as a principle exclude a combination of a CFSP and a non-CFSP legal basis. The Court held in the preliminary section of the judgment that a combination of Article 75 TFEU and Article 215 TFEU is impossible because of procedural incompatibilities. The Court concluded that 'Differences of that kind are such as to render those procedures incompatible'.[274] The specification 'differences of that kind' seems to indicate that the Court did not want to render a general statement, by principally excluding the possibility to use a dual legal basis.

In *Tanzania Agreement*[275] the Court adopted a centre of gravity test to determine the correct legal basis, in which the content and the context play a crucial role to determine the correct legal basis. As has been argued in the context of the assessment of the scope of the development cooperation policy competence as well, the application of an objectives-based centre of gravity test in order to determine the scope of the CFSP and its delimitation with other areas is ill-suited.[276] This is arguably the case for external action in general and international agreements, which often combine provisions in a wide variety of

---

271 C-91/05.
272 C-300/89.
273 G. De Baere, *Constitutional principles of EU external relations*, 287.
274 Case C-130/10, para. 48.
275 Case C-263/14, *Parliament/Council*, EU:C:2016:435.
276 G. De Baere, T. Van den Sanden, 105.

fields, making it difficult to determine the main aim or component on the one hand and the ancillary or incidental aims or components on the other hand.[277]

In *Small Arms and Light Weapons*,[278] the Court relied heavily on an objectives-based centre of gravity test to delimitate the CFSP and development cooperation from each other. While the Court assessed both the aim and content of the measure to determine the correct legal basis, it attached significantly greater importance to the measure's aim: the Court analysed in depth the objective of the measure, while the assessment of the content only led to further confirming the analysis on the objective.[279] Finally, the Court concluded that if the provisions of a CFSP measure, on account of both aim and content, had as their main purpose the implementation of a TFEU competence, and if they could properly have been adopted on this basis, they should have been adopted on this basis.[280] As already pointed out above, the disappearance of specific CFSP objectives makes the application of an objectives-based centre of gravity test to delimitate the CFSP from the non-CFSP difficult. Particularly as regards the analysis in the *Small Arms and Light Weapons* case, the distinction suggested by Advocate General Mengozzi between the CFSP objective of 'preserving peace and/or strengthening international security' and the development cooperation policy objective of 'social and economic development'[281] would no longer resolve the delimitation question between ordinary EU external action and the CFSP: both would fall under the general objectives of the Union's external action, under Articles 21(2)(c) and 21(2)(d) TEU, respectively.[282]

In the *Legal Basis for Restrictive Measures* and *Mauritius Agreement* cases, Advocate General Bot had suggested a striking interpretation of the delimitation question in light of the lack of specific CFSP objectives. He considered that the objectives set out in sub-paragraphs (a)–(c) 'are among those traditionally assigned to that [the CFSP] policy',[283] as the objectives defined in Article 21(2)(a)–(c) TEU are in essence the same as those assigned to the CFSP under ex Article 11(1) TEU. However, the objective in Article 21(2)(b) TEU to 'consolidate and support democracy, the rule of law, human rights and the principles of international law' also corresponds to the objective

---

277 M. Cremona, 'Balancing Union and Member State Interests: Opinion 1/2008, Choice of Legal Base and the Common Commercial Policy under the Treaty of Lisbon', 5 *European Law Review*, 2010, 688–691.

278 C-91/05.

279 Case C-91/05, para. 100.

280 Case C-91/05, para. 60..

281 Opinion of AG Mengozzi in Case C-91/05, point 189.

282 G. De Baere, T. Van den Sanden, 105.

283 Opinion of AG Bot in Case C-130/10, *Parliament v Council*, points 62–63.

assigned to development cooperation policy, as it was laid down in former Article 177(2) TEC, with the addition of the 'principles of international law'. The Advocate General further noted that the objectives defined in Article 21(2)(a)–(c) TEU are consistent with the provisions of the first sub-paragraph of Article 24(1) TEU. He concluded from this that action by the EU on the international stage that pursues one or more of the objectives referred to in Article 21(2)(a)–(c) TEU, in particular the objective of preserving peace and strengthening international security, must be regarded as falling within the sphere of the CFSP.[284] Advocate General Bot reiterated its reasoning in the *Mauritius Agreement* case.[285] Despite the fact that the Court did not analyse the choice of the substantive legal basis, as it argued that Parliament had not opposed the substantive legal basis,[286] the Advocate General did go into an assessment of the choice of the correct legal basis.[287] He considered it to be necessary to verify the substantive legal basis before determining the procedural legal basis.[288] In analysing the correct legal basis, Advocate General Bot reiterated his view that the objectives in Article 21(2)(a)–(c) TEU are 'among those that are traditionally assigned to the CFSP'.[289] To this he also added Article 21(2)(h) TEU, which concerns the promotion of an international system based on stronger multilateral cooperation and good global governance. However, that objective was added by the Treaty of Lisbon as a common objective of EU external action. The Advocate General also argued that Article 21(2) TEU should be read together with the more specific provisions applicable to each

---

284 Ibid., point 64.

285 Case C-658/11, *Parliament/Council*, EU:C:2014:2025.

286 The Court in Mauritius Agreement did not explicitly analyse the choice of the substantive legal basis of the decision. The Court's analysis to determine the appropriate procedure under Article 218 TFEU is entirely based on the symmetry between the internal and external division of competences with the aim of ensuring legal certainty. In that regard, Article 218(6)(a)(v) TFEU reflects externally the division of competences that applies internally. As the measure was based on the CFSP legal basis of Article 37 TEU, without a further assessment of the correctness of this legal basis by the Court, the agreement had to be based on the procedure for concluding agreements in the area of the CFSP. That is merely an application of the general rule that the substantive legal basis of a measure determines the procedures to be followed in adopting that measure.

287 The Advocate General stated that 'at the request of the Court at the hearing, the Parliament stated that, in its view, the contested decision should have been founded on the following substantive legal bases, namely, in addition to Article 37 TEU, Articles 82 TFEU, 87 TFEU and 209 TFEU': Opinion of AG Bot in C-658/11, point 40.

288 Opinion of AG Bot in C-658/11, point 20.

289 Opinion of AG Bot in Case C-658/11, points 86–87; cf Opinion of AG Bot in Case C-130/10, points 62–63.

policy in order to determine the Union policy to which a certain objective is more specifically related.[290]

The Advocate General's assessment cannot be followed. The analysis in which he links specific objectives that are part of the common external action objectives to the CFSP area is a clear example of 'path dependency', which refers to the practice of applying pre-Lisbon patterns to the post-Lisbon framework.[291] However, such an interpretation is *contra legem*: Article 21(2) TEU unequivocally regards the objectives as common to EU external action as a whole.[292] Linking certain objectives laid down in Article 21(2) TEU to a specific area of EU competence in order to determine the correct legal basis makes the insertion of the common external action objectives of Article 21(2) TEU redundant. While Advocate General Bot's suggestion to read Article 21(2) TEU together with the more specific provisions applicable to each policy could be a useful tool to further interpret the external action objectives, this cannot be applied in such a way as to limit certain objectives exclusively to one single policy. As argued above, the common external action objectives have an interpretative function but not a delimiting role. Article 21(3) TEU clearly states that the Union must 'respect the principles and pursue the objectives set out in paragraphs 1 and 2 in the development and implementation of the different areas of the Union's external action'. This indicates a mainstreaming requirement and emphasises the common character of the objectives laid down in Article 21(2) TEU. They can therefore not be used to link them to one specific competence area only in order to establish that area's competence boundaries.[293]

Contrary to the reasoning put forward by the Advocate General, the Court did not follow the Advocate General's reasoning that measures that pursue one of the objectives mentioned in Article 21(2)(a)–(c) TEU are CFSP measures. Although it reached the same conclusion in *Legal Basis for Restrictive Measures*, namely that Article 215 TFEU is the correct legal basis, it followed a different reasoning to assess the correct legal basis *in casu*. After establishing the link between Article 215(2) TFEU and the CFSP, it referred to Article 21(2)(c) TEU and Article 24(1) TEU to hold that measures aimed at

---

290 Opinion of AG Bot in Case C-658/11, point 88. On the basis of such an analysis, AG Bot concluded that the Mauritius Agreement fell within the scope of the CSDP: see points 88–105.

291 G. De Baere, 'From "Don't mention the Titanium Dioxide judgment" to "I mentioned it once, but I think I got away with it all right"', 555; G. De Baere, T. Van den Sanden, 106.

292 B. Van Vooren, 'The Small Arms Judgment in an Age of Constitutional Turmoil', 245; C. Hillion, R. Wessel, 582–584.

293 G. De Baere, T. Van den Sanden, 107.

preserving international peace and security can be used to combat international terrorism, as the latter constitutes a threat to international peace and security.[294] Interestingly, considering the lack of specific CFSP objectives, the Court did refer to the CSDP's objectives: it referred to the possibility in Article 43 TEU for CSDP missions to contribute to the fight against terrorism to support its claim that CFSP acts can be adopted to pursue this objective.[295] Subsequently the Court examined the aim and content of the measure to determine whether Article 215(2) TFEU is the correct legal basis. In that regard, the Court referred to the preamble of the contested regulation in order to determine its purpose.[296] Such an approach has been criticised because it might bring institutions to draft preambles so as to set the Court 'on the right track' on the choice of the correct legal basis.[297] This method to assess the appropriate legal basis of a measure has been referred to as a form of 'legislative hazard'.[298] Because of these difficulties which follow from an objectives-based reasoning, it is important that the choice of the correct legal basis in order to delimitate the CFSP from the non-CFSP is based on a theory that addresses aim, content, and context.[299] That is exactly what is emerging in the Court's case law: the analysis of the content and the context is materialising and coming at the forefront in the analysis of the appropriate legal basis.

Already in *Legal Basis for Restrictive Measures*, the Court did not follow an absolute objectives-based approach to determine the correct legal basis, but took into account the context and the wording as well.[300] First, the Court attached great importance to the connection that Article 215 TFEU has with the CFSP. Measures adopted on the basis of Article 215(2) TFEU necessarily find their origin in a CFSP instrument: they cannot be adopted, unless there is a CFSP Decision that lays the basis for the adoption of restrictive measures.[301]

---

294 C-130/10, para. 59–63.

295 C. Hillion, 'A powerless Court? The European Court of Justice and the Common Foreign and Security Policy', 62.

296 Case C-130/10, para. 68 and 70.

297 See, eg, N. Emiliou, 499. See also the suggestion in A. Dashwood, 'The Law and Practice of CFSP Joint Actions', in M. Cremona and B. de Witte (eds), *EU Foreign Relations Law: Constitutional Fundamentals*, Hart, 2008, 76.

298 M. Klamert, 'Conflict of legal basis: no legality and no basis but a bright future under the Lisbon Treaty?', 4 *European Law Review*, 2010, 502 and 505; M. Cremona, 'A reticent court? Policy objectives and the Court of Justice', 21–23.

299 G. De Baere, 'From "Don't mention the Titanium Dioxide judgment" to "I mentioned it once, but I think I got away with it all right"', 557; P. Van Elsuwege, 'The potential for inter-institutional conflicts before the Court of Justice: Impact of the Lisbon Treaty', in M. Cremona, A. Thies (eds), *The European Court of Justice and external relations law*, Hart, 2014, 118.

300 G. De Baere, T. Van den Sanden, 107.

301 C-130/10, para. 58.

The Court explicitly referred to Article 215 TFEU, as well as the old Articles 60 and 301 TEC, as providing a bridge between the CFSP and the non-CFSP in the adoption of restrictive measures.[302] Second, the Court took into account the 'system of interaction between the Security Council and the Union'[303] that exists in the adoption of restrictive measures: the Regulations that lay down restrictive measures are an example of instruments by which the Union gives effect to actions decided upon by the Security Council to preserve international peace and security.[304]

The importance of the context of a measure as a criterion to determine the centre of gravity is further strengthened in the *Tanzania Agreement* case. The Court first developed an analysis of the content of the measure, holding that the Agreement concerns the transfer of persons arrested and detained by EUNAVFOR to prosecute them in third countries, in a manner which is in accordance with international human rights standards.[305] The Court subsequently examined the aim of the measure, while it also established the aim on the basis of the context of the measure. The Court again referred to the preamble to further clarify the aim pursued by the measure to conclude that the agreement between the EU and Tanzania is an essential element to achieve the objectives of Operation Atalanta or EUNAVFOR.[306] The Court therefore explicitly linked the aim of the agreement to the achievement of the aims of Operation Atalanta, with which it is 'intimately linked'. As the Agreement would be 'devoid of purpose' without the Operation, it is 'merely ancillary to the EUNAVFOR action'.[307] As EUNAVFOR is undoubtedly part of CFSP action and considering the fact that the EU–Tanzania Agreement is inseparably linked[308] to the achievement of the Operation's aims of preserving international peace and security, the Agreement falls predominantly within the CFSP, according to the Court.[309] The analysis of the aim is therefore mainly established on an assessment of the context of the Agreement, namely its link with the CFSP. This connection is indeed quite straightforward, as the Agreement is set up to further implement the transfer of persons arrested and

---

302 C-130/10, para. 59.

303 C-130/10, para. 71.

304 C-130/10, para. 67

305 C-263/14, para. 45–46.

306 C-263/14, para. 48–49. Council Decision 2014/198/CFSP on the signing and conclusion of the Agreement between the European Union and the United Republic of Tanzania on the conditions of transfer of suspected pirates and associated seized property from the European Union-led naval force to the United Republic of Tanzania, OJ 2014 L108/1.

307 C-263/14, para. 51.

308 C-263/14, para. 53.

309 C-263/14, para. 53–55.

detained by EUNAVFOR. Also in other areas, more recently the context of a measure has emerged in the case law as an element in determining the centre of gravity.[310] Nevertheless, the application of a context criterion to assess the centre of gravity has been criticised in the literature.[311] Indeed, it is important to keep in mind that in some cases the choice between the 'context' or the 'content' criterion would be decisive for the outcome of the choice of legal basis, like in the *Mauritius Agreement* case:[312] while the decision takes place in a CFSP context, the provisions of the agreement would arguably relate more to the Area of Freedom, Security and Justice.[313] Moreover, it should be acknowledged that both in the *Legal Basis for Restrictive Measures* case[314] and in the *Tanzania Agreement* case,[315] the relationship with the CFSP was quite obvious. The *Legal Basis for Restrictive Measures* case concerned the issue of restrictive measures, which have an established link with the CFSP, while the *Tanzania Agreement* was necessarily linked to the actions in the framework of EUNAVFOR.

With the *Kazakhstan PCA* case,[316] the Court addressed the delimitation between development cooperation and CFSP in particular and confirmed the application of the *Portugal/Council* and *Philippines PCA* test to delimitate development cooperation and the CFSP. In this case, the Commission asked the Court to annul Council Decision (EU) 2017/477 on the EU position on the working arrangements of bodies set up by the EU–Kazakhstan PCA. The Commission had based the proposal for this decision Article 218(9) TFEU in conjunction with Article 37 TEU as its procedural legal basis and Articles 207 and 209 TFEU as its substantive legal basis. The Council, however, added

---

310 For example: Case C-81/13, *UK/Council*, EU:C:2014:2449, para. 38; Joined Cases C-626/15 and C-659/16, *European Commission/Council*, EU:C:2018:925, para. 76; 87–94.

311 S. Rodriguez Sanchez-Tabernero, 'The choice of legal basis and the principle of consistency in the procedure for conclusion of international agreements in CFSP contexts: Parliament v. Council (Pirate-Transfer Agreement with Tanzania)', 3 Common Market Law Review, 2017, 909.

312 C-658/11.

313 C. Matera, R. Wessel, 'Context or content? A CFSP or AFSJ legal basis for EU international agreements', Revista de Derecho, 2014, 1057; P. Van Elsuwege, 'Securing the institutional balance in the procedure for concluding international agreements: European Parliament v Council (Pirate Transfer Agreements with Mauritius)', 5 Common Market Law Review, 2015, 1396.

314 C-130/10.

315 C-263/14.

316 For a further analysis of this case, see: P. Van Elsuwege, G. Van der Loo, 'Legal basis litigation in relation to international agreements: Commission v. Council (Enhanced Partnership and Cooperation Agreement with Kazakhstan)', Common Market Law Review, 2019, 1333–1353.

Article 31(1) TEU and Articles 91 and 100(2) TFEU to the proposed legal bases. The Commission criticised in particular the addition of Article 31(1) TEU as a legal basis, which provides that CFSP decisions under Chapter 2 of Title V of the TEU are to be taken unanimously, except where that chapter provides otherwise. The Commission argued that, by contrast, a decision adopted pursuant to Article 218(9) TFEU is to be taken by qualified majority voting. The Court determined that as Article 218(9) TFEU does not lay down any voting rule, the applicable voting rule must be determined in each individual case by reference to Article 218(8) TFEU. Therefore, where a decision by which the Council establishes the position to be adopted on behalf of the European Union in a body set up by an agreement does not correspond to any of the cases in which the second subparagraph of Article 218(8) TFEU requires a unanimous vote, the Council must, in principle, in accordance with the first subparagraph of Article 218(8) TFEU read in conjunction with Article 218(9) TFEU, act by qualified majority when adopting that decision.[317] The first case in which the second subparagraph of Article 218(8) TFEU requires the Council to act unanimously concerns the situation where the agreement covers a field for which unanimity is required for the adoption of an EU act, thereby establishing a link between the substantive legal basis of a decision adopted under that article and the voting rule applicable to the decision's adoption. Such a field is the CFSP, since the first subparagraph of Article 31(1) TEU provides that decisions under Chapter 2 of Title V of the EU Treaty are to be taken unanimously, except where that chapter provides otherwise. Therefore, in order to determine whether a decision adopted within the framework defined in Article 218(9) TFEU covers such a field, it is necessary to refer to its substantive legal basis, the Court considered.[318] The Court then reiterates the theory and principles on choice of legal basis and concludes from this that a decision by which the Council establishes the position to be adopted on behalf of the European Union in a body set up by an agreement which concerns exclusively the CFSP must, in principle, be adopted unanimously. On the other hand, if such a decision comprises several components or pursues a number of objectives, some of which fall within the CFSP, the voting rule applicable for its adoption must be determined in the light of its main or predominant purpose or component. If the main or predominant purpose or component of the decision falls within a field in respect of which no unanimity is required for the adoption of an EU measure, that decision must be adopted by qualified majority.[319] The measures whose adoption was envisaged concern the functioning of the international

[317] C-244/17, para. 27.
[318] C-244/17, para. 29; 35.
[319] C-244/17, para. 38.

bodies set up on the basis of the PCA. Therefore, the field within which the contested decision falls must be determined in the light of the PCA as a whole, says the Court.[320]

With this, the Court went into the assessment of the substantive legal basis of the PCA as such and determined whether the choice of legal basis for the Council Decision on the signature and provisional application of the agreement had been correct. This Decision was based on the legal bases of Articles 37 and 31(1) TEU and Articles 91, 100(2) and 207 and 209 TFEU in conjunction with Article 218(5) and the second subparagraph of Article 218(8) TFEU. The Court held that although the PCA displays certain links with the CFSP, those links are not sufficient to require that the legal basis of the decision on the signing and provisional application of that agreement had to include Article 37 TEU.[321] First, the Court used a type of quantitative test to indicate that most of the provisions of the PCA fell within the CCP or development cooperation policy. Second, the Court determined that the provisions of the PCA that display a link with the CFSP, apart from being few in number in comparison with the agreement's provisions as a whole, were limited to declarations of the contracting parties on the aims and subjects that their cooperation must pursue and did not determine in concrete terms the manner in which the cooperation would be implemented.[322] Those provisions, of contributing to international and regional peace and stability and to economic development, were therefore not of a scope enabling them to be regarded as a distinct component of that agreement. On the contrary, they were incidental to that agreement's two main components constituted by the CCP and development cooperation.[323]

PCA Kazakhstan is therefore a crucial step in the case law on choice of legal basis in EU external action, in the delimitation between the CFSP and development cooperation and in the choice of legal basis for partnership and cooperation agreements in particular. The Court reconfirms the centre of gravity test to determine the choice of legal basis for international agreements in particular as well. It furthermore confirms that the specific form of the centre of gravity test, as laid down in *Portugal/Council* and *Philippines PCA*, to determine the scope of development cooperation and its agreements also applies to the delimitation with the CFSP. As such, the Court explicitly confirms the 'classical pattern' following which development cooperation policy agreements are traditionally

---

[320] C-244/17, para. 40. See also the case law cited: Case C-389/15, *Commission/ Council*, EU:C:2017:798, para. 64; Opinion 2/15, *EU-Singapore FTA*, EU:C:2017:376, para. 276.

[321] C-244/17, para. 43.

[322] C-244/17, para. 56.

[323] Case C-244/17, para. 44–46.

based on the development cooperation policy and CCP legal bases[324] – as long as the other elements respond to the test and are incidental, like the CFSP elements in the Kazakhstan PCA.

Both issues – the weight of the different criteria to determine the centre of gravity and the delimitation between development cooperation and CFSP – culminate in the *CEPA Armenia* case. As pointed out by the Advocate General, three years after *PCA Kazakhstan*, this case reflects a new stage in the dispute between the Commission and the Council regarding the appropriate legal basis for partnership agreements.[325] Like in *PCA Kazakhstan*, the case concerned the legal basis for the Council Decisions adopting the EU position to be expressed in the bodies set up by the Comprehensive and Enhanced Partnership Agreement between the European Union and the European Atomic Energy Community and their Member States, of the one part, and the Republic of Armenia, of the other part (CEPA Armenia). Initially, the Commission and the High Representative adopted a joint proposal, which also included Article 37 TEU as a substantive legal basis. However, after the *PCA Kazakhstan* case was rendered, the Commission submitted an amended proposal, in which the references to the High Representative and to Article 37 TEU as a substantive legal basis were deleted. That proposal was based on Article 218(9) TFEU as a procedural legal basis and on Articles 91, 100(2) and Articles 207 and 209 TFEU as substantive legal bases. As a reaction to the amended proposal, COREPER decided to split the act into two Council Decisions: i.e., Decision 2020/245 on the basis of Articles 91, 100(2) and Articles 207 and 209 TFEU as substantive legal bases and Article 218(8) and Article 218(9) TFEU as procedural legal bases, and Council Decision 2020/246 on the basis of Article 37 TEU and Articles 218(8) and 218(9) TFEU.

The Advocate General's Opinion gave a clear overview of how the Court approached the different elements of the centre of gravity test in its case law on the choice of legal basis and discussed in that respect *Opinion 1/78*, *Portugal/Council*, *Philippines PCA*, *Daiichi Sankyo*, *Conditional Access*, *PCA Kazakhstan*, *Tanzania Agreement*, and the *Antarctic MPAs*. On that basis, the Advocate General determined that the elements rank equally among the objective factors and that the importance attached to them depends on the specific case and is not based on a hierarchy.[326]

The Court confirmed this in its judgment by holding that the field covered by an act must be determined in each specific case having regard to all the objec-

---

[324] See above: M. Maresceau, 176–177.

[325] C-180/20, Commission/Council, EU:C:2021:495, point 1.

[326] Opinion in C-180/20, point 28.

tively identifiable factors pertaining to one or to the other of those criteria.[327] Following its previous reasoning in *PCA Kazakhstan*, the Court determined that, despite the Council having split the decision into two separate decisions, the field covered by the Partnership Agreement with Armenia and, hence, the appropriate substantive legal basis for the Council Decision has to be determined with regard to the Partnership Agreement as a whole.[328] Examining the content of the *CEPA Armenia*, the Court confirmed the *Portugal/Council* and *Philippines PCA* test on the characterisation of an agreement as a development cooperation agreement, which must be determined with regard to the agreement's essential object and not in terms of its individual clauses, provided that those clauses do not impose such extensive obligations in the specific areas that those obligations constitute objectives distinct from those of development cooperation. Applying this test to the *CEPA Armenia*, the Court used again a quantitative and a qualitative criterion. First, although Title II of the Agreement concerned subjects capable of falling within the CFSP, the Court determined that those provisions were few in number compared with the other articles of the agreement, most of which concern trade and development cooperation. Second, those provisions were for the main part limited to declarations by the contracting parties of a 'programmatic nature', which merely described the relationship between them and their common future intentions, without establishing a programme of action or determining the concrete terms governing their cooperation.[329]

As regards the aim of the *CEPA Armenia*, the Court referred to the Agreement's preamble, its objectives as listed in its Article 1, and the vast majority of its provisions, to determine that that agreement seeks principally to establish the framework for cooperation in matters of transport, trade, and development. The Court then linked this to the *Portugal/Council* and *Philippines PCA* test on the scope of development cooperation and its objectives to confirm that they are not limited to measures directly aimed at the eradication of poverty, but also pursue the general objectives of the European Union's external action, referred to in Article 21 TEU, including the objective of preserving peace, preventing conflicts, and strengthening international security as set out in Article 21(2)(c) TEU, and the objective of fostering the sustainable economic, social, and environmental development as set out in Article 21(2)(d) TEU. The Court reinforced this finding by additionally referring to its finding in *Small Arms and Light Weapons*, where it determined that the fight against the proliferation of small arms and light weapons can be seen

327 Para. 33.
328 Para. 38–40.
329 Para. 46.

as serving the objectives of the development cooperation policy.[330] Therefore, interestingly, the Court referred to the integration into development cooperation of the common external action objectives laid down in Article 21(2) TEU, while also explicitly referring in that regard to Article 21(2)(c) TEU, like it did in *Philippines PCA* to Article 21(2)(d) TEU. The Court went further into its analysis of the scope of the development cooperation objectives by confirming, with reference to *Portugal/Council* and *Philippines PCA*, the broad scope of the development cooperation objectives, in the sense that it must be possible for the measures required for their pursuit to concern a variety of specific areas, in particular in the case of an agreement establishing the framework of cooperation. The Court reiterated that to require a development cooperation agreement also to be based on other bases whenever the agreement touches on a specific area would in practice be liable to render devoid of substance the competence.[331]

Applying this to *CEPA Armenia*, the Court determined that, while some of the Agreement's aims may be linked to the CFSP, the enumeration of those specific aims is not accompanied by any programme of action or concrete terms governing cooperation in that field. As such, this is not capable of establishing that the CFSP constitutes one of the distinct components of the Agreement, outside the scope of those aspects connected with trade and development cooperation. With reference to *PCA Kazakhstan* and following the broad scope of the development cooperation objectives, the Court then found that common commercial policy, trade in transport services, and development cooperation constitute the centre of gravity of *CEPA Armenia* as its principal components, while the CFSP cannot be regarded as a distinct component of the Agreement but is, by contrast, incidental to the principal components. In this regard, the Court explicitly held that those principal components can also cover the elements of political dialogue in the Agreement, which may be linked to the CFSP.[332] Finally, the Court also addressed the context criterion. In this regard, the Court confirmed this criterion as relevant for the determination of the appropriate legal basis. Nevertheless, the Court determined that, in this specific case, there would be no specific link that would change its findings.[333]

On that basis, the Court concluded that the 'components or declarations of intention in the Partnership Agreement with Armenia which may be linked to the CFSP are not sufficient to constitute an autonomous component of that agreement'. On that basis, Decision 2020/246, based on Article 37 TEU and

---

[330] Para. 49.
[331] Para. 50–51.
[332] Para. 53.
[333] Para. 54–55.

Article 218(8) TFEU second subparagraph, must be annulled. At the same time, also Decision 2020/245 must be annulled, as on the basis of the Court's findings, that decision could also cover the incidental CFSP components and, hence, the Council could not justify adopting a separate decision on the CFSP components.[334]

With this recent line of case law, a general approach to the choice of the appropriate legal basis for instruments covering both the CFSP and other policy areas, which was lacking,[335] is emerging. In this approach, the legal basis is determined by the centre of gravity, which is identified 'all things considered',[336] providing a balance between the different objective factors to determine the legal basis,[337] their importance depending on the specific case – as pointed out by the Advocate General in *CEPA Armenia*. This balancing of the different factors addresses the difficulties caused by an objectives-based approach to determine the legal basis.[338] In this, the test on the scope of development cooperation is emerging as the standard for determining the centre of gravity and the appropriate legal basis, as it includes both the aim and content as objective factors, while allowing for the integration of the common external action objectives laid down in Article 21(2) TEU, without overstepping competence boundaries.[339] In that regard, the *Philippines PCA* test is a further completion of the centre of gravity test, as it provides more precise rules to determine the centre of gravity.[340] In *CEPA Armenia*, the Court provided a detailed assessment of the criteria, going into a rigorous assessment of both aim and content. In this regard, the Court not only further confirmed the scope of development cooperation, but also tested whether or not the CFSP provisions and objectives were sufficient to make the CFSP a distinct component of *CEPA Armenia* or whether, by contrast, they were incidental to the main components of development cooperation and CCP. Although not decisive in the specific case of *CEPA Armenia*, the Court also further established the context

---

334 Para. 56–58.

335 G. De Baere, 'From "Don't mention the Titanium Dioxide judgment" to "I mentioned it once, but I think I got away with it all right"', 557. S. Rodriguez Sanchez-Tabernero, 910.

336 A. Dashwood, 'Article 47 TEU and the Relationship between First and Second Pillar Competences', 101. Compare T. Corthaut, 'An Effective Remedy for All? Paradoxes and Controversies in Respect of Judicial Protection in the Field of the CFSP under the European Constitution', 2 *Tilburg Foreign Law Review*, 2005, 119–120.

337 G. De Baere, T. Van den Sanden, 108.

338 M. Klamert, 'Conflict of legal basis: no legality and no basis but a bright future under the Lisbon Treaty?', 505–506.

339 B. Van Vooren, 'The Small Arms Judgment in an Age of Constitutional Turnmoil', 246; G. De Baere, T. Van den Sanden, 108.

340 Opinion in Case C-180/20, point 31–32.

criterion as a relevant criterion to take into account when establishing the legal basis. With *CEPA Armenia* in particular, the Court therefore clearly confirmed the centre of gravity test, expressed in the test on the scope of development cooperation, as the standard to delimitate development cooperation and CFSP. The Court also provided clear criteria to do so with its detailed analysis on both aim and content of *CEPA Armenia.*

An important element in the delimitation between the CFSP and the non-CFSP that is not addressed in the Court's case law is Article 40 TEU. As already pointed out, the Treaty provision on the delimitation between the CFSP and the non-CFSP has changed fundamentally with the creation of the Treaty of Lisbon. In the *Legal Basis for Restrictive Measures* case, the Court did not refer to the provision. In *Tanzania Agreement*, Article 40 TEU is mentioned in the first paragraph of the Court's analysis in order to establish its jurisdiction.[341] The Court, however, did not include the provision in any way in its analysis. Also in *PCA Kazakhstan* and *CEPA Armenia*, the Court did not refer to Article 40 TEU. It is, nevertheless, clear that the Court's post-Lisbon case law does aim to respect the equal weight that is given to the CFSP in the post-Lisbon framework by Article 1 and 40 TEU and Article 1 TFEU. The *Legal Basis for Restrictive Measures*,[342] the *Mauritius Agreement*,[343] and *Tanzania Agreement*[344] cases prove that the prevalence of the TFEU competences has disappeared, as the CFSP was found to be the appropriate legal basis. In determining the legal basis, the Court implicitly necessarily also interprets the CFSP provisions and its scope.[345] Most importantly, by applying the centre of gravity test as a general principle of the theory on choice of legal basis to the delimitation between CFSP and non-CFSP, the Court applies the rationale of the non-affectation clause to the delimitation between CFSP and non-CFSP.[346] With the centre of gravity, the Court applies a neutral test, which gives the same value to the CFSP and the non-CFSP, without any precedence between both areas.[347] Therefore, the Court does apply the principle as enshrined in Article 40 TEU, without mentioning the provision. The application of the centre of gravity test and its specific expression in the

---

341 C-263/14, para. 42.

342 C-130/10.

343 C-658/11.

344 C-263/14.

345 C. Hillion, 'A powerless Court? The European Court of Justice and the Common Foreign and Security Policy', 60; C. Eckes, 'Common Foreign and Security Policy: the consequences of the Court's extended jurisdiction', 4 European Law Journal 2016, 500.

346 Contra: L. Lonardo, 'Commission v Council (Kazakhstan): the subject-matter question in EU external relations law, or the asymmetry of art.40 TEU', 3 E.L. Rev. 2020, 427–439.

347 Opinion C-180/20, point 35.

Philippines PCA test arguably also balances coherence and conferral: the inclusion in a measure of other objectives does not amount to a violation of Article 40 TEU, as this is in accordance with the common objectives in Article 21(2) TEU and the duty to ensure coherence laid down in Article 23(3) TEU and Article 7 TFEU. However, if the inclusion of these objectives does no longer amount to mere integration and these objectives are no longer incidental but rather amount to objectives distinct from the central objective, they require separate legal bases.[348]

3.3 Application of the Delimitation in the Adoption of Instruments on the Development Cooperation Policy–CFSP Nexus

Like in the sections on the development cooperation–environment and development cooperation–trade nexus, this section will evaluate whether and how the Treaty framework and case law on the development cooperation–CFSP nexus is reflected in the adoption of instruments. A first important question to address in this respect is the effect of the legal framework on the possibility to adopt instruments at the interface between development cooperation and the CFSP.

On the basis of the Treaty framework, the assessment is quite straightforward for international agreements. As confirmed by the Court, Article 218 TFEU sets out a single procedure of general application for concluding international agreements, which covers both CFSP and non-CFSP elements.[349] This follows from the wording of the article, which contains provisions on agreements relating to both areas. Article 218(3) and (6) TFEU clarify that the procedure applies to CFSP agreements as well, as these paragraphs explicitly refer to agreements that relate exclusively or principally to the CFSP. They therefore confirm that an international agreement can cover both CFSP and non-CFSP elements and be based on a dual CFSP and non-CFSP legal basis.[350] The procedural incompatibility that prevents the use of a dual legal basis is therefore absent in the procedure to conclude international agreements laid down in Article 218 TFEU. Further, Article 47 TEU grants the EU a single

---

[348] B. Van Vooren, 'The Small Arms judgment in an age of constitutional turmoil', 247.

[349] Case C-658/11, EU:C:2014:2025, para. 52; Case C-263/14, EU:C:2016:435, para. 55, Case C-244/17, para. 21. See further on the Court's recent case law on Article 218 TFEU as a single procedure of general application for concluding international agreements, its scope, and the powers of the different institutions thereunder: J. Heliskoski, 'The procedural law of international agreements: a thematic journey through Article 218 TFEU', Common Market Law Review, 2020, 79–118.

[350] P. Eeckhout, *EU External Relations Law*, 184.

legal personality. Both features enable the adoption of international agreements on a dual CFSP and non-CFSP legal basis when the agreement addresses both areas to an equal extent. The EU did conclude international agreements that are based on such a dual CFSP and non-CFSP legal basis. This is the case for the Treaty of Amity and Cooperation in Southeast Asia,[351] which is based on Articles 31(1) and 37 TEU and non-CFSP legal bases Articles 209, 212 and 218(6)(a) and (8), second subparagraph TFEU. The Cooperation Agreement on Partnership and Development between the European Union and its Member States and the Islamic Republic of Afghanistan[352] is based on Article 37 TEU and Articles 207, 209 and 218 paragraph 5 and the second subparagraph of paragraph 8 TFEU. The Political Dialogue and Cooperation Agreement concluded with Cuba[353] is based on Article 31(1) and Article 37 TEU and Articles 207, 209 and 218 paragraph 5 and the second subparagraph of paragraph 8 TFEU. Arguably, following the Court's judgment in *PCA Kazakhstan* and *CEPA Armenia*, the Cooperation Agreement on Partnership and Development with Afghanistan and the Political Dialogue and Cooperation Agreement with Cuba would not have to be based on the CFSP legal basis, as the CFSP elements are incidental to the development cooperation and CCP elements. Like in *PCA Kazakhstan* and *CEPA Armenia*, the CFSP provisions in the agreements with Cuba and Afghanistan are limited in number and relate to a few provisions on countering international crimes, conflict prevention, crisis management and peace-building, proliferation of weapons of mass destruction, and small arms and light weapons. As such, they could arguably not be regarded as distinct components of the agreements.[354] In *CEPA Armenia*, it is also relevant that the Court determined that the main components of CCP, trade in transport services, and development cooperation could also encompass the objectives on political dialogue.[355] In line with the current state of the Court's case law, a dual CFSP and non-CFSP legal basis, as enabled by the unified procedure laid down in Article 218 TFEU, would therefore be possible for international agreements but only for those agreements where CFSP and non-CFSP elements are equally present, without one being incidental to the other.

---

[351] Council Decision 2012/308/CFSP on the accession of the European Union to the Treaty of Amity and Cooperation in Southeast Asia, OJ 2012 L154/1.

[352] Cooperation Agreement on Partnership and Development between the European Union and its Member States, of the one part, and the Islamic Republic of Afghanistan, of the other part, OJ 2017 L67/3.

[353] Political Dialogue and Cooperation Agreement between the European Union and its Member States, of the one part, and the Republic of Cuba, of the other part, OJ 2016 L337I/3.

[354] C-244/17, para. 44–46, Case C-180/20, para. 45–46.

[355] Case C-180/20, para. 53.

As regards measures, the situation seems more complex. It follows from the confirmed application of the centre of gravity test that a measure addressing both development cooperation policy and the CFSP can be adopted on the predominant legal basis, as long as the other element is merely incidental. Despite the fact that the use of a dual legal basis is no longer principally excluded, it seems that the Court's statement in the *Legal Basis for Restrictive Measures* case[356] still prevents the adoption of comprehensive measures that are based on a dual development cooperation policy and CFSP legal basis, because of the procedural incompatibility. Article 209(1) TFEU clarifies that development cooperation policy measures are adopted on the basis of the ordinary legislative procedure, hence, by the Parliament and the Council by qualified majority. Article 24(1) TEU and Article 31(1) TEU determine that, as a rule, CFSP measures are adopted by the Council on the basis of unanimity. Hence, on the basis of the Court's case law in *Legal Basis for Restrictive Measures*, the adoption of a dual legal basis decision would still seem impossible.[357] The Court did not prevent the adoption of a combined CFSP and TFEU instrument as a principle in *Legal Basis for Restrictive Measures*, but it interpreted the requirements for a combination of these legal bases so narrowly that the use of a dual CFSP and non-CFSP legal basis is procedurally precluded.[358] Attempts in that regard to reconcile CFSP and non-CFSP procedures, namely by adopting measures on the basis of the ordinary legislative procedure, although with unanimity in the Council, would arguably contravene the CFSP's character as a specific area of external action and the current framework for delimiting the CFSP from the non-CFSP in the post-Lisbon framework.[359]

The procedural impossibility to adopt measures on a dual CFSP and non-CFSP legal basis prevents the institutions from taking measures that comprehensively address the CFSP and the non-CFSP to the same extent.[360] However, following the centre of gravity test and its specific application to determine the scope of development cooperation (objectives), it is also possible for development cooperation measures to integrate and address CFSP elements in a coherent manner, as long as they are incidental to the main development cooperation aim and component.

---

356 Case C-130/10, *Parliament/Council*, EU:C:2012:472.

357 C-130/10, para. 45–48.

358 C. Eckes, 'The CFSP and other EU policies: a difference in nature?', 545–546.

359 G. De Baere, 'From "Don't mention the Titanium Dioxide judgment" to "I mentioned it once, but I think I got away with it all right"', 558–559; T. Corthaut, 'Case C-166/07, European Parliament v Council of the European Union, Judgment of the Court of Justice ([Fourth] Chamber) of 3 September 2009, [2009] ECR I-7135', 1290.

360 C. Hillion, R. Wessel, 'Competence distribution in EU external relations after ECOWAS: clarification or continued fuzziness?', 580.

In the search for a coherent and integrated approach, the adoption of the Neighbourhood, Development and International Cooperation Instrument – Global Europe (NDICI-GE), under the multiannual financial framework 2021–2027, was crucial. Compared with the financing instruments under the previous multiannual financial framework, the NDICI-GE integrates several instruments into one overarching instrument. As such, it also encompasses a thematic programme on peace, stability, and conflict prevention and rapid response actions to contribute to peace, stability, and conflict prevention in situations of urgency, emerging crisis, crisis, and post-crisis, including those which may result from migratory flows and forced displacement, and to strengthening the resilience of states, societies, communities, and individuals, and to linking humanitarian aid and development action and, where relevant, peace-building. Most importantly, the NDICI-GE also integrates capacity-building in support of development and security for development (CBSD). Initially, a revision of the Instrument contributing to Stability and Peace (IcSP) set up CBSD. The Commission launched a proposal in 2016 in this regard in order to contribute to a genuine comprehensive approach: the Joint Communication of the Commission and the High Representative on Capacity Building in Support of Security and Development identified important gaps that prevented the EU from adopting a comprehensive approach in the context of supporting capacity-building in the security sector of partner countries. One of the gaps followed from the fact that no Union external action instrument was designed to cover 'a comprehensive financing to security capacity building in partner countries, in particular its military component'.[361] The amendment[362] added a new Article into Title II of Regulation 230/2014[363] in order to extend the capacity-building component under the IcSP to include, under exceptional circumstances, capacity-building of military actors. The ultimate objective of this extended funding was still to contribute to sustainable development and peaceful and inclusive societies, hence the term 'capacity building in support of development and security for development'. Article 9 NDICI-GE incorporates CBSD and clarifies that its objective is to contribute to sustainable development, which requires the achievement of stable, peaceful, and inclusive societies, therefore referring to the principle that there can be no development without stability. Interestingly, the NDICI-GE refers in its preamble to the delimitation between development cooperation and the CFSP

361 Joint Communication of the Commission and the High Representative on Capacity building in support of security and development, 8.

362 Regulation 2017/2306 of 12 December 2017 amending Regulation 230/2014 establishing an instrument contributing to stability and peace, OJ 2014 L335/6.

363 Regulation 230/2014 of 11 March 2014 establishing an instrument contributing to stability and peace, OJ 2014 L77/1.

in that regard. It determines that capacity-building of military actors in third countries is to be undertaken as part of the Union's development cooperation policy when it mainly pursues objectives in the field of development and, by contrast, as part of the CFSP when it mainly pursues objectives in the field of peace and security, in compliance with Article 40 TEU. In that regard, the preamble emphasises that the NDICI-GE respects the application of the procedures and the extent of the powers of the institutions under the Union's development cooperation policy and the Union's CFSP. Article 9 NDICI-GE further confirms that CBSD is to be used in exceptional cases only and under the conditions laid down in its third paragraph, where the objectives of the NDICI-GE cannot be met by recourse to non-military actors. It further determines that CBSD may cover in particular the provision of capacity-building programmes in support of development and security for development, including training, mentoring, and advice, as well as the provision of equipment, infrastructure improvements, and services directly related to that assistance. Importantly, the fourth paragraph lays down the limits of CBSD by clarifying that it cannot be used to finance capacity-building of military actors for purposes other than the delivery of development activities and security for development activities. It excludes explicitly the financing of recurrent military expenditure, the procurement of arms and ammunition, or any other equipment designed to deliver lethal force and training which is designed to contribute specifically to the fighting capacity of the armed forces. CBSD, as currently integrated in the NDICI-GE, is therefore an important measure that finds itself at the crossroads for development cooperation and the CFSP, enhancing a coherent approach in that regard. On the other hand, it is in accordance with conferral, through its pursuit of the development cooperation objectives: it is very clear that development is the ultimate aim. As such, it is a demonstration of the development cooperation policy–CFSP nexus, in which security creates the conditions for attaining the development cooperation policy objectives and vice versa. As such, it does respond to the centre of gravity test, in the sense that the CFSP is subordinate to the development cooperation objectives.

In relation to the outer limits for development cooperation measures, it is important to point at the limits imposed by Article 41(2) TEU, which excludes expenditure with military or defence implications from the EU budget. Measures with military or defence implications therefore need to be financed by the Member States outside the EU budget. For this reason, the Council has established the European Peace Facility (EPF).[364] The EPF finances – as an extra-budgetary fund – Union actions under the CFSP to preserve peace,

364 Council Decision 2021/509 of 22 March 2021 establishing a European Peace Facility, and repealing Decision (CFSP) 2015/528, OJ 2021 L102/14.

prevent conflicts, and strengthen international security, in accordance with Article 21(2) (c) TEU, in cases where, pursuant to Article 41(2) TEU, the operating expenditure arising from those actions is not charged to the Union budget. As such, the EPF is used for the financing of the common costs of (i) Union operations under Articles 42(4) and 43(2) TEU having military or defence implications and which, therefore, according to Article 41(2)TEU, cannot be charged to the Union budget, and (ii) assistance measures consisting of Union actions under Article 28 TEU where the Council decides unanimously, pursuant to Article 41(2) TEU, that the operating expenditure arising therefrom shall be charged to the Member States.[365] The EPF therefore also covers actions that were previously financed by the African Peace Facility, under the European Development Fund. As an extra-budgetary fund (see section above), the EDF was not subject to the limits imposed by the EU budget and could, as such, finance far-going measures on the development–CFSP nexus[366] that can currently no longer be financed by the NDICI-GE, pursuant to Article 41(2) TEU. The limit of Article 41(2) TEU is therefore a red line set by primary law to the integration of CFSP elements in development cooperation: military and defence measures cannot be financed by the external action instruments financed under the general budget of the EU.

As follows from the analysis above, from a coherence perspective, the Treaty of Lisbon has reinforced the demand to attain coherent EU external action, also in the nexus between CFSP and non-CFSP. The insertion of the common EU external action objectives in Article 21(2) TEU, the obligation to attain coherence laid down in Article 21(3) TEU and the institutional innovations that brought about the creation of the High Representative and the EEAS (see the analysis in Chapter 6) are all elements that need to further steer coherent EU external action. The delimitation rules, however, still prevent an entirely integrated approach. The Treaty of Lisbon granted the CFSP the same constitutional weight as the other external action competences and inserted in Article 40 TEU a mutual non-affectation clause that governs the delimitation between the CFSP and the non-CFSP. The CFSP, however, retains its character as a distinct area of Union external action with specific rules and procedures. In the *Legal Basis for Restrictive Measures* case,[367] the Court clarified that the incompatibility of the procedures still prevents the adoption

---

[365] Article 1 Council Decision 2021/509.

[366] For a detailed analysis, see European Commission, African Peace Facility Annual Report; M. Carbone, 'An uneasy nexus: development, security and the EU's African Peace Facility', European Foreign Affairs Review, 2013, 103–124; H. Merket, 'The EU and the Security-Development Nexus: Bridging the Legal Divide' (2013) 4 European Foreign Affairs Review, 83–102.

[367] C-130/10.

of fully integrated measures on a combined CFSP and a non-CFSP legal basis. This emphasises the importance of the centre of gravity for the adoption of measures and for concluding international agreements on the development cooperation–CFSP nexus and for the choice of their appropriate legal basis. In its case law on international agreements, the Court has further normalised the delimitation between development cooperation and the CFSP by applying the traditional rules on the choice of legal basis, and the centre of gravity test in particular, to agreements that also contain a CFSP section. After the Court's judgment in *PCA Kazakhstan* and *CEPA Armenia*, it is clear that the Court's test on the scope of development cooperation, as a specific expression of the centre of gravity test, also governs the nexus between development cooperation and the CFSP.

4. Conclusions on the legal scope of EU development cooperation policy and delimitation with other closely linked areas

EU development cooperation policy's broad legal scope supports and corresponds to what constitutes EU development cooperation policy on the basis of the area's policy documents: a multifaceted field. Although poverty reduction and eradication has been singled out as the primary objective of development cooperation policy, this objective has a broad scope as well, referring to various aspects of economic and social development. On the basis of Article 21(2) TEU and the specific Treaty articles on development cooperation policy, EU development cooperation policy should moreover be conducted in light of the common external action objectives as well. The main purpose of the primary poverty eradication aim must therefore be seen as to streamline this objective in all areas of external action and to steer the various aspects of development cooperation policy towards the attainment of this core objective of development cooperation policy. The reformulation of the Treaty objectives, as compared with previous Treaty texts, does not alter the legal scope of the development cooperation policy competence and its delimitation with other areas.

The Court's case law confirms the broad pre-Lisbon scope of development cooperation policy and its objectives. In the *Philippines PCA* case, the Court referred to the link between development cooperation policy and the pursuit of the common external action objectives in Article 21(2) TEU. As such, it emphasised the importance of coherence for the area of development cooperation policy: policy coherence for development. It determined that EU development cooperation policy is not limited to measures directly aimed at the eradication of poverty, as it also pursues the objectives referred to in Article 21(2) TEU, such as the objective, set out in Article 21(2)(d), of fostering the sustainable economic, social, and environmental development of developing countries with the primary aim of eradicating poverty. In *CEPA Armenia*, the Court further confirmed this and also referred to the objective of preserving peace, preventing conflicts, and strengthening international security as set out in Article 21(2)(c) TEU. As such, the Court confirmed its pre-Lisbon case law in *Portugal/Council* regarding the scope of EU development cooperation and its case law in *Small Arms and Light Weapons*, where the Court clarified that the objectives of Union development cooperation policy are not limited to measures directly related to the campaign against poverty but that they also contribute to the pursuit of that policy's economic and social development objectives.[1] By emphasising the link between the specific objectives and Treaty articles on development cooperation policy and the common external action objectives, the Court respects both the weight and function of the common external action objectives and the requirement of Article 208(1) TFEU, which requires that development cooperation be conducted in the framework of the common EU external action objectives. It moreover confirms the broad policy notion of development cooperation policy.

In its case law on the scope of EU development cooperation, the Court used a two-step test. First as regards the objectives, the Court confirmed that EU development cooperation's objectives are broad enough for measures required for their pursuit to concern a variety of specific matters. The Court emphasised that requiring a development cooperation agreement to be based on additional legal bases each time it touches on a specific matter would render the development cooperation competence and procedures 'devoid of substance'.[2] This is an important recognition by the Court that the development cooperation policy competence's scope should be protected as a fully fledged competence. Second, as regards the content, the characterisation of the agreement has to be determined having regard to its essential object and not in terms of individual clauses, provided that these do not impose such extensive obligations concerning the specific matters referred to that those obligations in fact constitute objectives distinct from those of development cooperation.[3] It is interesting to note that in its reasoning in *Philippines PCA*, like in *Philippines Border Management*[4] and *Small Arms and Light Weapons*,[5] the Court used the wide policy definition of 'poverty eradication', referring to the basic non-legally binding policy documents on Union development cooperation, as well as secondary EU law, to further support the choice of legal basis and the wide

---

1 Case C-91/05, para. 67.

2 Case C-268/94, para. 37.

3 Case C-268/94, para. 37–39.

4 The Court referred to the European Consensus to link development cooperation and security: Case C-403/05, para. 57.

5 The Court relied extensively on the European Union strategy to combat illicit accumulation and trafficking of small arms and light weapons adopted by the European Council on 15 and 16 December 2005 (Council document No 5319/06 PESC 31 of 13 January 2006) as well as on the European Consensus: Case C-91/05, para. 66, 69, 90–91.

scope of EU development cooperation policy.[6] This further enhances the link that exists between the policy scope and the legal scope of EU development cooperation policy.

The Court's case law on the scope of EU development cooperation therefore balances the aim and content criterion of the theory on choice of legal basis[7] and moreover reflects a specific expression of the centre of gravity test. This is further demonstrated by *Kazakhstan PCA* and *CEPA Armenia*, where the test on the scope of EU development cooperation also delimitates development cooperation from the CFSP. As a centre of gravity, the development cooperation policy competence is able to cover other areas of cooperation on the basis of its predominant character. When the other competence areas are no longer subordinate to the development cooperation policy competence, they can no longer be absorbed by the latter. In applying this specific centre of gravity test, the Court balanced the aim and content aspect of the test: while the first step of the test concerns the objective aspect, the second part of the test involves a content-based test. In *Philippines PCA*, the Court's case law represents a shift in the assessment of the second aspect of the test from the question of whether the cooperation was prescribed in concrete terms to the question of whether the provisions still need implementation. On the basis of this test, provisions on specific areas of cooperation can be covered by the development cooperation policy competence, even though they contain specific obligations and they are to some extent concrete as to how the cooperation in the specific area is to be carried out, as long as they still need to be implemented further before their concrete application. In the *Philippines PCA* case, this demonstrated that development cooperation can be used for relatively deep forms of cooperation.[8] While in *CEPA Armenia*, the Court formulated a slightly different variation of the content aspect, which seems to combine both the declaratory nature of the objectives and the fact that they still needed specific further implementation, the different expressions of the test, depending on the specificities of the case, would all relate to the substance and core of the Court's assessment: i.e., whether the provisions on other matters fall within the scope of EU development cooperation as the centre of gravity or whether, by contrast, the provisions impose such extensive obligations in the specific areas

---

6 See in the same sense B. Van Vooren as regards the *Small Arms and Light Weapons* case: B. Van Vooren, 'The Small Arms Judgment in an Age of Constitutional Turmoil', 235; M. Cremona, 'A reticent court? Policy objectives and the Court of Justice', 19.

7 Although not a relevant criterion for the specific case, the Court also confirmed in *CEPA Armenia* the context as a relevant criterion: Case C-180/20, para. 54–55.

8 M. Broberg, R. Holdgaard, 'Demarcating the Union's development cooperation policy after Lisbon: *Commission v. Council (Philippines PCFA)*', 564.

that they cover, that those obligations in fact constitute objectives distinct from those of development cooperation.[9]

As such, the case law on the scope of EU development cooperation would also balance coherence and conferral. The test on the scope of EU development cooperation allows for the integration of other specific matters into development cooperation, which is in line with the area's objectives as formulated in Article 208 TFEU and which supports the aim of attaining coherence and policy coherence for development in particular. Nevertheless, as soon as the other specific matters go as far as to become distinct objectives, they no longer fall under development cooperation as the centre of gravity and they would require the addition of their own legal basis. To further assess whether this is indeed the case, this book further determined the scope and limits of the development cooperation policy competence by analysing the delimitation between development cooperation policy and the strongly related areas of environment, the CCP, and the CFSP.

This analysis demonstrated that the delimitation of development cooperation with environment and with CFSP is in line with the test on the scope of EU development cooperation. The findings on the development–environment nexus demonstrated that the development cooperation policy competence indeed covers and absorbs environmental matters unless they constitute obligations so extensive that they are to be considered as distinct objectives. The Treaty itself enables the integration and mainstreaming of environmental protection: Article 11 TFEU lays down a duty to integrate environmental protection into the definition and implementation of the Union's policies, in particular with a view to promoting sustainable development. The Court's test defining the legal scope of development cooperation policy ensures the possible integration of environmental concerns in development cooperation policy by allowing development cooperation instruments to cover environmental protection issues and provisions. However, the delimitation respects the principle of conferral as well. As the analysis of international agreements and measures has demonstrated, first, only environmental measures that pursue development cooperation policy objectives can be covered by the development cooperation policy competence. Second, if that is the case, as soon as the provisions on environment contain obligations so extensive that they can be considered to be distinct objectives, and hence can no longer be seen as secondary or indirect, they need their own legal basis.

While one would assume that the development–CFSP would be the most problematic delimitation, the analysis above has demonstrated that the Court's

9 Case C-263/14, para. 47, Case C-377/12, para. 39; Case C-244/17, para. 46, Case C-180/20, para. 45.

case law has normalised this delimitation. The Treaty of Lisbon fundamentally changed the legal framework for external action and the delimitation between the CFSP and the non-CFSP. The delimitation between development cooperation policy and the CFSP is as such affected by two major innovations created by the Treaty of Lisbon: the common external action objectives formulated in Article 21(2) TEU, and the mutual non-affectation clause laid down in Article 40 TEU. The lack of specific CFSP objectives, which were laid down in former Article 11 TEU, steers to CFSP towards the common EU external action objectives. The mutual non-affectation clause laid down in Article 40 TEU gives the CFSP and the non-CFSP the same constitutional weight, which is in accordance with Article 1 TEU and Article 1(2) TFEU that state that both the TEU and the TFEU have the same legal value. At the same time, these provisions demonstrate the ambiguous character of the Treaty framework: the common objectives require both the CFSP and the non-CFSP to be steered towards the achievement of the same common objectives, while Article 24 TEU and Article 40 TEU demonstrate that the CFSP is still distinct as an area of external action and its delimitation with other areas.

In its case law, the Court uses a centre of gravity to assess the scope of the CFSP and to delimitate the CFSP from development cooperation. As such, the Court recognises the importance of the CFSP as a separate and distinct area that is to be equally protected, in accordance with the Treaty framework, and normalises the delimitation between CFSP and non-CFSP by applying the traditional rules on choice of legal basis. In *Tanzania Agreement*, the Court adopted a centre of gravity test to determine the correct legal basis, in which the content and the context in particular played a crucial role to determine the correct legal basis. There, the Court held that the EU–Tanzania Agreement fell predominantly within the CFSP, due to the agreement's inseparable link with the achievement of the objectives of the CFSP operation EUNAVFOR.[10] With *PCA Kazakhstan* and *CEPA Armenia*, the Court addressed the particular delimitation between development cooperation and CFSP and, as such, confirmed the application of the *Portugal/Council* and *Philippines PCA* test to delimitate development cooperation and the CFSP. With this, the test on the scope of development cooperation is emerging as the standard for determining the centre of gravity and the appropriate legal basis, considering that, as discussed above, the test includes both the aim and content as objective criteria, while allowing for the integration of the common external action objectives laid down in Article 21(2) TEU, without overstepping competence boundaries

[10] C-263/14, para. 53–55.

at the same time.[11] The Court's detailed assessment of the different criteria in *CEPA Armenia* is as such a reflection of determining the appropriate legal basis 'all things considered',[12] providing a balance between the different objective factors to determine the legal basis,[13] their importance depending on the specific case – as pointed out by the Advocate General in *CEPA Armenia.*

The delimitation between development cooperation and the CCP, by contrast, would not be in accordance with the test on the scope of EU development cooperation and would be characterised by an imbalance of coherence and conferral. As indicated above, the development–CCP nexus is characterised by the CCP's dominance over development cooperation, which follows from two characteristics of the development cooperation policy–CCP delimitation. First, as the analysis of the different types of agreement concluded with developing countries demonstrated, development cooperation policy agreements that cover a trade chapter necessitate the addition of the CCP legal basis. Second, trade measures have been adopted to attain development cooperation policy objectives: the GSP is a unilateral measure based on the CCP legal basis, while it clearly also pursues development cooperation policy aims. The CCP's dominance over the development cooperation policy competence by being omnipresent as a legal basis cannot be explained by the test on the scope of development cooperation policy. The analysis conducted above of the agreements demonstrates that the trade titles in the development cooperation policy agreements merely define the aims and subject of the cooperation. Hence, in accordance with the Court's case law, they would not constitute distinct objectives that require the addition of the CCP legal basis. It is moreover peculiar that in the different cases the Court tests the scope of the development cooperation competence as the centre of gravity, which enables it to include other specific matters, but merely accepts the presence of the CCP legal basis for the agreements in question. As such, the Court confirms the 'classical pattern' following which development cooperation policy agreements are based on both the development cooperation policy and CCP legal bases.[14]

Indeed, the explanation for the peculiar delimitation between CCP and development cooperation and the dominance of the CCP lies with the CCP. It can be explained by the specific nature of the CCP competence on the

---

11 B. Van Vooren, 'The Small Arms Judgment in an Age of Constitutional Turmoil', 246; G. De Baere, T. Van den Sanden, 108.

12 A. Dashwood, 'Article 47 TEU and the Relationship between First and Second Pillar Competences' 101. Compare T. Corthaut, 'An Effective Remedy for All? Paradoxes and Controversies in Respect of Judicial Protection in the Field of the CFSP under the European Constitution', 119–120.

13 G. De Baere, T. Van den Sanden, 108.

14 M. Maresceau, 176–177.

one hand and by historical reasons on the other hand. Like development cooperation policy, the CCP has a very broad scope. The CCP's very broad scope follows from the scope of its objective, trade liberalisation,[15] and the Court's corresponding broad interpretation of the competence. The Court has not only included measures that pursue CCP aims under the area's scope but also measures that are of a commercial nature, regardless of the aims that they pursue.[16] This has expanded the CCP's scope and explains why measures such as the GSP[17] fall under the CCP, while they clearly pursue a development cooperation policy aim, and why trade chapters in development cooperation policy agreements bring about the addition of the CCP legal basis. From a historical perspective, the CCP predates the development cooperation policy. As a result, and as discussed above, early international agreements and measures at the interplay of development cooperation policy and the CCP have been based on the CCP alone or on the CCP legal and the flexibility clause or later on the dual CCP–development cooperation policy competence. The fact that the CCP legal basis was therefore consistently present in development cooperation agreements and measures explains to an important extent the ongoing domination of the area over the development cooperation policy competence.

The patterns in delimiting the CCP and the development cooperation policy competence are consistent: the CCP competence is consistently present, in the dual legal basis or as the sole legal basis, despite the strong development cooperation policy objectives of international agreements or measures. However, the fact that the CCP's dominance over the development cooperation competence cannot be explained by the test on the scope of development cooperation and the centre of gravity would create an imbalance between the two competences. Such would, in turn, arguably affect both coherence and conferral.

15 Article 206 TFEU.

16 Case 45/86, *Commission/Council*, ECLI:EU:C:1987:163.

17 Regulation 978/2012 of 25 October 2012 applying a scheme of generalised tariff preferences and repealing Council Regulation (EC) No 732/2008, OJ 2012 L303/1.

PART II

Division of competences and cooperation between actors

5. The nature of EU development cooperation and vertical division of competences and cooperation between the Union and the Member States in development cooperation policy

This chapter discusses the legal nature of EU development cooperation and how the competence of the EU and those of the Member States in the area relate to each other. Seen from the vertical division of competences between the Union and the Member States, EU development cooperation policy originated as a policy complementary to Member State policy. Its origin still influences the policy today and is also reflected in its legal nature. In the vertical division of competences, development cooperation policy is of a distinct nature, as it can be referred to as an irregular shared or non-pre-emptive shared competence, amounting to a special subcategory of shared competence. The first part of the chapter explains this distinct nature and the effects it has on the division of competences between the EU and its Member States.

The management of the division of competences between the European Union and its Member States in the area of development cooperation policy is to a great extent governed by the principle of sincere cooperation, as formulated in Article 4(3) TEU. The second part of the chapter examines how this principle is able to influence the relationship between the EU and Member States' actions in development cooperation policy. First, the applicability of the principle in the area of development cooperation policy will be clarified, as well as its link with other constitutional principles and mechanisms of EU law to further explain how they relate to the development cooperation policy competence. Second, the obligations stemming from the principle of sincere cooperation policy are analysed in depth to answer how they govern the management of the vertical division of competences in development cooperation policy. In this respect, a distinct analysis is made of the positive obligations to act and the negative obligations to abstain, both flowing from the principle of sincere cooperation as laid down in Article 4(3) TEU.

The distinction between positive and negative obligations stemming from the principle of sincere cooperation is meaningful, both in light of the complementary nature of the development cooperation competence, and in order to respond to the questions that this chapter aims to answer: (i) how are conflicts prevented and resolved; and (ii) what cooperation and coordination mechanisms apply? This chapter therefore further questions how the duty of positive cooperation manifests itself in development cooperation policy and what consequences it brings about, as well as what limits the principle of sincere cooperation entails to Member State action in the area of development cooperation policy.

1. THE COMPLEMENTARITY OF EU DEVELOPMENT COOPERATION POLICY

The idea that EU development cooperation policy complements the Member States' own development cooperation policies, rather than replacing the bilateral policies,[1] has been present from the creation of EU development cooperation policy and still influences its nature today. The complementary nature and the difficulty to create an EU development cooperation policy of its own has led to the conclusion that EU development cooperation policy was fragmented, bilateral, and ad hoc, which negatively influenced the effectiveness of the EU's common development cooperation policy.[2] Policy documents therefore emphasised the necessary link between complementarity and coordination from early on.[3] The Maastricht Treaty developed the separate legal basis for development cooperation policy in the Treaties,[4] while at the same time it incorporated the requirements of complementarity and coordination. The Maastricht Treaty provisions on development cooperation policy reflect the so-called triple C principles:[5]

(i) Coherence between policies that have an impact on third countries and the objectives of development cooperation;
(ii) Complementarity between Member State and EU activities in development cooperation policy;

---

1 Commission Memorandum on a Community policy for development co-operation, 27 July 1971, 8; 22.

2 M. Holland, M. Doidge, *Development policy of the European Union*, 2012, Palgrave, 184, 189.

3 Memorandum from the Commission on a Community policy on development cooperation, 2 February 1972, 20–21.

4 Before an explicit legal basis on development cooperation policy was inserted in the Treaties, development cooperation policy acts were based on the flexibility clause.

5 M. van Reisen, 'The enlarged European Union and the developing world: what future?' In A. Mold (ed.), *EU development policy in a changing world. Challenges for the 21st century*, Amsterdam University Press, 2007, 47.

(iii) Coordination of actions between the Member States and the EU;
(iv) The Treaty of Amsterdam introduced a fourth principle: consistency between the policies of the CFSP and development cooperation policy.

These principles can still be found in the current Treaty articles, in Article 208(1) TFEU, Article 209(2) TFEU, and Article 210 TFEU respectively. The Treaty articles on development cooperation policy formulated the EU's development cooperation policy as complementary to the Member States' policy. With the Treaty of Lisbon, however, the language of the Treaty articles changed. The current provisions hold that EU and Member State development cooperation policy 'complement and reinforce *each other*' and need to be 'achieved through coordination and consultation and the possibility of joint action'. This seems to imply a more balanced relationship and seems to grant the development of the EU's development cooperation policy more weight. Article 210 TFEU moreover gives the Commission a leading coordinating role.

In the development cooperation policy of the EU, complementarity and coordination are two sides of the same coin. On the one hand, the fact that EU and Member State policy develop as complementary parts in parallel makes coordination necessary in order to ensure that development cooperation policy's objectives can be attained. On the other hand, coordination makes complementarity possible: well-developed and well-functioning coordination arrangements, in particular division of labour arrangements, make it possible that both the EU and the Member States develop their development cooperation policy in a complementary manner. From a policy perspective, coordination efforts are rooted in the idea of aid effectiveness and avoiding aid fragmentation.[6] Fragmentation is seen as an important obstacle to the effectiveness of development cooperation.[7] One of the most important negative consequences is the emergence of scattered activities, with a duplication of efforts on the one hand and the creation of funding gaps on the other hand. Coordinated delivery of development aid would reduce transaction and management costs, fill funding gaps and avoid duplication of efforts, ensure transparency and participation, and rationalise objectives and procedures.[8] The reform process

---

6 Council conclusions – EU Common Position for the Fourth High Level Forum on Aid Effectiveness 1 December 2011 (Busan Conclusions): https://www.consilium.europa.eu/uedocs/cms_data/docs/pressdata/EN/foraff/126060.pdf.

7 OECD Busan Outcome Document, http://www.oecd.org/development/effectiveness/49650173.pdf, para. 25; M. Carbone, 'Between EU actorness and aid effectiveness: the logics of EU aid to Sub-Saharan Africa', 3 International Relations, 2013, 343.

8 M. Barry, B. Boidin, 'La coordination de l'aide: un objectif aux présupposées contestables', 4 European Journal of Development Research, 2012, 648.

of EU development cooperation in the late 1990s and early 2000s therefore not only led to a stronger common EU development cooperation policy, based on shared objectives and principles, but also to a new emphasis on the promotion of a more coordinated development policy.[9]

The EU is by definition vulnerable to negative consequences caused by aid fragmentation concerns, as its development cooperation policy consists of a common policy, as well as the bilateral policies of all its Member States. Because of this structure, there is great scope for complementarity within the Union.[10] It seems that, aware of this risk, the EU has aimed to take the lead in aid coordination and division of labour initiatives, also inspiring initiatives at the international level.[11] The 2000 Communication 'The European Community's Development Policy' referred to the role of the Commission to promote coordination and ensure complementarity between Union and Member State activities and to the need to establish a division of labour and sectoral approaches.[12] The European Consensus further develops and emphasises the need to 'Work better together'. Improving effectiveness and impact through greater coordination and coherence is relevant at different levels in that respect: it concerns common positions in international fora, cooperation at country level through joint programming, joint implementation, joint monitoring, while the section also addresses aid modalities and pooling of funds.[13] Moreover, the European Consensus as such, as a Joint Statement by the Council, the Representatives of the Member State governments, the European Parliament and the European Commission, which sets out the common vision on development cooperation, is in itself an expression of complementarity. In this respect, the Consensus indicates that it is the framework for a common approach to development policy that will be applied by the EU institutions and the Member States, while fully respecting each other's distinct roles and competences. Actions by the

---

9 M. Carbone, 'Preserving policy autonomy: EU development cooperation from Maastricht to Lisbon', 233.

10 Communication from the Commission to the Council and the European Parliament, Translating the Monterrey Consensus into practice: the contribution by the European Union, SEC(2004)246, 14.

11 E.g.: Council Conclusions of July 1974, November 1976; Resolution on Coordination, May 1993; Conclusions on Coordination of Aid Policies, June 1995; Conclusions on Complementarity between Development Policies and actions of the Union and those of Member States, 1996; Council Conclusions on Operational Coordination, March 1998; Guidelines for strengthening the operational coordination between the Community and the MS in the field of development cooperation, May 2000.

12 Communication The European Community's Development Policy, 14, 29.

13 European Consensus, 38–41.

EU and its Member States will be mutually reinforcing and coordinated to ensure complementarity and impact.[14]

Therefore, complementarity inherently refers to two notions, which both determine the nature of the EU development cooperation policy competence. First, complementarity refers to the fact that both the EU and the Member States develop their own development cooperation policies. Legally speaking, this refers to the fact that both levels exercise their competence in the area, without the possibility of being pre-empted. This refers to the so-called parallel or irregular shared nature of the development cooperation policy competence, which will be addressed in the next section. Second, complementarity concerns the requirement that EU and Member State development cooperation policy not only develop next, in parallel, to each other, but that they also complete each other. Both levels agree to exercise their competence in such a way that the development cooperation policy objectives can be attained, despite the fact that both levels are competent without being able to be pre-empted. This second aspect is governed by the principle of sincere cooperation and will be discussed in Section 3 below.

2. NATURE OF THE COMPETENCE: IRREGULAR SHARED COMPETENCE

2.1 Identification of the Irregular Shared Nature

There are several elements that demonstrate the particular legal nature of development cooperation policy. First, the specific Treaty articles on EU development cooperation clearly point in this direction. Article 208(1) TFEU states that the Union's development cooperation policy and that of the Member States complement and reinforce each other, while Article 209(2) TFEU confirms the EU's competence to conclude international agreements in the area of development cooperation policy to be without prejudice to Member States' competence to negotiate in international bodies and to conclude agreements. Article 211 TFEU further clarifies that 'within their respective spheres of competence, the Union and the Member States shall cooperate with third countries and with the competent international organisations'.

It is, nevertheless, Article 4(4) TFEU that demonstrates most clearly the distinct legal nature of EU development cooperation policy. The Treaty of Lisbon has established a clear classification of the different categories of Union competences,[15] which is particularly important to assess the vertical

---

14 European Consensus, 4.

15 Article 2 TFEU.

division of competences. The different categories of competences are laid down in Articles 2–6 TFEU, which determine the different categories of competences, their main characteristics in defining Union competence, and a list of competence areas that belong to the different categories.[16] Article 2(6) TFEU clarifies that the scope of and arrangements for exercising the Union's competences are further determined by the provisions of the Treaties relating to each area. In Article 4, development cooperation and humanitarian aid are singled out in a specific paragraph which determines that in these areas, the Union has competence to carry out activities and conduct a common policy; however, the exercise of that competence does not result in Member States being prevented from exercising theirs. Only humanitarian aid and research, technological development, and space are granted the same separate character in the Article on shared competences. This formulation of the development cooperation policy competence in the Treaties establishes the distinct nature of EU development cooperation policy in the vertical division of competences between the Union and the Member States.

In the pre-Lisbon era, the Court of Justice confirmed the complementary nature of EU development cooperation policy in the *Lomé IV* case, also sometimes referred to as the *EDF* case.[17] At the time during which the case was rendered, the relations between the EU and the ACP states were governed by the Fourth ACP-EEC Convention, or the so-called Lomé IV Convention. The key issue in the case concerned the legitimacy of the set-up of the European Development Fund (EDF) outside the general EU budget: the question was raised whether the Member States were entitled to set up the 7th EDF outside the EU framework, while making use of the EU institutions. The 7th EDF was established by the Internal Agreement on the measures and procedures required for implementation of the Fourth ACP-EEC Convention[18] concluded between the Member States, while implementation took place in the form of a Council Regulation, not pursuant to the EU framework but pursuant to the Internal Agreement. Under Article 32 of the Internal Agreement, an implementing financial regulation had to be adopted by the Council, acting by a qualified majority on the basis of a draft of the Commission and the opinions of the European Investment Bank (EIB) and the Court of Auditors. Though not

---

16 In that respect, Article 3 and Article 6 TFEU lay down an exhaustive list of competence areas, while Article 4(2) TFEU on the shared competences contains a non-exhaustive list. Article 4(1) TFEU holds that the competences that are not listed under Article 3 and 6 TFEU fall under the shared competences, making the shared competences the residuary category of competences.

17 Case C-316/91, *Parliament/Council*, EU:C:1994:76.

18 Internal Agreement on the measures and procedures required for implementation of the Fourth ACP-EEC Convention, OJ 1991 L229/301.

required by Article 32 Internal Agreement, the Parliament was consulted by the Council on the basis of the Commission's draft. The European Parliament subsequently sought the annulment of the Financial Regulation,[19] arguing that the regulation should have been adopted on the basis of former Article 209 EC Treaty. It claimed that it followed from the wording of Article 231 Fourth Lomé Convention, reiterated in Article 1 of the Financial Protocol, that the Union as such has undertaken an obligation of international law distinct from those of the Member States towards the ACP countries. Therefore, the expenditure provided for in the Fourth Lomé Convention constituted Union expenditure and should hence have been part of the general budget of the Union.

The Court held that the Union's competence in development aid is not exclusive. It followed Advocate General Jacobs in this regard, who stated that because of the lack of indications that EU policy in the area of development cooperation policy was exclusive, it could be accepted that the EU and the Member States shared competence in that field.[20] The Court further held that it followed from the fact that the Union's competence was not exclusive that Member States were accordingly entitled to enter into commitments themselves towards third countries, either collectively or individually, or even jointly with the EU.[21] As the competence to implement the Union's financial assistance was shared by the EU and its Member States, it was for them to choose the source and methods of financing. That choice was made by concluding the Internal Agreement, according to the Court.[22] The Court moreover added that this conclusion was not altered by the fact that the procedure of the financial regulation was very closely related to EU acts. No provision of the Treaty prevented Member States from using, outside its framework, procedural steps drawing on the rules applicable to Union expenditure and from associating the EU institutions with the procedure set up.[23] Recent case law in the framework of the European Stability Mechanism confirmed that the EU institutions can act outside of the EU's framework, while they remain bound by EU law in such instances.[24] In the *Lomé IV* case, the Court based its findings

[19] Financial Regulation 91/491/EEC of 29 July 1991 applicable to development finance cooperation under the Fourth ACP-EEC Convention, OJ 1991 L 266/1.

[20] Opinion of Advocate General Jacobs in Case C-316/91 *Parliament/Council*, EU:C:1993:872, point 40. The *Pringle* case recently indeed reiterated that the EU's competence should be presumed to be non-exclusive, unless there are clear indications to the contrary: Case C-370/12 *Pringle*, EU:C:2012:756, paras 120–121.

[21] Case C-316/91, para. 26.

[22] Case C-316/91, para. 35–36.

[23] Joined Cases C-181/91 and C-248/91, *Parliament/Council and Commission*, EU:C:1993:271.

[24] C-370/12, *Pringle*, EU:C:2012:756; Joined Cases C-105/15 P and C-109/15 P, *Mallis*, EU:C:2016:702; Joined Cases C-8/15 P to C-10/15 P, *Ledra Advertising*, EU:C:2016:701.

on Article 130x EC, which provided for the EU and the Member States to coordinate their policies on development cooperation policy, to consult each other on their aid programmes, and to take joint action. The Court, however, did not go into an analysis of Article 130y EC. Previously the Court had stated in the *Bangladesh* case that also in the area of humanitarian aid the competence of the Community is not exclusive and that the Member States were not prohibited from exercising collectively their competence in that field.[25] Therefore, already in 1994 the Court cleared the extra-budgetary status of the EDF and, as discussed above, in line with this, subsequent EDFs have indeed been set up on the basis of Internal Agreements concluded between Representatives of the Member State governments meeting within the Council. The EDF set-up as an extra-budgetary fund financed by direct contributions from Member States is therefore a typical expression of the complementary nature of EU development cooperation.

Within the Court, it was Advocate General Kokott in Case *C-13/07* who referred to the term 'parallel competences' when classifying the EU development cooperation policy competence in relation to the Member States' competence in this field. The case, however, involved not an issue of development cooperation policy but concerned the EU's position on Vietnam's accession to the WTO. In analysing the nature of Article 133(5) EC, inserted by the then newly adopted Treaty of Nice, the Advocate General aimed to distinguish this Article from Article 181 EC on development cooperation policy in order to conclude that Article 133(5) did not bring about a parallel but a concurrent competence. The Advocate General argued that previous case law, the *Lomé IV* case in particular, has interpreted Article 188 EC as the expression of a parallel competence.[26] The Advocate General considered a parallel competence between the Union and the Member States to be consistent with the 'meaning and purpose' of development cooperation, namely 'the more development aid, the better'. She added that this conclusion did not limit in any way the priority of EU law, nor the requirement for the Member States to coordinate their development policies with the Union's.[27]

Apart from Advocate General Kokott in *C-13/07*, the Court never referred to the term 'parallel competences', nor did the Treaties ever include such a reference. In order to determine the specific nature of the development cooperation policy competence, certain authors use the term parallel competences,[28] while

25 Joined Cases C-181/91 and C-248/91, para. 16.

26 Advocate General Kokott in Case C-13/07, *Commission/Council*, EU:C:2009:190, point 68.

27 Advocate General Kokott in Case C-13/07, point 70.

28 E.g.: G. De Baere, *Constitutional principles of EU external relations*, 62; R. Schütze, 'Lisbon and the federal order of competences: a prospective analysis' 5

others refer to irregular shared competences,[29] non-pre-emptive shared competence,[30] or simply to 'a special category of shared competences'.[31] It seems that the term irregular shared or non-pre-emptive shared competence would best reflect the competence's legal nature. Referring to a parallel competence might create the impression that Member States can never be prevented from acting, as two perfectly parallel sets of rules cannot conflict with each other.[32] However, as will be analysed in further detail below, arguably the exercise of Member State competence in the area of development cooperation policy cannot be restricted on the basis of pre-emption, as argued in the next section, but the exercise of Member State competence can by contrast be limited by the principle of sincere cooperation.

2.2 Implications of the Irregular Shared Character

As indicated above, Article 4(4) and Article 209(2) TFEU indicate that the EU's competence in the field of development cooperation policy is without prejudice to Member State competence and that the exercise of EU competence cannot prevent Member States from exercising theirs. The wording of these provisions, together with Article 211 TFEU, which refers to EU and Member State action within their respective spheres of competence, demonstrates that the application of the theories through which the EU can gain exclusive competence on the international scene is excluded in the area of development cooperation. Exclusivity is linked to primacy, as both are

---

European Law Review, 2008, 709; A. Dashwood, 'Conflicts of competence in responding to global emergencies' in Antoniadis, Schütze and Spaventa (eds), *The European Union and Global Emergencies: A Law and Policy Analysis*, Hart, 2011, 37; G. De Baere, 'EU external action' in Barnard, Peers (eds), *European Union Law*, OUP, 2014, 722; M. Broberg, R. Holdgaard, 'EU development cooperation post-Lisbon: main constitutional challenges', 361.

29 M. Klamert, *The principle of loyalty in EU law*, OUP, 2014, 163.

30 M. Cremona, 'External relations and external competence of the European Union: the emergence of an integrated policy', P. Craig, G. De Burca, *The evolution of EU law*, 2011, 253; M. Estrada-Canamares, 'A legal approach to joint programming in development cooperation policy: cooperation in action led by Union Delegations', CLEER Working Papers 2014/6, 57.

31 A. Rosas, 'Exclusive, shared and national competence in the context of EU external relations: do such distinctions matter?' in I. Govaere, E. Lannon, P. Van Elsuwege, S. Adam (eds), *The European Union in the world: Essays in honour of Marc Maresceau*, Nijhoff, 2014, 19.

32 As Schütze explains, the use of the word 'parallel' may give the impression that Member State action is unlimited, as two perfect parallels never meet and never come into conflict with each other: R. Schütze, 'Lisbon and the Federal Order of Competences', 717.

theories of pre-emption, in the internal and the external sphere respectively.[33] As such, both principles function as conflict rules. Primacy solves conflicts in the internal sphere by requiring that EU rules take precedence over any conflicting national rule, which should be disapplied by national courts and administrations, while the adoption of conflicting national rules is prevented.[34] As the external reflection of primacy, exclusivity prevents Member States from taking international actions, based on the underlying rationale that these actions damage the EU's interests. As on the international scene a conflict cannot be solved by disapplying conflicting Member State rules because of the international character of Member State external action and the involvement of third parties, exclusivity prevents the Member States from acting in the first place.[35] Exclusivity therefore implies that the Member States can only act when they are authorised to act or when they are implementing EU legislation. Apart from these two specific circumstances, the Member States cannot act because the EU's exclusive competence prevents them from acting. The EU has exclusive competence in a few areas where the Treaties explicitly grant the Union exclusive competence, as formulated in Article 3(1) TFEU, the *a priori* exclusive areas. Furthermore, Article 3(2) TFEU formulates instances in which the EU can obtain exclusive competence to conclude an international agreement in areas which are not *a priori* exclusive but which become exclusive: (i) when its conclusion is provided for in a legislative act of the Union, or (ii) is necessary to enable the Union to exercise its internal competence, or (iii) in so far as its conclusion may affect common rules or alter their scope. This feature of the development cooperation policy competence determines its distinct nature: it cannot become exclusive through the different options addressed by Article 3(2) TFEU, contrary to the regular shared competences. As an irregular shared competence, the development cooperation policy competence therefore forms a category separate from the regular shared competences in the broader category of non-exclusive competences.[36]

The wording of the Treaty articles on development cooperation policy prevents one of the three options in Article 3(2) TFEU triggering EU exclusive

---

33 For an in-depth analysis of pre-emption in EU internal and external action, see: A. Arena, 'Exercise of EU competences and pre-emption of member states' powers in the internal and the external sphere: towards 'Grand Unification'?', 1 Yearbook of European Law 2016, 29–105.

34 Case 106/77, *Simmenthal*, EU:C:1978:49, para. 17; Case 103/88, *Fratelli Costanze*, EU:C:1989:256, para. 33; C-10/97 and C-22/97, *IN.CO.GE*, EU:C:1998:498, para. 20.

35 J. Heliskoski, *Mixed agreements as a technique for organizing the international relations of the European Community and its member states*, Kluwer, 2001, 30; G. De Baere, *Constitutional principles of EU external relations*, 33.

36 Ibid., 39.

competence in this area. The exclusion of possible exclusive competence in development cooperation policy nevertheless focuses in the first place on the last option, which provides for the exclusive competence to follow from the exercise of Union competence. With the expression in Article 4(4) TFEU that the exercise of EU competence cannot prevent Member States from exercising theirs, the Treaty clearly excludes this possibility to trigger EU exclusive competence in the area of development cooperation policy. The exclusivity mechanism that applies on the basis of a risk of affecting common rules or altering their scope refers to the so-called *ERTA* principle.[37] In the *ERTA* case the Court held that the Member States no longer have the right acting individually or collectively to enter into international agreements that would affect common rules adopted by the EU to implement a common policy. In case such common rules exist, only the EU is capable of taking actions arising out of international agreements with third countries, affecting the whole sphere of application of the EU legal system.[38] This principle is linked with the exercise of EU competence: it entails that Member States can no longer enter into international obligations, by themselves outside the EU framework, that fall within the scope of common rules, meaning within an area which is already largely covered by such rules, as this would affect the common rules established.[39] For this reason, although the term was never explicitly used by the Court,[40] the *ERTA* principle is also referred to in literature as a pre-emption rule, as the adoption of EU measures pre-empts the Member States.[41] As such,

---

[37] See for the impact of the ERTA judgment on the field of EU external action: T. Verellen, 'The ERTA doctrine in the post-Lisbon era: Note under judgment in Commission v Council (C-114/12) and Opinion 1/13', Columbia Journal for European Law, 2015, 383–410; M. Chamon, 'Implied exclusive powers in the ECJ's post-Lisbon jurisprudence: the continued development of the ERTA doctrine, Common Market Law Review, 2018, 1101–1142.

[38] Case 22/70 *Commission/Council*, EU:C:1971:32, para. 17–18.

[39] Opinion 2/91, EU:C:1993:106, para. 25; Case C-467/98, *Commission/Denmark*, EU:C:2002:625, para. 82; Case C-475/98, *Commission/Germany*, EU:C:2002:630, para. 108, Opinion 1/03, EU:C:2006:81, para. 133; C-114/12, *Commission/Council*, EU:C:2014:2151, 68–71; Opinion 1/13, EU:C:2014:2303, 73.

[40] See, however, Advocate General Sharpston, who does refer to a pre-emption principle laid down in Article 2(2) TFEU (see below): Opinion of Advocate General Sharpston in Opinion procedure 2/15, point 59. Other Advocates General have also referred to pre-emption in their opinions: Advocate General Colomer in Case C-478/07, Budweiser, EU:C:2009:52, point 93; Advocate General Jääskinen in Opinion 1/13 and Advocate General Bot in C-66/13, Green Network, EU:C:2014:156, point 37, as referred to in A. Arena, 31.

[41] For an examination and different views on different expressions of a pre-emption concept in EU law, see: J. Weiler, 'The external legal relations of non-unitary actors: Mixity and the federal principle' in J. Weiler (ed.), *The Constitution of Europe:*

it functions as a conflict-avoiding rule: pre-emption is linked with exclusivity in line with the idea that exclusive competences are created in order to avoid conflicts between the Union and the Member State level and to safeguard the uniformity and effectiveness of Union law.[42]

Before the Treaty of Lisbon, there was still discussion on the exact nature of the development cooperation policy competence and doubts were raised whether the application of *ERTA* was entirely excluded in the area of development cooperation policy. Advocate General Jacobs argued in the *EDF* case that the rationale behind the development of the *ERTA* test, the damaging effect of external Member State action on common EU rules, could not be at issue in the area of development cooperation policy. He determined that in the field of development aid to third States, the risk that action undertaken by the Member States may have adverse consequences on action undertaken by the Community is much less than it is in other areas: if the Member States undertake an obligation to provide development aid, that in itself cannot affect any internal rules adopted by the EU. His subsequent conclusion about the question whether *ERTA* is applicable or not is quite ambiguous: he determined that it can therefore not be concluded that once the Community undertook an obligation by entering into an international agreement, the Member States were necessarily excluded from undertaking that obligation jointly with the Community.[43] It therefore seems that the Advocate General did not rule out the applicability of the *ERTA* principle in the area of development cooperation policy as such but that he took the view that the nature of the actions that are being undertaken in this area prevent that the *ERTA* principle is triggered in practice.

Do the new clothes have an emperor? and other essays on European integration, CUP, 1999; R. Schütze, 'Supremacy without pre-emption? The very slowly emergent doctrine of community pre-emption', Common Market Law Review, 2006, 1023–1048; Waelbroeck, 'The emergent doctrine of Community pre-emption – Consent and redelegation', in T. Sandalow and E. Stein, *Courts and free markets: Perspectives from the United States and Europe*, OUP, 1982, 551, as referred to in T. Verellen, 'The ERTA doctrine in the post-Lisbon era: Note under judgment in Commission v Council (C-114/12) and Opinion 1/13', Columbia Journal for European Law, 2015, 383–410; A. Arena, 'Exercise of EU competences and pre-emption of member states' powers in the internal and the external sphere: towards "Grand Unification"?', 1 Yearbook of European Law 2016, 29–105. For a comparative study with the pre-emption principle in US constitutional law, see: K. Lenaerts, *Le juge et la constitution aux Etats-Unis d'Amérique et dans l'ordre juridique européen*, Bruylant, 1988, 176–185; 525–566.

42 P. Eeckhout, 'Bold constitutionalism and beyond' in M. Poiares Maduro, L. Azoulai, *The past and future of EU law: The classics of EU law revisited on the 50th anniversary of the Rome Treaty*, 2010, 219–220.

43 Advocate General Jacobs in Case C-316/91, points 49–50.

The Advocate General's rather ambiguous conclusion has been subsequently interpreted by authors, such as O'Keeffe, to conclude that the application of *ERTA* was in principle not excluded but that it was very unlikely that the *ERTA* test comes into play in the area of development cooperation policy.[44] Interestingly, O'Keeffe referred to Declaration 10 on Article 109, 130r and 130y EC, included in the Treaty of Maastricht, which stated that 'The Conference considers that the provisions of Article 109(5), Article 130r(4), second subparagraph, and Article 130y do not affect the principles resulting from the judgment handed down by the Court of Justice in the AETR case.' According to O'Keeffe, it followed from Declaration 10 that even in the areas where the applicable Treaty articles define the EU competence as being 'without prejudice to Member States' competence' – as is the case in development cooperation policy – the adoption of common rules internally will create exclusive competence externally in the relevant field.[45] The *ERTA* rule applied, according to him, *a fortiori* when this rule was expressly preserved, as is the case in the Declaration.[46] In the *Portugal v Council* case, Advocate General La Pergola adopted a similar reasoning by arguing that the Declaration confirmed that Member States do not have the power to undertake obligations with third countries which affect common rules adopted by the EU or alter their scope.[47]

In the pre-Lisbon era, Declaration 10 was indeed liable to cause confusion about the exact nature of the development cooperation policy competence and about the question whether the application of *ERTA* was entirely excluded or not. Certain authors nevertheless still take the Declaration into account in the post-Lisbon era to interpret the nature of the development cooperation policy competence. Lenaerts and Van Nuffel seem to try to reconcile the formulation of the Treaty on development cooperation policy with Declaration 10. They emphasise that the EU's development cooperation policy and that of the Member States are to complement and reinforce each other, while Member States' freedom to act is restricted by measures adopted by the Union at internal level or agreed upon at international level, referring to Declaration 10.[48] Nonetheless, they add that the *ERTA* effect, in the sense that Member States no longer have the competence to conclude an agreement because it would affect Union rules, may have different consequences in the area of development

---

[44] D. O'Keeffe, 'Exclusive, concurrent and shared competence', in Dashwood, Hillion (eds), *The general law of EC external relations*, Sweet & Maxwell, 2000, 27, 32, 34.

[45] Ibid., 27.

[46] Ibid., 34.

[47] Advocate General La Pergola in Case C-268/94, *Portugal/Council*, EU:C:1996:207, point 18.

[48] K. Lenaerts, P. Van Nuffel, *European Union law*, Sweet & Maxwell, 2011, 994.

cooperation policy than in the area of the other regular shared competences, which would result from the formulation of Article 4(4) TFEU.[49] Klamert, on the other hand, refers to development cooperation policy as an irregular shared competence of a 'generally non-pre-emptive nature'. Hence, according to him, the Member States are not necessarily precluded from also entering into obligations with third states once the EU has concluded an international agreement. The exercise of competence by the Union, the adoption of development policy measures as such, cannot preclude Member State action.[50] However, according to Klamert, Member State action is only possible under the condition that these obligations do not affect or alter the scope of the Union agreement, which does seem to refer to the criteria established in *ERTA*.[51] Schütze does refer to development cooperation policy as a parallel competence but asks what the exact consequences of this categorisation are. He accepts that development cooperation policy constitutes a separate category of competences, distinct from the regular shared competences, as Article 4(4) TFEU contradicts the fundamental characteristic of a shared competence as defined in Article 2(2) TFEU. However, in his perspective, two perfectly parallel competences should never meet, which is contrary to the assessment that an EU legal act always has a potentially limiting effect on the powers of the Member States, especially when Member States' action would hinder or impede the EU's action. Moreover, he questions why two parallel levels of rules that supposedly are not able to meet require explicit cooperation and coordination obligations as formulated in Article 210 TFEU.[52]

This final step in Schütze's reasoning is particularly interesting and reflects the reasoning defended in this book: while the application of *ERTA* exclusivity is excluded in the irregular shared development cooperation policy competence, this does not imply that Member States can act in this area without limits. As will be analysed below, this is, however, the effect of the principle of sincere cooperation and not of exclusivity. Development cooperation policy is an irregular shared competence, a 'special sub-category of shared competences'[53] or a 'non-pre-emptive shared competence'[54] because the pre-emptive effect of the *ERTA* test is excluded: the mere fact that the EU has acted does

---

49 Ibid., 1022.

50 M. Klamert, *The principle of loyalty in EU law*, 167.

51 Ibid., 165.

52 R. Schütze, 'Lisbon and the federal order of competences: a prospective analysis', 709.

53 A. Rosas, 19, also referring to A. Dashwood, 'Mixity in the era of the Treaty of Lisbon', in C. Hillion, P. Koutrakos, *Mixed Agreements Revisited*, Hart, 2010, 361.

54 M. Cremona, 'External relations and external competence of the European Union: the emergence of an integrated policy', 253.

not preclude Member State action in that field. Both the EU and the Member States have competence to act internationally without one preventing the other from acting.[55] As such, the exercise of EU competence does not prevent the Member States from taking action. That follows from the wording of the development cooperation competence's specific Treaty articles, which, in their post-Lisbon formulation, no longer leave scope for any doubt about the exclusion of the *ERTA* principle in development cooperation policy. Article 209(2) TFEU holds that the EU's competence to conclude international agreements in the area of development cooperation policy 'shall be without prejudice to Member States' competence to negotiate in international bodies and to conclude agreements'. Article 211 TFEU states that the Union and the Member States are to cooperate with third countries and with the competent international organisations 'within their respective spheres of competence', while Article 208(1) TFEU clarifies that EU development cooperation policy and that of the Member States 'complement and reinforce each other'. The aim is therefore for EU and Member State policies to reinforce each other, without pre-empting the Member States from exercising their competence.[56] Broberg's argument can be followed, who argues that if EU development cooperation policy would be an exclusive competence, the complementarity obligation in Article 208(1) TFEU would be redundant. On the other hand, if development cooperation policy would fall in the category of regular shared competences, the rule of pre-emption for shared competences would entail that Member State competence is complementary to that of the Union, while Article 208 TFEU classifies them as mutually complementary.[57]

In addition to the specific Treaty articles on development cooperation policy, it is Article 4(4) TFEU that undoubtedly confirms the irregular shared nature of the development cooperation policy competence, which implies that it is a shared competence without a pre-emptive effect. This article determines that the EU has the competence to carry out activities and conduct a common policy in the areas of development cooperation and humanitarian aid but 'the exercise of that competence shall not result in Member States being prevented from exercising theirs'. The wording of Article 4(4) TFEU clearly indicates that it aims to exclude the application of Article 2(2) TFEU and of the *ERTA* principle. By singling out development cooperation policy in the categorisation of competences by mentioning it in a separate paragraph of Article 4 TFEU, this article recognises the distinct nature of the development cooper-

---

55 G. De Baere, 'EU external action', 722.

56 M. Estrada-Canamares, 57.

57 M. Broberg, R. Holdgaard, 'EU development cooperation post-Lisbon: main constitutional challenges', 361.

ation competence as an irregular shared competence with a non-pre-emptive effect. Other Treaty articles which also refer to the fact that EU action in the area applicable will be 'without prejudice to Member State competence', such as Article 191(4) TFEU, are not explicitly singled out in the categorisation of competences.[58] The Treaty, moreover, no longer includes a Declaration similar to Declaration 10, which confirms the application of *ERTA* in certain areas.[59] Current Protocol N. 25 on the exercise of shared competence[60] is also silent on this issue. Given the fact that it was one of the aims of the Treaty of Lisbon to clarify the division of competences, in the area of external action in particular, the explicit distinct categorisation of development cooperation policy in Article 4(4) TFEU emphasises its irregular shared nature. Advocate General Sharpston explains the relationship between Article 2(2) TFEU – to which she refers as the EU's 'right of pre-emption' – and Article 4 TFEU accurately: Article 4 TFEU determines the existence of the competences that are identified as shared between the Union and the Member States, while the pre-emption principle embedded in Article 2(2) TFEU concerns the exercise of these competences.[61] The latter article clarifies that a shared competence implies that both the EU and the Member States are competent to legislate and adopt legally binding acts in the area. However, the Member States exercise their competence to the extent that the Union has not exercised its competence and are able to again exercise their competence to the extent that the Union has decided to cease exercising its competence. It therefore follows from Article 2(2) TFEU that the EU has exclusive competence to the extent that it has occupied the field.[62] With regard to the particular area of development cooperation policy, formulated in the separate paragraph 4 of Article 4 TFEU, this effect on the nature of the competence is excluded. The development cooperation

---

58 Also note that the Court has strictly limited the applicability of Article 191(4) TFEU in *Opinion 2/00*, with the requirement that substantive measures in the field of environmental protection need to be based on Article 192(1) TFEU. After *Opinion 2/00*, the Commission no longer referred to Article 191(4) TFEU as the legal basis for international environmental agreements. This was confirmed by the Court in the *Mox Plant* case (Case C-459/03), where it stated that then Article 175(1) EC Treaty was 'the appropriate legal basis for conclusion, on behalf of the Community, of international agreements on protection of the environment': G. De Baere, 'Mercury rising: the European Union and the international negotiations for a globally binding instrument on mercury', 642–643.

59 See contra: Klamert, who argues that since the wording of the relevant Treaty provisions has not changed, this Declaration must still be considered as a guideline for their interpretation: M. Klamert, *The principle of loyalty in EU law*, 166.

60 Protocol N. 25 on the exercise of shared competence OJ 2012 C326/307.

61 Opinion of Advocate General Sharpston in Opinion 2/15, points 60–61.

62 Opinion of Advocate General Sharpston in Opinion 2/15, point 59.

policy competence is therefore a non-exclusive competence on the basis of the Treaty:[63] the specific Treaty provisions on development cooperation policy, Article 209(2) TFEU and Article 211 TFEU, and the specific subcategorisation of the competence in Article 4(4) TFEU determine the competence's non-pre-emptive character.

The irregular shared development cooperation policy competence not only distinguishes itself from the category of shared competences but from the supporting competences as well. It follows from Article 2(6) TFEU that the exercise of Union competences is determined by the Treaty articles corresponding to each specific area. Paragraph 4 on the development cooperation competence is explicitly part of Article 4 on shared competences, and determines that the Union can develop a common policy in the area of development cooperation policy. The *Portugal v Council* case moreover confirmed that the EU has the capacity to develop a common development cooperation policy of its own: the Court rejected Portugal's argument that the EU lacked the competence to develop a distinct development cooperation policy that went beyond merely coordinating Member States' policies.[64] A crucial difference between the irregular shared development cooperation policy competence and the supporting competences is furthermore the level and form of required cooperation. Supporting competences also include cooperation provisions. However, this cooperation focuses rather on cooperation among the Member States, contrary to the requirement in development cooperation policy, which requires the Member States and the Union to cooperate and coordinate with each other, with the Commission taking a leading role in this respect.[65] Finally, development cooperation is also not a distinct competence such as the CFSP, which is mentioned separately in Article 2(4) TFEU, without being embedded in the categorisation of competences in Articles 3–6 TFEU. The development cooperation policy competence is therefore a shared competence, with the prerequisite that the exercise of EU competence cannot prevent the Member States from exercising theirs. As such, exclusivity is irrelevant for the management of the vertical division of competences in development cooperation policy. Rather, the management of the division of competences between the Union and the Member States and the prevention and solution of conflicts between them takes place on the basis of the principle of sincere cooperation, as will be discussed in the next section.

---

[63] G. De Baere, *Constitutional principles of EU external relations*, 62.

[64] Case C-268/94, para. 36.

[65] M. Klamert, *The principle of loyalty in EU law*, 171. Klamert has moreover argued to extend the principles expressly provided for development cooperation and health to the entire field of supporting competences, including areas such as culture.

3. THE MANAGEMENT OF THE VERTICAL DIVISION OF COMPETENCES IN EU DEVELOPMENT COOPERATION POLICY: THE PRINCIPLE OF SINCERE COOPERATION

3.1 The Principle of Sincere Cooperation and Coherence and Exclusivity as Related Principles

Currently, the principle of sincere cooperation is laid down in Article 4(3) TEU, which emphasises the mutual character of the duty, by stating that 'pursuant to the principle of sincere cooperation, the Union and the Member States shall, in full mutual respect, assist each other in carrying out tasks which flow from the Treaties'. Apart from this mutual duty, it further refers to the Member States as the main addressees of the duty by stating that:

> the Member States shall take any appropriate measure, general or particular, to ensure fulfilment of the obligations arising out of the Treaties or resulting from the acts of the institutions of the Union. The Member States shall facilitate the achievement of the Union's tasks and refrain from any measure which could jeopardise the attainment of the Union's objectives.

The principle of sincere cooperation in its current form therefore still covers two obligations which the Member States should fulfil, apart from assisting the EU (and vice versa) in carrying out tasks which flow from the Treaties: (i) a positive obligation to act in order to fulfil the Treaty obligations or obligations flowing from acts of the institutions, as well as to facilitate the achievement of the Union's tasks, and (ii) a negative obligation to abstain from measures which could jeopardise the attainment of the Union's objectives.

The principle of sincere cooperation constitutes the basis of several other constitutional principles and mechanisms of EU law,[66] while certain duties also

---

[66] For that reason, it has been referred to as 'a qualified expression of the pacta sunt servanda principle' (P. Koutrakos, *EU international relations law*, Hart, 2006, 184–185), a federal principle (G. De Baere, *Constitutional principles of EU external relations*, 253), a multifaceted legal principle aimed at coherence and effectiveness (B. Van Vooren, *EU external relations law and the European Neighbourhood Policy: A paradigm for coherence?*, 2012, 100; see also: E. Neframi, 'The duty of loyalty: rethinking its scope through its application in the field of EU external relations', 2 Common Market Law Review, 2010 359; S. Hyett, 'The duty of cooperation: a flexible concept', in Dashwood and Hillion, *The general law of EC external relations*, Sweet & Maxwell, 2000, 248–253), or a constitutional principle governing the entire EU legal system (C. Hillion, 'Mixity and coherence in EU external relations: The significance of the duty of cooperation'; G. De Baere, T. Roes, 'EU loyalty as good faith', 5). It is for example also the basis for cooperation between the Court of Justice and national courts:

follow from the principle as such.[67] These constitute both negative and positive obligations.[68] It is in the area of EU external action in particular that the principle has brought about increasingly strict obligations incumbent on the Member States.[69] In the field of EU external action, the principle of sincere cooperation finds a particular expression as the principle or duty of cooperation,[70] which follows from the more general principle of sincere cooperation laid down in Article 4(3) TEU.[71] In EU external action, this specific expression follows from the requirement of unity in the international representation of the Union,[72] which demonstrates the importance of the duty for EU external action.[73] In this sense, the duty of cooperation is a mechanism to ensure the requirement of unity, and hence the coherence, of the international representation of the Union.[74] Initially, the duty of cooperation in EU external action was developed in the framework of mixed agreements, where it had particular importance.[75] In the *Mox Plant* case, the Court affirmed that the duty of close cooperation in mixed agreements is a specific expression of and finds its origins in the broader principle of sincere cooperation as formulated in the Treaty.[76] Despite

---

K. Lenaerts, 'La vie après l'avis: exploring the principle of mutual (yet not blind) trust', 3 Common Market Law Review, 2017, 805–840.

[67] M. Klamert, *The principle of loyalty in EU law*, 234–241.

[68] J. Heliskoski, *Mixed agreements as a technique for organizing the international relations of the European Community and its member states*, 62.

[69] G. De Baere, T. Roes, 'EU loyalty as good faith', 1.

[70] Ruling 1/78, paras 33–34; M. Cremona, 'Case C-246/07, Commission v. Sweden (PFOS), judgment of the Court of Justice (Grand Chamber) of 20 April 2010', 5 Common Market Law Review, 2011, 1652; Cremona, 'External relations and external competence: the emergence of an integrated policy', 170; G. De Baere, EU external action; M. Klamert, *The principle of loyalty in EU law*, 33; E. Neframi, 'The Duty of Loyalty: Rethinking its Scope Through its Application in the Field of EU External Relations', 323–359, 325; A. Rosas, 35.

[71] C-246/07, para. 69.

[72] Ruling 1/78, para. 34–36; Opinion 2/91, para. 36; Opinion 1/94, EU:C:1994:384, para. 108; and Case C-25/94 *Commission/Council*, EU:C:1996:114, para. 48; Case C-246/07, para. 73.

[73] M. Cremona, 'Defending the Community interest: The duties of cooperation and compliance', in M. Cremona, B. de Witte, *EU Foreign Relations Law: Constitutional Fundamentals*, Hart, 2008,157.

[74] C. Hillion, 'Mixity and coherence in EU external relations: The significance of the duty of cooperation', 90.

[75] Joined Cases C-300/98 and C-392/98, *Dior and Others*, EU:C:2000:688, para. 36–38.

[76] Case C-459/03, para. 174–175. It has been argued that by linking the duty of cooperation with the broader principle of sincere cooperation as formulated in the Treaties in *Mox Plant*, rather than to refer to the requirement of unity in the international representation of the Union, the Court firmly confirmed the constitutional foundation of the duty of cooperation between the Union and the Member States in external

the fact that the duty of cooperation was mainly established in the specific context of mixed agreements, the *PFOS* case clarified that the principles and duties flowing from the duty of cooperation developed in the framework of mixed agreements also apply in general in the sphere of EU external action.[77]

The principle of sincere cooperation is not a goal in itself: according to Article 4(3) TEU it is directed at achieving the Union's tasks and the attainment of its objectives, as well as coherent international action in pursuit of its EU Treaty objectives.[78] The broad principle of sincere cooperation and the principle of coherence are indeed necessarily linked on a fundamental level. In essence, they both aim to ensure that the Union's objectives are attained. As such, they have in common that they bring about far-reaching legal obligations towards the objectives enshrined in the Treaties. As discussed in Chapter 1, the principle of coherence covers a negative and a positive dimension: the negative dimension aims to avoid contradictions, gaps, and conflicts, while the positive element of coherence aims to create synergies. As such, the negative dimension of coherence relates to conflict resolution and competence delimitation.[79] This distinction is crucial in the management of the vertical axis of development cooperation policy. The analysis on the irregular shared nature of the EU development cooperation policy competence in Section 2 above has demonstrated that the exclusivity theories do not apply to development cooperation policy. Rather, in development cooperation policy, conflicts are avoided and resolved and synergies created by the application of the negative and the positive dimension of the broad principle of sincere cooperation (see below the analysis of the positive duty to cooperate and the negative duty to abstain).

While related, exclusivity and sincere cooperation are conceptually different. The exclusivity principle as formulated in the *ERTA* case is based on and is a specific application of the broader principle of sincere cooperation as formulated in Article 4(3) TEU. The rationale behind the *ERTA* principle is that the Union's tasks and the objectives of the Treaty would be compromised if Member States were able to enter into international commitments containing rules capable of affecting rules adopted by the Community or of altering their scope.[80] The Court explicitly made the link with the principle of sincere coop-

---

relations: C. Hillion, 'Mixity and coherence in EU external relations: The significance of the duty of cooperation', 92.

77 M. Cremona, 'Case C-246/07, Commission/Sweden (PFOS)', 1652.

78 B. Van Vooren, *EU external relations law and the European Neighbourhood Policy: A paradigm for coherence?*, 100, referring to Opinion 1/94, para. 108.

79 M. Cremona, 'Coherence through law: What difference will the Treaty of Lisbon make?', 14–16.

80 C-22/70, para. 20–22; Opinion 2/91, para. 11; Case C-467/98, para. 110–112; Opinion 1/03, para. 116–119.

eration in the *ERTA* case.[81] However, although the *ERTA* principle stems from the principle of sincere cooperation, it was developed into a doctrine of its own, which should be kept conceptually distinct from the principle of sincere cooperation as such. The crucial difference between both concepts is that they operate on a different level. *ERTA* pre-emption is a question of determining competence:[82] it is one of the ways through which the Union acquires exclusive competence.[83] The principle of sincere cooperation, by contrast, does not operate on the level of the vertical or horizontal division of competences, but it regulates the *exercise* of those competences.[84] The *Commission/Luxemburg* and *Commission/Germany* cases on the principle of sincere cooperation made clear that Member States are bound by obligations flowing from the principle of sincere cooperation, even while they are still competent to act. The principle of sincere cooperation is therefore able to create specific obligations incumbent on the Member States *in the exercise of their competence.*[85] As *ERTA* exclusivity is triggered by the fact that existing EU rules would be affected or their scope altered, it seems that the *ERTA* rule's function is rather to preserve the effectiveness of the existing EU *acquis* than to facilitate the development of a common policy,[86] while sincere cooperation aims to serve both objectives. Put differently, while the duty of cooperation aims to ensure that EU Treaty objectives are attained, exclusivity intends to protect the EU's powers from being affected.[87]

This can be further explained by distinguishing the scope of Union competences from the scope of Union law.[88] The scope of Union competences is limited by the powers as conferred to the Union institutions in the Treaties.[89] However, the scope of Union law is a broader notion as it is linked to the attainment of the Treaties' objectives: these are pursued by Union actions but also by positive Member State action, as well as by Member States refraining

---

81 Case C-22/70, para. 77, 87. M Cremona, 'Defending the Community interest: the duties of cooperation and compliance', 159.

82 S. Weatherill, *Law and integration in the European Union*, Clarendon 1995, 136–137.

83 Article 3(2) TFEU.

84 G. De Baere, 'EU external action', 36–37; See C. Hillion, '*Tous pour un, un pour tous!* Coherence in the External Relations of the European Union', 28.

85 C. Hillion, 'Mixity and coherence in EU external relations: the significance of the duty of cooperation', 99.

86 R. Holdgaard, 'The European Community's implied external competence after the Open Skies cases', 3 European Foreign Policy Review, 2003, 370.

87 B. Van Vooren, *EU external relations law and the European Neighbourhood Policy: A paradigm for coherence?*, 116.

88 G. De Baere, 'External action', 36–37.

89 Article 5(2) TEU, Article 13(2) TEU.

from exercising certain powers in light of these aims.[90] The obligations flowing from the principle of sincere cooperation are therefore determined by the scope of Union law, rather than by the scope of Union competences, the latter operating at the level of the division of competences between the Union and the Member States.[91] This can be linked to the functioning of the principle of exclusivity on the one hand and the duty of cooperation on the other hand: the duty of cooperation is broader because it functions in relation to the attainment of the EU objectives (i.e., in the scope of Union law), while exclusivity more strictly relates to EU competences (i.e., in the scope of Union competences). The EU's tasks and objectives, as mentioned in Article 4(3) TEU, and the corresponding Member States' obligations flowing from the duty of sincere cooperation should therefore be assessed in the context of Union law.[92]

The application of the principle of sincere cooperation and the *ERTA* principle are therefore triggered in different instances: exclusivity arises when EU competences are affected, while the duty of cooperation brings about obligations for the EU and the Member States when EU law – in terms of its objectives and not in the more strict sense of its competences – is affected.[93] Arena refers in this respect to the distinction between 'constitutional external-sphere pre-emption' and 'legislative external-sphere pre-emption', both flowing from the broad principle of sincere cooperation. While constitutional external pre-emption grants the EU exclusive competence because Member State action would affect common EU rules, i.e. the *ERTA* effect, legislative external pre-emption applies in all areas of EU action and prevents Member States from taking actions that conflict with common EU rules. The latter, however, does not lead to exclusivity.[94] This is essential in the management of the vertical division of competences in development cooperation policy: while it is not subject to exclusivity theories, a duty of abstention can follow from the principle of sincere cooperation as such. This is analysed in detail in Section 3.4 below.

Several cases have demonstrated the distinction between *ERTA* exclusivity and sincere cooperation. In the *Kramer* case the Court recognised the existence of Member State competence in the absence of Union legislation, while it required the Member States to exercise that competence in line with Union

---

[90] A. Dashwood, 'The Limits of European Community Powers', 21 ELRev, 1996, 114.

[91] M. Cremona, 'Defending the Community Interest: the Duties of Cooperation and Compliance', 167.

[92] Ibid., 126.

[93] B. Van Vooren, *EU external relations law and the European Neighbourhood Policy: A paradigm for coherence?*, 77.

[94] A. Arena, 64–65.

law obligations, in particular the duty of sincere cooperation. It held that the Member States are under a duty not to enter into any commitment which might hinder the Union in carrying out its tasks, as well as the obligation to proceed by common action and use all their political and legal means to ensure the participation of the Union in the relevant agreements.[95] In the *Commission/Luxemburg* case, the Court explicitly dismissed the exclusivity claim on the basis of *ERTA* put forward by the Commission,[96] while it did consider there to be a violation of the principle of sincere cooperation (see further below). Regulation 847/2004 was developed in the aftermath of the *Open Skies* cases and is a rare example of a legal instrument that codifies the duty of cooperation between the Union and the Member States in a specific situation.[97] It demonstrates the distinction between sincere cooperation and exclusivity very well: its preamble clarifies that a cooperation procedure is established 'without prejudice to the division of competences between the Community and the Member States'.[98]

The positive duty of cooperation, flowing from the principle of sincere cooperation, relates to the position dimension of coherence by ensuring synergy. In *Commission v Germany* the Court referred explicitly to the function of the duty of sincere cooperation as a means to achieve coherence: the rationale of the duty of cooperation is 'to facilitate the achievement of the EU's tasks and to ensure the coherence and consistency of the action and its international representation'.[99] This too can be linked to the distinction between the scope of EU law and the scope of EU competences. The duty of sincere cooperation functions in the context of the scope of EU law by requiring that the EU and the Member States must attain the Treaty objectives, which is not limited to the scope of EU competences. This duty nevertheless brings about less restricting positive and negative legal obligations than is the case when EU exclusivity is triggered.[100]

Hillion indicates a shift in recent case law on the principle of sincere cooperation that strengthens the link with the principle of coherence. While earlier

---

95 Cases 3, 4, 6/76, Kramer 1976, EU:C:1976:114, paras. 39, 45.

96 Case C-266/03, para. 38–51.

97 For an analysis of the Regulation as a case study of proceduralisation in EU external relations, see: P. Koutrakos, G. De Baere, 'The interactions between the European Court of Justice and the legislature in the European Union's external relations' in P. Syrpis, *The Judiciary, the Legislature and the EU Internal Market*, CUP, 2012, 262–266.

98 Recital 5 of Regulation 847/2004/EC on the negotiation and implementation of air services agreements between Member States and Third Countries, OJ 2004 L157/7.

99 Case C-433/03, para. 66.

100 B. Van Vooren, *EU external relations law and the European Neighbourhood Policy: A paradigm for coherence?*, 100.

case law linked the duty of cooperation with the unity in the international representation of the Union, in the framework of mixed agreements in particular, it seems to follow from more recent case law that the rationale behind the principle of sincere cooperation is based more on coherence and consistency in international representation than on unity in international representation.[101] In that regard, an increasing number of studies point at the absence of an automatic causal link between a more unified representation and a higher level of effectiveness at the international stage.[102] This shift from the requirement of unity in international representation to coherent international representation proves to be more viable in the context of the development cooperation policy competence, considering its complementary nature.

3.2 Applicability of the Principle of Sincere Cooperation to Development Cooperation Policy

The principle of sincere cooperation is of general application, from which it follows that it necessarily also applies to the development cooperation policy competence. In the current Treaty framework, the principle is laid down in the TEU under the title 'Common provisions', confirming its scope of general application. The Court has also confirmed the general application of the duty of cooperation, irrespective of the exclusive or shared nature of the competences or whether the Member States operate in the area of their retained competences.[103] It held that in all the areas corresponding to the objectives of the Treaty, the principle requires Member States to facilitate the achievement of the Union's tasks and to abstain from any measure which could jeopardise the attainment of the objectives of the Treaty.[104] The duty may therefore impose certain duties on the Member States, even if they are acting wholly or partly

---

[101] C. Hillion, 'Mixity and coherence in EU external relations: the significance of the "duty of cooperation"', 88–92.

[102] T. Delreux, S. Keukeleire, 'Informal division of labour in EU foreign policymaking', Journal of European Public Policy, 2016, 14; M. Smith, 'The European Union at the human rights council: speaking with one voice but having little influence', 2 Journal of European Public Policy, 2010, 224, 241; D. Thomas, 'Still punching below its weight? Coherence and effectiveness in European Union foreign policy', 3 Journal of Common Market, 2012, 457, 474.

[103] Ruling 1/78, paras 34–36; Opinion 2/91, para 36; Opinion 1/94, para. 108; Opinion 2/00 para 18; Case C-266/03, paras 57–59; Case C-433/03, para. 63–65; Case C-246/07.

[104] Opinion 1/03, para. 119, C-459/03, para. 174.

within the scope of their own competences.[105] In the *PFOS* case,[106] Sweden was exercising its own competence when it breached the duty of sincere cooperation, while in the *Commission/Luxembourg*[107] and *Commission/Germany*[108] cases too, the Member States were bound by the duty, although they were still competent to act. The finding that sincere cooperation is of general application and therefore applies to Member State actions, even when they act within their own competences or when they operate outside of the Treaty entirely, is further supported by case law concerning the duties incumbent on the Member States in the framework of mixed agreements. In this context, the Court has repeatedly held that the duty of cooperation applies 'where it is apparent that the subject matter of an agreement or convention falls in part within the competence of the Community and in part within that of the Member States'.[109] The Court has confirmed that the principle of sincere cooperation is particularly crucial in mixity but that its application extends to EU external action more generally speaking.[110]

The question is nonetheless what exact consequences the principle brings about in the area of development cooperation policy and what obligations and restrictions it is able to set to Union and Member State action in the field. The central question is whether the complementary nature of the competence entails that stricter or, by contrast, less strict limitations can be set to Member State action. It has been argued that the limits set by the principle of sincere cooperation are more severe in the case of exclusive Union competence than they are in the area of shared competence.[111] Following this reasoning, the limits in the area of irregular shared competences would be even less strict. The question is whether this is indeed the case or whether, on the contrary, the non-pre-emptive character of the competence justifies stricter limitations on

---

105 Kuijper et al., *The law of EU external relations: Cases, materials and commentary on the EU as an international legal actor*, 2nd edn, OUP, 2015, 197; C. Hillion, 'Mixity and coherence in EU external relations: the significance of the duty of cooperation', 99.

106 Case C-246/07, *Commission v Sweden*, EU:C:2010:203.

107 Case C-266/03 *Commission/Luxembourg*, EU:C:2005:341.

108 Case C-433/03, *Commission/Germany*, EU:C:2005:462.

109 See Ruling 1/78; Opinion 2/91, para 36; Opinion 1/94, para 108; Opinion 2/00, para 18.

110 B. Van Vooren, *EU external relations law and the European Neighbourhood Policy: A paradigm for coherence?*, 100, referring to Case C-266/03, para. 58; P. Eeckhout, *EU external relations law*, 215.

111 G. De Baere, 'O, where is faith? O, where is loyalty? Some thoughts on the duty of loyal co-operation and the Union's external environmental competences in the light of the PFOS case', 3 European Law Journal 2011, 414.

Member States set by the principle of sincere cooperation in the exercise of their competences. The following sections will answer these questions.

3.3 Positive Aspect: Duty of Cooperation and Coordination

3.3.1 General requirements flowing from the positive duty of cooperation

As formulated in Article 4(3) TEU, the positive duty of cooperation contains several obligations: (i) the Union and the Member States need to assist each other, in full mutual respect, in carrying out tasks which flow from the Treaties, (ii) the Member States are required to take any appropriate measure, general or particular, to ensure fulfilment of the obligations arising out of the Treaties or resulting from the acts of the institutions of the Union, and (iii) the Member States are to facilitate the achievement of the Union's tasks. The first part of the provision therefore covers a reciprocal obligation, incumbent on both the Union and the Member States, while the latter two obligations require Member States to positively act towards the achievement of the Union's obligations and tasks.

The case law focusing on the positive aspect of the principle of sincere cooperation has defined the duty of cooperation in more general terms, underlining the importance of the principle in the relations between the EU institutions[112] and between the EU and its Member States. However, the case law has done so without specifying which concrete obligations result from the principle or without clarifying how the EU and the Member States should precisely fill in their duties in practice.[113] A few cases provide elements in this respect. *Ruling 1/78* is the first expression of this duty in the external sphere and, although it was formulated in the framework of the EURATOM Treaty, the Court has confirmed its application in the framework of the EU.[114] In this case, the Court stated that Article 103 EAEC requires the Member States to communicate to the Commission all draft agreements or contracts relating to matters within the scope of the Treaties. The Commission may object, in which case the Member States may ask for a ruling by the Court. Referring to Article 192 EAEC, which was identical to Article 4(3) TEU, the Court held that the draft convention at issue could be implemented only in a sphere of close association between the institutions and the Member States, both in the process of negotiation and conclusion and in the fulfilment of the obligations entered into.

---

112 This issue will be addressed in Chapter 6.

113 A. Delgado Casteleiro, J. Larik, 'The duty to remain silent: limitless loyalty in EU external relations?', 4 European Law Review, 2011, 529.

114 Opinion 2/91, para. 36.

The implementation of the agreement moreover required close cooperation between the Member States and the institutions.[115] The Court, however, did not clarify what this cooperation should entail in practice. It did demarcate the areas of the agreement to be implemented by the EU.[116] It can therefore be said that it seems that the Court considered the duty of cooperation to be fulfilled when the Member States and the EU have both implemented successfully their parts of the agreement.[117]

Opinion 2/91 is particularly important, as it is the first case where the Court clarified that the duty of cooperation originates in the requirement of unity in the international representation of the EU.[118] It furthermore repeated its statement formulated in *Ruling 1/78*, underlining the importance of close association between the institutions and the Member States in the process of negotiation, conclusion, and in the fulfilment of the obligations entered into.[119] A particular aspect in *Opinion 2/91* is the fact that the Convention at stake, Convention 170 of the International Labour Organization concerning safety in the use of chemicals at work, is covered by EU competence but the EU itself was unable to become a party to the Convention, since it was only open to states. The Court emphasised that in such a case cooperation between the EU and the Member States is 'all the more necessary', since the Union must act 'through the medium of the Member States'.[120] As to how the necessary cooperation needed to be achieved, the Court merely stated that 'all the measures necessary' needed to be taken,[121] leaving it to the Member States and the Union to decide what this entails in practice.[122]

In *Opinion 1/94* too, the Court again underlined the essential role that cooperation plays in the implementation of an international agreement,[123] although it did not suggest any concrete means in order to achieve the cooperation. In the *FAO* case, the Court reiterated its statement that in the process of negotiation and conclusion and in the fulfilment of the commitments entered into, the Member States must take all necessary steps to ensure the best possible cooperation.[124] Important in this case is that the Court recognised that informally concluded inter-institutional agreements are able to materialise

---

115 Ruling 1/78, para. 34.
116 Ruling 1/78, para. 36.
117 A. Delgado Casteleiro, J. Larik, 527.
118 Opinion 2/91, para. 36.
119 Opinion 2/91, para. 36.
120 Opinion 2/91, para. 37
121 Opinion 2/91, para 38.
122 A. Delgado Casteleiro, J. Larik, 528.
123 Opinion 1/94, para. 108.
124 Case C-25/94, para. 48.

and codify the duty of cooperation and that these agreements are of a binding nature.[125] By establishing rules on voting, speaking, or attending meetings in the FAO, the EU and the Member States fulfilled the duty of cooperation.[126] The emergence of inter-institutional agreements like these find their origin in the freedom left to the EU and the Member States as to how to achieve the cooperation *in concreto*. It follows from this case that the Court approved this approach. However, it remains unclear how the duty of cooperation should be implemented in practice when there is no inter-institutional agreement or whether the conclusion of inter-institutional agreements or soft law instruments is the preferred way to achieve cooperation.[127] What is clear is that an inter-institutional agreement does not act as a condition for the duty of cooperation to be binding: the duty creates legal consequences by itself, without the need to be further formalised.[128]

There is moreover case law in which the Court found a breach of the positive duty of cooperation on the part of the Member States. In *Case 141/78* the Court found the UK to be in breach of the duty of cooperation in a case concerning fishing and the conservation of maritime waters. A particular duty to cooperate applied in this case: a regulation required that fishing measures had to be notified to the other Member States and to the Commission, while a Council Resolution demanded that, as long as a common EU policy on the conservation in maritime waters was lacking, Member States should seek Commission approval before taking unilateral measures.[129] By not respecting these specific duties, the UK violated the duty to cooperate.[130]

From the *Mox Plant* case follows a duty of prior information and consultation. The Court held that it followed from the obligation of close cooperation within the framework of a mixed agreement that Ireland had a duty to inform and consult the competent EU institutions prior to instituting dispute settlement proceedings concerning the MOX plant within the framework of the Convention for the Protection of the Marine Environment of the North-East Atlantic.[131] That was in particular the case because the Commission had already argued that the dispute relating to the MOX plant was a matter falling within the exclusive jurisdiction of the Court and Ireland had not even yet fulfilled its duty of information and consultation until the court proceedings were

---

[125] Case C-25/94, para. 50; P. Eeckhout, *EU External Relations Law*, 246.

[126] Case C-25/94, para. 49.

[127] A. Delgado Casteleiro, J. Larik, 529.

[128] Joined Cases C-300/98 and C-392/98, C. Hillion, 'Mixity and Coherence in EU external relations: the significance of the duty of cooperation', 96.

[129] Case 141/78, *French Republic/United Kingdom*, EU:C:1979:225, para. 7.

[130] Case 141/78, para. 9, 12.

[131] Case C-459/03, para. 179.

brought.[132] Therefore, Ireland had not only violated the exclusive jurisdiction of the Court, but also its duty of cooperation.

The *Commission/Luxemburg* and *Commission/Germany* cases are relevant for both the positive duty of cooperation and the negative duty to abstain. The latter will be discussed in the next section, while this section focuses on the positive aspect. The cases concerned the negotiation of international agreements on inland waterways, both by the EU and by Member States bilaterally. The Council had authorised the Commission to negotiate a multilateral agreement on the rules applicable to the transport of passengers and goods by inland waterway between the EU and several states in Eastern Europe. Following this decision, the Commission called on the Member States to suspend their bilateral processes to conclude agreements on inland waterways with the same states. Both Germany and Luxemburg had initiated such bilateral treaty-making processes with these countries. The Commission lodged separate proceedings against both Member States. Luxembourg had negotiated, concluded, ratified, and implemented the contested bilateral agreements without cooperating or consulting with the Commission. In the case of Germany, the agreements were already signed before the Council Decision authorising the negotiation of the agreement was adopted, but Germany still ratified and implemented those agreements. The Commission argued that the Member States had compromised the implementation of the decision because the negotiation of the agreement by the Commission and the subsequent conclusion by the Council is inevitably made more difficult by interference from the Member States. Moreover, this would have weakened the EU's negotiating position because the EU and its Member States appeared fragmented.[133] The Court held that Member States are 'subject to special duties of action and abstention in a situation in which the Commission has submitted to the Council proposals which, although they have not been adopted by the Council, represent the point of departure for concerted EU action'.[134]

The *Commission/Luxemburg* and *Commission/Germany* cases are also important because they further clarify the moment when the application of the duty of cooperation is triggered, expressed by the point of departure for concerted Union action. According to the Court:

> a decision authorising the Commission to negotiate a multilateral agreement marks the start of such a concerted EU action at international level and requires for that purpose, if not a duty of abstention on the part of the Member States, at the very least

---

[132] Case C-459/03, para. 178, 181.

[133] Case C-266/03, para. 53.

[134] Case 804/79, *Commission/United Kingdom*, EU:C:1981:93, para. 28; Case C-433/03, para. 65, Case C-266/03, para. 59.

> a duty of close cooperation in order to facilitate the achievement of the Community tasks and to ensure the coherence and consistency of the action and its international representation.[135]

The Court held that by negotiating, concluding, ratifying, and implementing, in the case of Luxemburg, or ratifying and implementing, in the case of Germany, the agreements *without cooperating or consulting with the Commission*, Luxemburg and Germany had failed to fulfil their obligations under Article 4(3) TEU.[136] The Court held that consultation was all the more necessary, since a gentleman's agreement annexed to the Council Decision called for close coordination between the Commission and the Member States. The agreement moreover designated the Commission as the spokesperson during the negotiations and the Member States could not 'handicap the Commission' in this regard.[137]

The conclusion that can be drawn from the *Commission/Luxemburg* and *Commission/Germany* cases is not entirely straightforward: it is not clear whether informing and consulting the Commission would have sufficed to avoid a breach of the duty of cooperation.[138] The facts in the Luxemburg case are rather straightforward: Luxemburg had not consulted the Commission at all, and although the negotiations had already started before the Council Decision was adopted, the agreements were signed and ratified after that date. A breach of the positive duty of cooperation is therefore rather clear. Several authors have argued that this is different for the *Commission/Germany* case and have questioned whether informing and consulting in the ratification and implementation phase would have remedied the breach or whether the duty to cooperate would have boiled down to a duty to abstain that can only be alleviated by an authorisation for the Member States to act.[139] The latter aspect will be discussed in the next section on the negative obligations flowing from the principle of sincere cooperation. Because of this ambiguity, it is difficult to draw a clear-cut conclusion from these cases for the consequences that the positive duty of cooperation brings about, despite a clear duty of prior information and consultation from the moment there is concerted EU action, as well as an emphasis on the Commission's role as primary negotiator.

The analysis of the case law on the positive duty of cooperation would point at the Court defining the duty of cooperation in a rather open-ended manner,

---

135 Case C-433/03, para. 66; CaseC-266/03, para. 60.

136 Case C-266/03, para. 61; Case C-433/03, para. 73.

137 Case C-266/03, para. 62; Case C-433/03, para. 70.

138 A. Delgado Casteleiro, J Larik.

139 B. Van Vooren, *EU external relations law and the European Neighbourhood Policy: A paradigm for coherence?*, 118.

emphasising its importance in the relationship between the Union and the Member States but without specifying how the duty should be materialised concretely.[140] The particular circumstances of a case are essential to assess whether a breach took place, making it difficult to draw general conclusions and leading to the assessment that the duty's consequences differ from case to case. What seems possible to conclude from the above analysed case law is, first, the necessity of close association between the institutions and the Member States in the negotiation, conclusion, and fulfilment of the obligations flowing from mixed agreements.[141] Second, the Court recognises that the duty of cooperation can be further materialised in inter-institutional agreements, which are moreover of a binding nature.[142] Third, a duty of prior information and consultation applies from the moment there is concerted EU action and applies at all stages of Member State action.[143] However, as will be further developed in the next section, the duty arguably applies even before there is a specific concerted EU action:[144] it can be argued that a genuine duty of sincere cooperation, in particular in the area of irregular shared competence, implies that a duty to inform and consult applies as soon as a Member State aims to take action in an area which falls under the scope of Union law.

3.3.2 Specific application in development cooperation policy

This section will assess in further detail how the positive duty of cooperation operates in the area of development cooperation policy. Of particular interest in this regard is the explicit expression of the positive duty of cooperation in the Treaty articles, as well as in secondary legislation and soft law in the area of development cooperation policy.

On the basis of the scope of application of the principle of sincere cooperation, a duty to inform and consult is incumbent on the Member States as soon as the Member State is about to take action in an area which falls under the scope of Union law. That the duty to inform and consult is incumbent on the Member States before taking action follows from the *Mox Plant* case.[145] There the Court held that as the Convention's provisions at issue in the dispute come within the scope of Union competence, Ireland had violated its duty of cooperation – the duty of prior information and consultation in particular – in this case

---

140 A. Delgado Casteleiro, J. Larik, 529.

141 Ruling 1/78, para. 34.

142 Case C-25/94, para. 50.

143 Case 804/79, para. 28; Case C-433/03, para. 65, Case C-266/03, para. 59.

144 The next section on the negative duty to abstain will discuss this notion in further detail.

145 M. Cremona, 'Defending the Community interest', 167.

in the specific form of exclusive jurisdiction for the Court of Justice.[146] This more far-going duty to inform and consult is justified and necessary in order to effectively ensure the fulfilment of the obligations arising out of Union law and to achieve the Union's tasks, as required by Article 4(3) TEU.[147] That this is not confined to the context of concluding international agreements[148] is confirmed by the *PFOS* case.

Arguably, another active positive duty that is more far-going than a duty of prior information and consultation that applies to Member States is the obligation for Member States to take early steps to eliminate the risk of conflict between Member State action and Union action and to adjust their bilateral actions while the Union process of decision-making is advancing.[149] While it can be said that these further-going positive obligations incumbent on the Member States apply generally, this is *a fortiori* the case for the area of the complementary irregular shared development cooperation competence because of the enhanced demand for positive cooperation in this area. In the area of development cooperation policy, the principle of sincere cooperation is explicitly expressed in the form of an enhanced demand for positive cooperation.[150] This enhanced duty of cooperation finds expression in the Treaty articles, as well as in secondary legislation and in soft law in the area of development cooperation policy.

In Article 210 TFEU, the principle of sincere cooperation explicitly manifests itself as a duty of coordination and cooperation.[151] It states that:

> 1. In order to promote the complementarity and efficiency of their action, the Union and the Member States shall coordinate their policies on development cooperation and shall consult each other on their aid programmes, including in international organisations and during international conferences. They may undertake joint action. Member States shall contribute if necessary to the implementation of Union aid programmes.
> 2. The Commission may take any useful initiative to promote the coordination referred to in paragraph 1.

The enhanced positive duty of cooperation is an essential characteristic of the management of the EU–Member State relations in development cooperation policy, both in formulation and in their relations with third countries and other

---

146 Case C-459/03, para. 126.
147 M. Cremona, 'Defending the Community interest', 165.
148 Ibid., 165.
149 C. Hillion, 'Mixity and coherence', 101.
150 M. Cremona, 'Coherence through law: what difference will the Treaty of Lisbon make?', 17.
151 M. Klamert, *The principle of loyalty in EU law*, 18.

international actions. As indicated in Article 210 TFEU, in order to ensure the complementarity and efficiency of EU and Member State action, the positive duty of cooperation in the area of development cooperation policy is an essential rule in the management of the relationship between the Union and its Member States. The statement that 'The term cooperation denotes a process just as much as it describes a relationship between different actors'[152] is therefore especially true for the area of development cooperation policy.

This supports the argument that a positive duty of information and consultation always applies. The duty of prior information and consultation arguably amounts to an obligation of result. As argued above, Member States find themselves under this obligation as soon as they are about to act in a field which falls under the scope of Union law. The act of informing and consulting as such is an obligation of result. However, the obligation to reach a common Union position is merely an obligation of conduct, in the context of which Member States must employ their best endeavours to reach a common position.[153] They are, however, not under an obligation of result to reach a common position and to align themselves with the Union position, as will be further illustrated below when discussing the different forms of cooperation and coordination that follow from Article 210 TFEU and that are further developed in secondary legislation and soft law.

Coordination between EU and Member State actions

Article 210 TFEU requires the EU and the Member States to coordinate their policies on development cooperation policy and to consult each other on their aid programmes, while also enabling the possibility to develop joint action. The second paragraph gives the European Commission the mandate to take any useful initiative to promote the coordination. The NDICI-Global Europe further emphasises and concretises the need for coherence by including the need for coordination between the Union and the Member States as a general principle. Article 8(7) NDICI-Global Europe determines in that regard that the Union and the Member States need to coordinate their policies and programmes and, in that regard, should regularly consult each other on their programmes, including in international organisations and during international conferences. The Union moreover fosters inclusiveness and collaboration with Member States, seeking to maximise added value and taking into account experience and capacities, thus reinforcing shared interests, values, and common goals.

152 M. Klamert, *The principle of loyalty in EU law*, 33.

153 C. Hillion, 'Mixity and coherence in EU external relations: the significance of the duty of cooperation', 104.

In this respect the Union should encourage the exchange of best practices and knowledge-sharing among Member States' bodies and experts.

On this basis, the EU takes up a leading role in coordinating Union and Member State development policies, aimed at a successful exchange of information and ideas and in order to stimulate policy convergence.[154] An important role in this respect is indeed attributed to the Commission and the EU Delegations, considering the Commission's specific role in the formulation and implementation of EU development cooperation policy.[155] Its leading role in coordination follows from its global presence, its role in policy coherence, and its specific competences and expertise in the field.[156] The European Commission, and the delegations in the field, are sometimes also referred to as an 'honest broker', referring to the fact that it is less influenced by specific foreign policy interests, while Member States often have specific historical, political, or economic ties with a developing country.[157] In parallel with the Commission at headquarter level, the EU delegations in particular are of key importance in order to ensure the necessary coordination among EU donors, as well as between EU donors on the one hand and the partner country and other donors on the other hand.[158] The partner country level is moreover important for the implementation of aid and establishing the frameworks for development cooperation policy.[159]

Coordination entails in the first place systematic information-sharing.[160] Article 27(3) TEU requires the EEAS to work in cooperation with the diplomatic services of the Member States, which is further emphasised in Article 5(9) EEAS Decision, which states that the Union delegations work in close cooperation and share information with the diplomatic services of the Member States. Despite the one-way formulation in Article 5(9) EEAS Decision, the Member States are also under the obligation to share information with the Delegation. This follows from their positive duty of sincere cooperation to cooperate with

---

154 Communication from the Commission to the Council and the European Parliament, Translating the Monterrey Consensus into practice: the contribution by the European Union, 14.

155 The role of the Commission in EU development cooperation, as well as the role and structure of EU delegations, will be analysed in more detail in Chapter 6.

156 European Consensus, point 46.

157 T. Lethinen, 'The coordination of European development cooperation in the field: myth or reality?' ECDPM, 2003, 18; M. Holland, M. Doidge, 186.

158 Translating the Monterrey Consensus into practice: the contribution by the European Union, SEC(2004) 246, 9; S. Bartelt, 17.

159 Council conclusions 14 May 2012 on the Commission Communication regarding the future approach to EU budget support to third countries.

160 Translating the Monterrey Consensus into practice: the contribution by the European Union, SEC(2004) 246, 9.

the Union, which is further expressed in Article 32(3) TEU, which covers the specific obligation of the diplomatic missions of the Member States and the Union delegations to cooperate.[161] Apart from information-sharing, there are several formal and informal coordination structures in place that not only aim to exchange information but also aim to facilitate cooperation on the ground.[162] Assessments of such coordination efforts often mention their pragmatic and often informal character.[163] The advantage of informal arrangements would be that they can bring about more efficient policy-making.[164] This could arguably be the case for EU development cooperation policy, considering its original complementary nature, which results in Member States having traditionally more room for developing their own policy. Informal and flexible coordination structures and division of labour make it possible to bring together the Member States that are most committed towards a particular issue in development cooperation policy in a quick and flexible manner and to steer cooperation forwards.[165] It is, however, important to keep the division of labour and cooperation structures open to all interested Member States. The presence of informal and flexible mechanisms in development cooperation policy can furthermore be explained by the complexity of the issues that need to be dealt with in this area and their interrelationship with other, more political foreign policy issues, which are traditionally linked to the informal sphere.[166]

Coordination and cooperation between the EU and its Member States takes on different forms, depending on the specific area of cooperation, the country where the cooperation is established, as well as the number of Member States present and active in the third country. The cooperation takes the form of (formal or informal) bilateral meetings with Member States, ad hoc consultations based on needs or requests, as well as formal structures – such as coordination groups, working groups, task forces – which meet on a regular basis, or a combination of these different forms. The Heads of Cooperation of the

---

161 B. Van Vooren, 'A legal-institutional perspective on the European External Action Service', Common Market Law Review, 2011, 497; S. Blockmans, C. Hillion, 48. In the past, the information-sharing stemming from the side of the Member States has been criticised, claiming that the information flow between EU delegations and Member State diplomatic missions is mainly a one-way flow: B. Van Vooren, R. Wessel, 'External Representation and the European External Action Service: Selected Legal Challenges', in S. Blockmans, R. Wessel (eds), *Principles and Practices of EU External Representation*, CLEER Working Paper Series, 2012, 74.

162 T. Lethinen, 19.

163 Translating the Monterrey Consensus into practice: the contribution by the European Union, SEC(2004) 246, 9; T. Lethinen, 11.

164 T. Delreux, S. Keukeleire, 4.

165 Ibid., 14.

166 Ibid., 13.

EU delegation and of the several Member State embassies meet regularly to discuss cooperation policies and topical issues. The EU and the Member States moreover coordinate their political analyses in the framework of the Heads of Mission meetings, which take place regularly and which address issues related to development cooperation policy.[167]

In order to ensure aid effectiveness, the EU has also adopted more far-going measures than mere coordination. Arguably, effectiveness can only be ensured and fragmentation avoided when the number of actors is effectively reduced through a division of labour, delegated cooperation, and joint initiatives.[168] These will be discussed in the following subsections.

Division of labour and delegated cooperation

Following the EU's engagement in the international initiatives on aid effectiveness, the EU has developed division of labour initiatives. Influenced by the original complementary nature of EU development cooperation policy, the EU adopted an ambitious view on aid effectiveness commitments. The complementarity of EU development cooperation policy – which initially could be regarded as a disadvantage for integration in this area – arguably gave the EU the opportunity to manifest itself as a leader in aid coordination and division of labour in development cooperation policy at the international stage. This enabled the EU to play a leading role at the international conferences on aid effectiveness in Paris and Accra and boosted the EU's position on the international development cooperation scene.[169] Following the Monterrey Consensus in March 2002 and in light of the subsequent High Level Forum on Aid Effectiveness in Paris in March 2005, the Commission released a Communication concerning the EU's contribution to the aid effectiveness agenda, covering issues of coordination and division of labour. The Communication explains that a division of labour is necessary in order to avoid a concentration of cooperation and aid in certain sectors and countries, while other, especially challenging, sectors and countries are underinvested.[170]

---

[167] T. Lethinen, 17.

[168] S. Delputte, J. Orbie, 'The EU and donor coordination on the ground: perspectives from Tanzania and Zambia', 5 European Journal of Development Research, 2014, 676–691.

[169] M. Carbone, 'Between EU actorness and aid effectiveness: the logics of EU aid to Sub-Saharan Africa', 342. For the EU's role in shaping the post-2015 SDG framework: T. Van den Sanden, 'The EU perspective on the post-2015 development framework and the legal scope of EU development cooperation', *Studia Diplomatica* 2014, 79–91.

[170] Translating the Monterrey Consensus into practice: the contribution by the European Union, SEC(2004) 246, 14.

After playing an influential role at the Paris High Level Forum,[171] the EU endorsed a Code of Conduct on Complementarity and Division of Labour in 2007.[172] The EU Code of Conduct is a soft law instrument and, hence, it is not legally binding. It calls itself a 'voluntary and flexible' instrument, which should be applied in a 'pragmatic' and 'self-policing' way.[173] The Code targets complementarity at both sector and country level: countries and sectors with substantial overlaps or, on the other hand, gaps require specific attention. It recognises, however, that Member State decisions on country and sector allocation remain national decisions, which the Member States are free to take. The Code intends to lead EU donors to concentrate their aid in a partner country by focusing on a maximum of three sectors, apart from addressing cross-cutting issues. The division of labour in that regard is based on comparative advantage and aims to identify a lead donor in each priority sector, which is in charge of the donor coordination in the given sector, possibly complemented by burden-sharing arrangements.[174] The focus should, moreover, ideally limit the amount of active donors to a maximum of three to five per sector. Apart from sector concentration in a given partner country, the Code of Conduct also aims to concentrate donors' action by establishing cooperation with a limited number of priority countries.[175] In organising the division of labour, the Code gives the EU the role to assist the partner country, and the EU should in any event always play an active role in promoting complementarity and division of labour.[176]

Linked to division of labour in ensuring aid effectiveness is delegated cooperation. This generally refers to the implementation by one donor on behalf of another. In that regard, delegated cooperation also builds on comparative advantages and sharing and maximising capacities. Co-financing is an important means in this regard, in which the EU can be both the receiver and the provider of funds. On the latter, NDICI-Global Europe provides in that regard that financing under the instrument can be provided through contributions to international, regional, or national funds, such as those established or managed by the EIB, by Member States, by partner countries and regions, by international organisations, or by other donors. Article 26(4) NDICI-Global Europe

---

171 M. Carbone, 'Between EU actorness and aid effectiveness: the logics of EU aid to Sub-Saharan Africa', 346.

172 EU Code of Conduct on Complementarity and Division of Labour in Development Policy, COM(2007) 72 final – Conclusions of the Council and of the Representatives of the governments of the Member States meeting within the Council, 15 May 2007.

173 EU Code of Conduct, 8.

174 EU Code of Conduct, 12–15.

175 EU Code of Conduct, 16.

176 EU Code of Conduct, 11.

moreover provides for parallel or joint co-financing. Individual Member States which do not have sufficient capacity on the ground in a country or particular sector, or which do not have a local presence, may see co-financing as a good option to efficiently provide support to that country or sector.[177] EU Trust Funds can also be seen as a form of delegated cooperation. The Commission can establish EU Trust Funds for emergency and post-emergency actions necessary to react to a crisis, or for thematic actions, under an agreement concluded with other donors. The Parliament and the Council are consulted, for trust funds for emergency and post-emergency actions, or need to give their approval, for thematic trust funds, on the establishment of EU Trust Funds. The establishment of EU Trust Funds needs to follow from the added value of the Union intervention in the form of a trust fund, the political visibility for the Union and managerial advantages that they bring, they do not duplicate other existing funding channels or similar instruments and their objectives are in line therewith.[178] On this basis, the EU Emergency Trust Fund for stability and addressing root causes of irregular migration and displaced persons in Africa (EUTF for Africa) was created to address the root causes of instability, forced displacement, and irregular migration, and to contribute to better migration management.[179] Finally, implementation of EU development cooperation financing through indirect management is also an important means of delegated cooperation. Article 26(1) NDICI-Global Europe provides for the possibility for the Commission to implement financing under NDICI-Global Europe either directly by the Commission, by Union delegations, or by executive agencies, or indirectly through the entities listed by the Financial Regulation. In line with the Financial Regulation, this can be done by Member State organisations, which can be a public law body or a body governed by private law with a public service mission.[180]

---

[177] EU Toolkit for the Implementation of Complementarity and Division of Labour in Development Policy, European Commission, 2009, 21.

[178] Article 234 Regulation 2018/1046 of 18 July 2018 on the financial rules applicable to the general budget of the Union, amending Regulations (EU) No 1296/2013, (EU) No 1301/2013, (EU) No 1303/2013, (EU) No 1304/2013, (EU) No 1309/2013, (EU) No 1316/2013, (EU) No 223/2014, (EU) No 283/2014, and Decision No 541/2014/EU and repealing Regulation (EU, Euratom) No 966/2012, OJ 2018 L193/1.

[179] EUTF for Africa constitutive agreement via: https://ec.europa.eu/trustfundforafrica/sites/default/files/original_constitutive_agreement_en_with_signatures.pdf.

[180] Article 62(1)(c) Regulation 2018/1046.

Joint programming and implementation

In recent years, the EU has increasingly focused on joint initiatives in order to not only avoid gaps and duplications but also to create synergies.[181] The European Consensus provides for the promotion and strengthening of joint programming at country level as a voluntary, flexible, and inclusive initiative, specific to the country context. The rationale behind joint programming is that all development donors that share the same principles and have the political will to work together replace their individual country strategies with joint assistance strategies. In this regard, the EU and its Member States agree to adopt a common multiannual programming document for their cooperation towards a particular partner country or region.[182] While it is in principle the partner country taking the lead joint programming exercise, ensuring inclusiveness and ownership of the partner country, the EU will act as a driving force.[183] The fact that the EU, the Commission and the EU Delegations in particular, is leading the joint programming exercise is in line with Article 210(2) TFEU. In line with the 2016 Council Conclusions that called on a further strengthening of joint programming, the NDICI-Global Europe determines that joint programming is the preferred approach for country programming. In that regard, Article 14(4) NDICI-Global Europe provides for the replacement of the Union's and Member States programming documents by a joint programming document. This document should also contain a division of labour between the Union and the Member States. Joint programming shall be open to other relevant donors and actors if the Union and the Member States consider this to be relevant.

Apart from joint programming, the EU also aims to strengthen joint implementation.[184] Joint implementation is grounded in joint responses, analyses, and monitoring.[185] It is inclusive and open to all EU partners who agree and can contribute to a common vision, including Member States' agencies and their development financial institutions, the private sector, civil society, and academia. When assessed to be relevant, it can also include those of like-minded governments, the United Nations, and other international and

---

[181] Communication from the Commission to the Council and the European Parliament: Increasing the impact of EU aid: a common framework for drafting country strategy papers and joint multiannual programming, COM(2006) 88 final,

[182] Council Conclusions of 14 November 2011 on an EU common position for the Fourth High Level Forum on aid effectiveness, 6.

[183] Council Conclusions of 14 November 2011 on an EU common position for the Fourth High Level Forum on aid effectiveness, Annex on Joint Multiannual Programming.

[184] Council Conclusions, Stepping up Joint Programming, 12 May 2016.

[185] European Consensus on Development, 39.

regional organisations and financial institutions. Joint implementation also refers to modalities, such as co-financing and delegated cooperation which are discussed above, but also to non-financial means of implementation. In line with this, joint programming and joint implementation are also embedded in the Team Europe approach, which provides a common framework to support partner countries in the fight against the COVID-19 pandemic and its consequences. It brings together (resources from) the EU, its Member States, their diplomatic network, finance institutions including national development banks, and implementing agencies, as well as the European Investment Bank and the European Bank for Reconstruction and Development.[186]

From the above analysis, it follows that an increased demand for positive cooperation applies in the area of development cooperation policy, and the EU and the Member States use various forms to concretise this duty. Having discussed the *FAO* case above, it follows from this case that the Court approves the specification of the positive duty of cooperation in the form of an inter-institutional agreement. Regulation 847/2004,[187] which was adopted as a result of the *Open Skies* cases,[188] is another example of a concretisation of the principle of sincere cooperation in a formalised instrument. It is therefore a legitimate practice to concretise the duty of cooperation in (soft law) instruments, as is the case for development cooperation policy. As already highlighted above, this does not entail that a specification of the duty of cooperation in subsequent instruments is a prerequisite for its binding nature and to bring about legal consequences.[189] Despite this certain level of formalisation or concretisation of the cooperation arrangements between the EU and Member States in development cooperation, these remain of a voluntary, soft law nature.

There is arguably a clear relationship between the increased demands for positive cooperation that apply in the area of development cooperation policy and the irregular shared or complementary nature of the competence. First, the

---

[186] Joint Communication to the European Parliament, the Council, the European Economic and Social Committee and the Committee of the Regions, Communication on the Global EU response to COVID-19, JOIN/2020/11 final; Council Conclusions, Team Europe, 23 April 2021.

[187] Regulation 847/2004 of 29 April 2004 on the negotiation and implementation of air service agreements between Member States and third countries, OJ 2004 L157/7.

[188] Cases C-466/98, *Commission/United Kingdom;* C-467/98, Commission/Denmark; C-468/98, Commission/Sweden; C-469/98, Commission/Finland; C-471/98, Commission/Belgium; C-472/98, Commission/Luxembourg; C-475/98, Commission/Austria and C-476/98, Commission/Germany.

[189] Joined Cases C-300/98 Christian Dior and C-392/98 Assco gerüste 2000, C. Hillion, 'Mixity and Coherence in EU external relations: the significance of the duty of cooperation', 96.

coordination and cooperation structures are intended to enhance the complementarity and efficiency of EU action. In an area where pre-emption does not apply, it is the duty to cooperate that makes it possible to attain the objectives of the Union's development cooperation policy. Second, a well-developed relationship between the Union and its Member States on the basis of coordination and cooperation arrangements serves the complementarity of the area. Well-functioning coordination structures and division of labour arrangements make it possible that development cooperation objectives are attained, while both the EU and the Member States develop their development cooperation policies in parallel, without there being a need for the Member States to be pre-empted in the division of competences.

The exact extent to which a Member State can follow its own policies and distance itself from an EU position is also governed by the negative aspect of the principle of sincere cooperation, the duty of abstention, in the next subsection.

3.4 Negative Aspect: Duty of Abstention

3.4.1 General requirements

The final part of Article 4(3) TEU demands that Member States refrain from any measure which could jeopardise the attainment of the Union objectives. More recent case law has shown that this negative aspect of the duty of sincere cooperation can impose on the Member States a duty to abstain, separate from the exclusivity theory and hence solely based on the duty of sincere cooperation.

As discussed above, in the *Mox Plant* case, by instituting proceedings before the Arbitral Tribunal, Ireland had violated both the exclusive jurisdiction of the Court and the duty of prior information and consultation.[190] The *Commission/Luxemburg*[191] and *Commission/Germany*[192] cases on international agreements regarding transport on inland waterways too have been discussed in the part on the positive duty of cooperation. However, the *Commission/Germany* case in particular is also relevant when assessing the negative aspect of the duty of sincere cooperation. Again turning to the facts of the case, Germany had, contrary to Luxembourg, consulted the Commission when negotiating and concluding its bilateral agreements with third countries on inland waterways. This nevertheless took place before the Council adopted the decision authorising the Commission to negotiate an EU inland waterways agreement, which

[190] C-459/03, para. 133, 182.
[191] Case C-266/03, *Commission/Luxembourg*, EU:C:2005:341.
[192] Case C-433/03, *Commission/Germany*, EU:C:2005:462.

marks the start of a concerted Union action and which triggers the application of the duty of cooperation. While Germany had complied with the duty before its application was triggered, it disregarded its duty after that point by ratifying the agreements without consulting the Commission.[193] Germany therefore jeopardised the implementation of the Council Decision, as well as the accomplishment of the EU's tasks and the attainment of its objectives, according to the Court.[194] However, what would the duty to inform and consult have entailed in the case of Germany: would merely informing the Commission have sufficed to respond to the duty of cooperation's requirements, or would the duty to consult call for a request for authorisation? Moreover, it could be argued that if the Commission would have responded in a negative sense, this would have implied a duty to abstain for Germany. A few authors have criticised the Court's case law for this reason because the duty to inform and consult would essentially boil down to a duty of abstention: the Member States are prevented from acting, unless they are authorised by the Commission.[195]

The *IMO* case is interesting to consider when discussing a duty to abstain on the basis of the principle of sincere cooperation.[196] In the *IMO* case, Greece had submitted a proposal to the Maritime Safety Committee of the International Maritime Organization (IMO) on the creation of checklists to monitor compliance with certain rules on maritime safety. The Court considered that Greece's proposal could lead to the adoption by the IMO of new rules, which would have an effect on the EU's Regulation that integrated the rules on maritime safety at issue into EU law,[197] as the latter is intended to implement these rules into the EU legal order. As a consequence, Greece's proposal was likely to affect the provisions of the Regulation, constituting a violation of the Treaty articles on sincere cooperation and transport policy.[198] The Court moreover held that a possible violation of the principle of sincere cooperation by the Commission could not influence this conclusion, as Greece had argued that the Commission had infringed its duty of cooperation by refusing to put Greece's proposal on the agenda of the Maritime Safety Committee's agenda, while the Commission was the chair. The Court agreed that the Commission 'could have endeavoured' to submit the proposal, allowing it to be discussed, which could not

---

[193] C-433/03, para. 68.

[194] C-433/03, para. 69.

[195] A. Delgado Casteleiro, J. Larik, 532–533; B. Van Vooren, *EU external relations law and the European Neighbourhood Policy: A paradigm for coherence?*, 118.

[196] For a case note on this case, see: M. Cremona, 'Extending the reach of the AETR principle: comment on Commission v Greece', European Law Review, 2009, 754–767.

[197] Regulation 725/2014 of 31 March 2004 on enhancing ship and port facility security, OJ 2004 L129/6.

[198] Case C-45/07, *Commission/Greece (IMO)*, EU:C:2009:81, para. 21–23.

be regarded as a strong obligation of result on the side of the Commission.[199] However, the Court emphasised, a violation by the Commission of the duty of cooperation did not entitle a Member State to take initiatives likely to affect EU rules.[200] Further, Greece's argument that its proposal was allowed on the basis of a gentlemen's agreement adopted by the Council allowing Member States to submit proposals when no common position has been established was also rejected by the Court. According to the Court, the gentlemen's agreement only allowed Member State action when its position was coordinated at EU level beforehand. In this case, however, no coordination took place. Moreover, the gentlemen's agreement was not able to affect the division of competences.[201] Finally, the Court concluded by stating that the non-membership of the EU in an international organisation did not amount to an authorisation for the Member States to assume obligations likely to affect EU rules aimed at the attainment of the Treaty's objectives. Rather, in line with Opinion 2/91,[202] the Member States should act jointly in the EU's interest when the EU itself is not a member of the international organisation.[203]

Some authors have seen *IMO* as a case that established rather far-going consequences, with the duty of sincere cooperation imposing a duty of abstention on the Member States.[204] The Court's reasoning in the case can indeed lead to confusion because it links the *ERTA* pre-emption formulation with a violation of the principle of sincere cooperation: it refers to the 'affectation' test, without referring to *ERTA*, to conclude that there is a violation of the principle of sincere cooperation.[205] However, it should be clear that the duty of abstention incumbent on Greece in this case stems from *ERTA* exclusivity and not from the principle of sincere cooperation as such: Greece's obligations might have affected the regulation in question in the meaning of the *ERTA* case law.[206] It therefore violated the EU's exclusive competence in the field: the Member States can no longer act in an area of exclusive competence. The reference to the principle of sincere cooperation should therefore be understood as referring to the principle as the basis of *ERTA* exclusivity. The duty of abstention, however, did not follow from the principle of sincere cooperation as such.

---

199 A. Delgado Casteleiro, J. Larik, 535; C. Hillion, 'Mixity and coherence in EU external relations', 113.

200 Case C-45/07, para. 24–26.

201 Case C-45/07, para. 27–29.

202 Opinion 2/91, EU:C:1993:106.

203 Case C-45/07, para. 30–31.

204 A. Delgado Casteleiro, J. Larik, 533.

205 C-45/07, para. 26, 30, 33.

206 B. Van Vooren, *EU external relations law and the European Neighbourhood Policy: A paradigm for coherence?*, 119; M. Cremona, 'Extending the reach of the AETR principle: comment on Commission v Greece', 763.

Therefore, the case which sets the standard for a duty of abstention based on the principle of sincere cooperation as such is the *PFOS* case. This case concerns Sweden's breach of the principle of sincere cooperation by unilaterally proposing to add the chemical PFOS to an annex of the international Stockholm Convention on Persistent Organic Pollutants (POPs). Because the facts of the case are particularly relevant to fully understand its importance and the consequences of this case, a closer look at them is necessary.[207] In August 2004, the Commission presented a proposal for a Council decision on the authorisation to submit, on behalf of the Community and the Member States which are parties, proposals to have a certain number of chemicals included in the relevant Annexes to the Aarhus Protocol and/or the Stockholm Convention. PFOS was not included in the proposal. Sweden announced its wish to establish a common proposal to list PFOS in the relevant Annex to the Stockholm Convention at the Council Working Party in September 2004 and offered the possibility of it unilaterally presenting such proposal. The Commission had already expressed its legal objections to the unilateral listing of PFOS in the Stockholm Convention. In March 2005, the Council adopted conclusions covering a common position on the substance to be proposed for listing in the Annexes, which covered up to three additional substances. The addition of substances to the Stockholm Annex is linked to the Aarhus Protocol: the list of substances under the Aarhus Protocol is the basis for adding substances to the Stockholm Convention. At the subsequent first meeting of the Conference of the Parties to the Stockholm Convention held in May 2005, the EU and its Member States proposed two substances, chlordecone and hexabromobifenyl, for listing in the Annexes. In July 2005, the Council's Working Party met again, and according to the minutes of that meeting, the members agreed that the listing of certain substances should be proposed at the second Conference of the Parties, but no agreement was reached on which substances and the discussion on the issue was postponed. With regard to PFOS, this Working Party observed that work was ongoing on the identification of control measures at EU level: as soon as the Commission had submitted a proposal on those control measures PFOS should be proposed for inclusion in the Aarhus Protocol. The economic consequences of a proposal to include PFOS in the Stockholm Convention were also discussed: the inclusion of PFOS could lead to the need for additional financial aid to developing countries. In July 2005, Sweden submitted in its name and on its own behalf a proposal to list PFOS in Annex A of the Stockholm Convention. In July 2015, Coreper discussed the amended draft Council decision and authorised the Commission to submit a proposal, together with the Member States, to amend the Annexes to the

[207] Case C-246/07, para. 29–49.

Aarhus Protocol by adding PFOS to the Protocol once the Commission had submitted a proposal for a Directive on restrictions on the marketing and use of perfluorooctane sulfonates. In December 2005, the Commission submitted such a proposal, which resulted in Directive 2006/122/EC.[208] The Commission argued that Sweden's unilateral submission to propose to list PFOS had split the international representation of the EU and had compromised the unity of its international representation and therefore constituted a violation of the principle of sincere cooperation. Sweden had proposed the listing, although it was aware that work in this respect was ongoing, which was a condition for international action by the EU and its Member States.[209] Sweden, by contrast, argued that there were no EU rules in respect of PFOS at the time of its proposal to add PFOS to Annex A, and since it operated in an area of shared competence, both the Member States and the EU could propose to add PFOS to the Annex. It further argued that there was no common position reached as regards PFOS at the Council meeting in July 2005. According to Sweden, the principle of good cooperation entails that Member States must make any effort to cooperate with the EU institutions. It argued that it responded to this requirement: it gave sufficient information to and consulted with the EU and the Member States, while it also tried to obtain common action before launching its unilateral proposal.[210]

The Court started its reasoning by reiterating, and therefore confirming, the principles it developed in earlier case law on the principle of sincere cooperation. First, it held that the fact that the case concerned an area of shared competence did not preclude application of the principle of sincere cooperation: the 'duty of genuine cooperation' is of general application and does not depend on the question whether the EU competence is exclusive or shared.[211] The Court further repeated its statement on the duty of cooperation in the framework of mixed agreements: when an agreement falls partly within EU and partly within Member State competence, it is essential to ensure close cooperation between the Member States and the EU institutions, both in the negotiation and conclusion as well as in the fulfilment of the commitments entered into. This obligation flows from the requirement of unity in the international representa-

---

[208] Directive 2006/122/EC of 12 December 2006 on the approximation of the laws, regulations and administrative provisions of the Member States relating to restrictions on the marketing and use of certain dangerous substances and preparations (perfluorooctane sulfonates), OJ 2006 L372/32.

[209] Case C-246/07, para. 44–45.

[210] Case C-246/07, para. 61–63.

[211] Case C-266/03, para. 58; Case C-433/03, para. 64; Case C-246/07, para. 71–72. See also above.

tion.[212] The Court followed its reasoning by referring to the special duties of action and abstention incumbent on the Member States when the Commission has submitted to the Council proposals which, although they have not been adopted by the Council, represent the point of departure for concerted EU action.[213] The adoption of a decision authorising the Commission to negotiate a multilateral agreement on behalf of the EU marks the start of a concerted EU action at international level and requires in that regard, if not a duty of abstention on the part of the Member States, at the very least a duty of close cooperation with the EU Member States.[214]

Turning to the case at hand, the Court determined that the Council had not adopted any formal decision on adding substances to the Stockholm Convention's Annex at the time when Sweden submitted its proposal. However, in line with the established case law, it was crucial to determine whether there was at the time an EU strategy which was not to propose the listing of PFOS immediately.[215] The Court further clarified that a common position should not need to have a specific form for it to be a common position. Nevertheless, it must be able to establish its content to the requisite legal standard.[216] The Court determined that there was at the time when Sweden launched its proposal a common strategy not to propose, at that time, to list PFOS in Annex A to the Stockholm Convention.[217] The Council decided to not include PFOS in the EU and Member States' proposal during the first meeting of the Conference of the Parties. Economic considerations were part of the EU strategy at that time. PFOS would be nominated for inclusion in the Aarhus Protocol, the basis for adding substances to the Stockholm Convention, as soon as the Commission had submitted a proposal for EU legislation on control measures on that substance and, according to the Court, this was indeed what happened.[218] As regards the Stockholm Convention itself, the Court determined that the Council's Working Party of July 2005 agreed that some substances should be nominated at the Second Conference of the Parties. There was, however, no agreement on the substances to be proposed and the discussion of this issue was postponed. Nevertheless, the Court underlined that this did not amount to a decision-making vacuum or a waiting period equivalent to the absence of a decision. The Council's Working Party did not intend to reach

212 Ruling 1/78, para. 34–36; Opinion 2/91, para. 36; Opinion 1/94, para. 1008; Case C-25/94, para. 48; Case C-246/07, para. 73. See also above.

213 Case 804/79, para. 28; Case C-266/03, para. 59; Case C-433/03, para. 65.

214 Case C-266/03, para. 60; Case C-433/03, para. 66; C-246/07, para. 75.

215 C-246/07, para. 76.

216 C-246/07, para. 77.

217 C-246/07, para. 89.

218 C-246/07, para. 80–85.

a decision in July 2005 but thereafter, which was confirmed by subsequent events.[219] Therefore, there was clearly a common strategy not to propose, at that time, to include PFOS in the Annex to the Stockholm Convention. As a consequence, by unilaterally proposing to add PFOS to Annex A to the Stockholm Convention, Sweden dissociated itself from a concerted common strategy within the Council.[220]

The Court, moreover, attached particular importance to the fact that Sweden's unilateral proposal had consequences for the Union: under the Stockholm Convention's provisions, a proposal to add a substance to the Annex would have had consequences for the Union as it would have been bound by the amendment.[221] The Court furthermore again reiterated the special duties of action an abstention on the Member States as soon as the Commission has submitted to the Council proposals which, regardless of whether they were adopted by the Council or not, represent the point of departure for concerted Union action.[222] The Court added that this would be especially true when the situation concerned a unilateral proposal, which dissociated the Member State in question from a concerted common strategy within the Council, such as in this particular case. The Court finalised its reasoning by stating that such a situation was likely to compromise the principle of unity in the international representation of the Union and its Member States and therefore constituted a violation of the principle of sincere cooperation.[223]

The *PFOS* case has received a lot of attention and criticism in literature. One of the main critiques is that the Court has blurred the distinction between exclusivity and the principle of sincere cooperation by establishing a duty of abstention in an area of shared competence, which flows from the duty of sincere cooperation as such. The most severe criticism has been expressed by Van Vooren, and Delgado Casteleiro and Larik, the latter referring to a 'duty to remain silent' when analysing the *PFOS* judgment, while Van Vooren equates the outcome of *PFOS* with 'de facto pre-emption'.[224] Delgado Casteleiro and Larik question the difference between the consequences that the *PFOS* case brings about, compared with the *IMO* case[225] in the area of exclusive competence, a distinction the Court itself makes in its *PFOS* judgment.[226] They raise

219 C-246/07, para. 86–87.

220 C-246/07, para. 91.

221 C-246/07, para. 92–101.

222 Case C-266/03, para. 60; Case C-433/03, para. 66. See also above.

223 C-246/07, para. 103–104.

224 B. Van Vooren, *EU external relations law and the European Neighbourhood Policy: A paradigm for coherence?*, 116.

225 Case C-45/07, *Commission/Greece*.

226 C-246/07, para. 72; A. Delgado Casteleiro, J. Larik, 538.

the question whether the fact that the lack of a clear Union position prevents the Member States from acting – as it follows from the *PFOS* judgment, according to the authors – entails that Member States require an authorisation in order to be able to act. That, however, would overthrow the distinction between shared and exclusive EU competence in the authors' view.[227] Van Vooren agrees that the duty of cooperation always generally applies between the EU and the Member States, but he argues that as soon as there is concerted EU action, the obligations flowing from the duty of cooperation are reinforced: it follows from *PFOS* that from that point on, the duties of information and consultation turn into a duty of abstention.[228] He criticises the abolishment of a clear distinction between pre-emption and the principle of sincere cooperation because Sweden should have waited until there was a clear EU decision not to act: the decision that there would be no concerted EU action would have enabled unilateral Member State action. This amounts to 'de facto pre-emption', according to the author.[229] The author further criticises the temporal scope of application of the principle of sincere cooperation, as established in *PFOS*.[230] It follows from earlier case law that the point in time which triggers the application of the duty of sincere cooperation is the moment when there is 'concerted Union action'. While the further clarification of this moment expressed in the *Commission v Luxembourg* and *Commission v Germany* cases[231] – when the Commission makes a proposal to the Council – is rather easy to define, the *PFOS* case further extends this to a vaguely defined moment in time, according to the authors. The starting point of 'concerted EU action' can now follow from the discussion of an issue in a Council Working Party and can be based on Council Conclusions and minutes of the Working Party's meetings.[232] The 'requisite legal standard' required by the Court is therefore 'largely illusory' and 'of no practical utility', the criticism says.[233] A more nuanced critique is put forward by *Cremona*, who accepts that there is a duty of abstention incumbent on the Member States as soon as a common position has been reached, but she argues that imposing an obligation on the Member States that is stricter than an obligation to work together towards a common position before this point

---

227 A. Delgado Casteleiro, J. Larik, 539.

228 B. Van Vooren, *EU external relations law and the European Neighbourhood Policy: A paradigm for coherence?*, 124.

229 B. Van Vooren, *EU external relations law and the European Neighbourhood Policy: A paradigm for coherence?*, 123–125.

230 See also: G. De Baere, 'O, where is faith? O, where is loyalty?', 416.

231 Case C-266/03, para. 60; Case C-433/03, para. 66.

232 A. Delgado Casteleiro, J. Larik, 538.

233 B. Van Vooren, *EU external relations law and the European Neighbourhood Policy: A paradigm for coherence?*, 122.

undermines the existence of Member State competence. Moreover, considering the far-going consequence that a common position brings about, this author argues that a common position should be established in a Council decision or a collective decision of the Member States, in light of legal certainty.[234]

The above-mentioned criticism on the *PFOS* case stems from a legitimate concern: it is indeed necessary that the distinction between *ERTA* exclusivity – an issue concerning the existence of a competence – and the principles flowing from the principle of sincere cooperation – concerning the exercise of a competence – is maintained (see above).[235] It is moreover necessary to avoid creeping EU competences through the functioning of the principle of sincere cooperation.[236] However, the criticism put forward by Delgado Casteleiro and Larik and by Van Vooren needs further nuance. In essence, these critiques do not consider the particular circumstances and context of the *PFOS* case, which, following De Baere's reasoning on the *PFOS* judgment,[237] are essential to understand the outcome and the consequences of the case. A general duty to cooperate is always incumbent on the parties, but as soon as a concerted position is established, an enhanced duty to cooperate is triggered,[238] which in certain situations – but not always – requires a duty of abstention. *In casu* Sweden had to respect a duty of abstention, but this follows from the particular circumstances of the case and cannot be transformed into a general rule. There was a Union position not to add PFOS at that time, which Sweden contravened with its action. However, there is even a more crucial element present in the particular circumstances of the case that made Sweden's action amount to a violation of the principle of sincere cooperation: the specific procedural rules that applied in the Stockholm Convention's framework led to the fact that Sweden's unilateral action was able to bind the Union against its own will.[239] According to De Baere, it follows from the *PFOS* case that as soon as a Union decision or strategy not to act is established, the Member States are under a duty of abstention under two conditions: (i) the Union's inaction constitutes a Union position, the content of which is established to the requisite legal standard and is not a sign of obstruction of the EU decision-making process, and (ii) the unilateral Member State action possibly leads to measures which

[234] M. Cremona, 'Case C-246/07, Commission v. Sweden (PFOS)', 1664.

[235] B. Van Vooren, *EU external relations law and the European Neighbourhood Policy: A paradigm for coherence?*, 125.

[236] For the distinction between the scope of EU competences and the scope of EU law: see above.

[237] G. De Baere, 'O, where is faith? O, where is loyalty?', 417.

[238] B. Van Vooren, *EU external relations law and the European Neighbourhood Policy: A paradigm for coherence?*, 124.

[239] C-246/07, para. 100; A. Rosas, 36.

bind the Union and therefore cause damage to the Union (more on the latter aspect: see below).[240]

As to the above-mentioned criticism on the temporal scope of the principle of sincere cooperation, it can indeed be argued that this scope has been broadened by the *PFOS* judgment.[241] However, as was argued above, a general duty of cooperation always applies, even before a concerted Union action is established. In that regard, as long as the principle of sincere cooperation mainly covers a positive duty of cooperation and only exceptionally a duty of abstention, the broadening of the starting point which triggers an enhanced duty of cooperation is not that problematic.

What principles can be derived from the case law on the negative aspect of the principle of sincere cooperation, the duty to abstain, that might be relevant for the analysis in the framework of the specific development cooperation policy competence? The Court reiterated that the principle of sincere cooperation is of general application in the external actions of the Union, irrespective of the nature of the competences of the EU. It may impose certain duties on the Member States, even if they are acting wholly or partly within the scope of their own competences.[242] This is not only important in the context of mixed agreements or mixed action in international organisations, but also in light of the distinct nature of a competence, such as the irregular shared nature of development cooperation policy. The *PFOS* case is the first case to clarify that a duty of abstention can follow – as argued above, only in particular circumstances – from the principle of sincere cooperation as such, irrespective of *a priori* or *ERTA* exclusivity.[243] The *PFOS* case moreover demonstrates that the duty of sincere cooperation also applies to political decision-making, outside the context of the negotiation, conclusion, or management of a mixed agreement.[244] Member States are not only bound by a formal Council decision, but also by other acts on the Union level providing the starting point for concerted action, such as a certain strategy for Union action.[245] As the Court held, a common position should not need to have a specific form for it to be a common position.[246] This is particularly relevant for development cooperation policy, an area which is by its nature more linked with informal and polit-

---

240 G. De Baere, 'O, where is faith? O, where is loyalty?', 417.

241 G. De Baere, 'O, where is faith? O, where is loyalty?', 416; A. Delgado Casteleiro, J. Larik, 538; B. Van Vooren, *EU external relations law and the European Neighbourhood Policy: A paradigm for coherence?*, 122.

242 Case C-266/03, para. 58; Case C-433/03, para. 64; Case C-246/07, para. 71–72.

243 G. De Baere, 'O, where is faith? O, where is loyalty?', 417.

244 M. Cremona, 'Case C-246/07, Commission v. Sweden (PFOS)', 1651.

245 M. Klamert, *The principle of loyalty in EU law*, 113.

246 C-246/07, para. 77.

ical processes. Finally, the particular element leading to Sweden's violation, the fact that the unilateral action could bind the Union,[247] is an expression of the fact that Member State action can cause damage to the Union, violating the principle of sincere cooperation.[248] This criterion is of particular importance in the functioning of the principle of sincere cooperation as a principle that can potentially set limits to Member State action in the area of development cooperation policy, an issue which will be further examined in the next section.

3.4.2 Application to development cooperation policy

The Court's conclusion in the above-mentioned cases depends largely on the factual circumstances and context of the cases. The lack of case law in the area of irregular shared competences does not make a straightforward answer to the question of the implications of the principle of sincere cooperation's application in this area any easier. This is particularly important as regards the negative aspect of the duty of sincere cooperation, the duty to abstain, as the latter has potentially the most far-going consequences for the exercise of Member State competence and the management of the vertical axis. It is difficult to identify the exact duties and legal consequences incumbent on Member States derived from the duty of cooperation, as the limits that follow from the principle depend to a large extent on the international legal and political context of the specific action in which the Union and the Member States operate.[249] Each situation therefore requires an individual assessment as to what the duty of cooperation specifically entails, taking into account policy considerations as well as the nature of Union law in the specific field.[250] Nevertheless, it would arguably be possible to identify a bottom line to which the Member States need to respond in order not to violate the principle of sincere cooperation's negative obligation. This bottom line would also apply to the category of the non-pre-emptive or irregular shared competence development cooperation policy.

It follows from the final part of Article 4(3) TEU that the negative duty of abstention covers two elements. The phrase states that 'the Member States shall [...] refrain from any measure which could jeopardise the attainment of the Union's objectives'. Hence, two aspects need to be present to amount to a violation of the negative aspect of the principle of sincere cooperation: (i) to put in jeopardy (ii) the attainment of the Union's objectives. First, as the

---

[247] C-246/07, para. 92–101.

[248] G. De Baere, 'O, where is faith? O, where is loyalty?', 417.

[249] G. De Baere, 'EU external action', 36–37; B. Van Vooren, *EU external relations law and the European Neighbourhood Policy: A paradigm for coherence?*, 100.

[250] M. Cremona, 'Defending the Community interest: the duties of cooperation and compliance', 164.

negative aspect of Article 4(3) TEU is oriented towards the attainment of the Union's objectives, it is essential to determine what the Union's objectives are in the context of the principle of sincere cooperation. Both Klamert[251] and Cremona[252] have referred to the broad notion of 'Union interest' and to the unity of international representation and consistency and coherence of Union action in this respect. This links to what Neframi has formulated as 'the ultimate external action objective'. She argues that it follows from that case law that the duty of abstention incumbent on the Member States serves both the specific objective of the action but also the ultimate external action objective of an effective international action in the interest of the Union.[253]

That line of argument cannot be followed. The duty of cooperation is indeed a means to attain unity of the international representation, as well as consistent and coherent Union action, which is ultimately linked to efficient external action. However, these underlying aims cannot function as an objective in the sense of the duty of abstention as formulated in the final sentence of Article 4(3) TEU. Only specific objectives that are reflected in a particular strategy can constitute objectives on which a duty of abstention can be based. The *PFOS* case further supports this argument. In the *PFOS* case, Sweden had argued that its action did not intend to obstruct the Union's environmental policy objectives. The Court, however, did not assess Sweden's behaviour in light of the broad overall environmental objectives but rather on the basis of the specific strategy adopted in the Council on the particular issue. This included an assessment covering other objectives than the strict environmental ones – such as the discussion of the effects of the addition of PFOS to the Convention on developing countries – as well as considerations in relation to the EU's broader strategy within the Stockholm Convention.[254] Therefore, based on the *PFOS* case, it can be argued that the 'Union objectives' include not only the objectives formulated in the Treaties but also the political formulation of these objectives in the form of a specific strategy adopted by the Council, which can also cover a balancing of several objectives.[255] Assessing the duty of abstention on the basis of mere general objectives such as the unity of external representation or coherent external action would limit Member

---

[251] M. Klamert, *The principle of loyalty in EU law*, 123; 291.

[252] M. Cremona, 'Defending the Community interest: the duties of cooperation and compliance', 127; M. Cremona, 'Case C-246/07, Commission v. Sweden (PFOS)', 1653.

[253] E. Neframi, 'Vertical division of competences and the objectives of the European Union's External action', in M. Cremona, A. Thies (eds), *The European Court of Justice and external relations law*, Hart, 2014, 92.

[254] Case C-246/07, para. 39.

[255] M. Cremona, 'Case C-246/07, Commission v. Sweden (PFOS)', 1653.

States' action disproportionally: a duty to abstain can only be based on specific objectives that are reflected in a particular strategy.

The second criterion that is necessary in order to have a violation of the negative aspect of the principle of sincere cooperation is, as formulated by Article 4(3) TEU, to put in 'jeopardy' the Union's objectives. On the basis of the concretisation of the principle in legal provisions, case law, and following other authors, it seems that this would entail whether Member State action impedes, hinders, undermines, or damages the Union's action.[256] First, Regulation 847/2004 on the negotiation and implementation of Air Service Agreements between Member States and Third Countries,[257] which codified the duty of cooperation between the Union and the Member States in the aftermath of the *Open Skies* cases, states that the Commission will notify the Member States if Member State negotiations are 'likely to be incompatible' with Union law and are 'likely to undermine the objectives of Union negotiations'. Moreover, the Member States can be authorised to conclude the agreement, provided that 'this does not harm the object and purpose of the Community common transport policy'.[258] A parallel can also be drawn with the specific duty of cooperation in the context of the CFSP, laid down in Article 31(1) TEU. The Article states that when a Member State issues a qualified abstention 'in a spirit of mutual solidarity, *the Member State concerned shall refrain from any action likely to conflict with or impede Union action* based on that decision and the other Member States shall respect its position'.[259] The Treaty article on the specific duty to cooperate in the CFSP therefore explicitly includes the criterion of conflicting with or impeding Union action. Even in the intergovernmental area of the CFSP,[260] Member State action can be governed on the basis of this criterion.

Second, Advocates General Maduro and Tizzano respectively have argued that the decisive criterion to assess whether the duty of cooperation was violated should be whether the exercise of Member State competence was 'liable seriously to compromise the exercise of a Union competence'[261] or 'likely

[256] R. Schütze, 'Lisbon and the federal order of competences: a prospective analysis', 709; G. De Baere, 'O, where is faith? O, where is loyalty?', 410.

[257] Regulation 847/2004 of 29 April 2004 on the negotiation and implementation of air service agreements between Member States and Third Countries, OJ 2004 L157/7.

[258] Article 4(3) Regulation 847/2004/EC.

[259] Emphasis added.

[260] See Chapter 3 on the delimitation with the CFSP for a specific analysis of the CFSP's distinct nature in EU external action.

[261] Advocate General Maduro in Case C-205/06, *Commission/Austria*, EU:C:2009:118; Case C-249/06, *Commission/Sweden*, EU:C:2009:119, point 36–42; Case C-246/07, point 38.

to limit, if not undermine, a common action'.[262] The Court has also used the criterion. It follows from the *Kramer* case that the Member States are under a duty not to enter into any commitment which 'might hinder the Union in carrying out its tasks'.[263] In the *Commission/Luxemburg* case, the Court considered prior consultation with the Commission all the more necessary because of a gentlemen's agreement which stated, *inter alia*, that the representatives of the Member States must take no action which is 'likely to handicap the Commission in its work'.[264] In the *PFOS* case in particular, this was essentially the core criterion which led to Sweden's action's incompatibility with the duty of sincere cooperation: because of the particular context of the Stockholm Convention, Sweden's unilateral action could harm the EU because it could bind the EU.[265] Because of the fact that the Union and its Member States are not entitled to exercise rights under the Convention concurrently, a vote by Sweden would have undermined the position of the Union.[266]

The latter has led De Baere to refer to the criterion of 'hindering or impeding the Union's action'[267] and the question whether Member State action is 'liable to cause damage to the Union'.[268] Klamert formulates it as 'undermining the effectiveness'[269] and refers to the duty to abstain incumbent on the Member States in case of conflicting actions with Union action as a 'pro-Union approach'.[270] Schütze refers to national measures that 'hinder or impede the EU scheme',[271] and Hillion to the requirement that Member States refrain from 'taking actions which would compromise the effectiveness of EU provisions',[272] while Cremona refers to an 'obstruction of the Union interest'.[273]

This 'bottom line' which triggers the duty to abstain on the basis of the duty of sincere cooperation as such is reminiscent of rule pre-emption and obstacle pre-emption.[274] Arena places both rule and obstacle pre-emption

---

262 Advocate General Tizzano in Case C-433/03, point 83.

263 Cases 3, 4, 6/76, para. 45.

264 Case C-266/06, *Commission/Luxemburg*, EU:C:2008:295, para. 62.

265 G. De Baere, 'O, where is faith? O, where is loyalty?', 410.

266 M. Klamert, *The principle of loyalty in EU law*, 114.

267 G. De Baere, 'EU external action', 36–37.

268 G. De Baere, 'O, where is faith? O, where is loyalty?', 417.

269 M. Klamert, *The principle of loyalty in EU law*, 165.

270 M. Klamert, *The principle of loyalty in EU law*, 166–167.

271 R. Schütze, 'Lisbon and the federal order of competences: a prospective analysis', 717.

272 C. Hillion, 'Mixity and coherence in EU external relations: the significance of the duty of cooperation', 108.

273 M. Cremona, 'Defending the Community interest: the duties of cooperation and compliance', 164.

274 J. Weiler, 'The Community system: The dual character of supranationalism', YEL 1981, 90; R. Schütze, 'Supremacy without pre-emption? The very slowly emer-

under the common denominator of conflict pre-emption.[275] These types of pre-emption also follow from the existence of a material conflict between EU and Member State measures.[276] Rule pre-emption then refers to the situation in which external actions plainly contradict a specific EU rule, while obstacle pre-emption applies when an action interferes with the proper functioning or impedes the objectives of a specific EU rule.[277] Conflict pre-emption would then be the type of pre-emption which is most in line with sincere cooperation, its source of existence. The *ERTA* exclusivity rule, by contrast, relates more to field pre-emption, while *ERTA* pre-emption and sincere cooperation operate on a different level as conceptually different notions (see above). This difference manifests itself in the negative duty of abstention as well: a negative duty of abstention flowing from the principle of sincere cooperation as such arises not when unilateral Member State action would affect common rules in the *ERTA* sense, but when it contradicts Union norms or when it would jeopardise the attainment of the objectives of the Union.[278] The criticism that a duty of abstention on the basis of the principle of sincere cooperation as such amounts to pre-emption[279] does not correspond with the conclusion that *ERTA* pre-emption and a duty of abstention on the basis of the principle of sincere cooperation as such are triggered in different circumstances. A duty of abstention only follows from the principle of sincere cooperation as such if unilateral Member State action would contradict or undermine Union action. Common Union rules are, however, affected in the *ERTA* sense even if they do not strictly contradict them.[280] *ERTA* therefore applies irrespective of the fact whether unilateral Member State action complies with Union law.[281] As well illustrated by De Baere: in the *ERTA* reasoning, the 'harmful effect is presumed by the mere fact of Member State action in an area covered by common

gent doctrine of community pre-emption', 1035–1038; A. Arena, 29–105. See also: M. Chamon, 'Implied exclusive powers in the ECJ's post-Lisbon jurisprudence: the continued development of the ERTA doctrine, Common Market Law Review, 2018, 1101–1142.

275 Arena, 71.

276 R. Schütze, 'Supremacy without pre-emption? The very slowly emergent doctrine of Community pre-emption', 1041.

277 A. Arena, 71.

278 E. Neframi, 'Vertical division of competences and the objectives of the European Union's External action', 93.

279 B. Van Vooren, *EU external relations law and the European Neighbourhood Policy: A paradigm for coherence?*, 116–125; A. Delgado Casteleiro, J. Larik, 540–541.

280 Opinion 2/91, para. 25–26; Opinion 1/03, para. 120; Opinion 1/13, para 86; Opinion 3/15, para 113.

281 G. De Baere, *Constitutional principles of EU external relations*, 43–51; 71–72.

rules, even if it appears perfectly in accordance with agreed Union policy'.[282] By contrast, a duty of abstention on the basis of sincere cooperation as such always follows from Member State action which contradicts Union action in the sense that the former would undermine, hinder, or impede the latter. While in the area of regular shared competences, any Member State action is prevented on the basis of *ERTA* when common Union rules exist because any Member State action in this light is presumed to be harmful to the Union,[283] this does not apply in the area of development cooperation policy. Because of the irregular shared nature of the development cooperation competence, Member States can only be prevented from exercising their competence on the basis of the principle of sincere cooperation if their action would contradict, undermine, hinder, or impede a specific Union action.

In this respect, it can be useful to draw a parallel between the duty of abstention on the basis of the principle of sincere cooperation and primacy (see also above). Both have in common that their application is triggered by a conflict between Member State and Union action. By contrast, *ERTA* exclusivity applies as soon as common rules are affected or their scope altered, regardless of the question of a real conflict between Member State and Union action. Primacy is then the conflict rule which is traditionally applicable to solve conflicts between the Union and the Member States in the internal Union order: in the event of a conflict between EU and national law, EU law prevails. Conflicting national rules are subsequently disapplied by national courts and administrations, while the adoption of conflicting national rules is prevented.[284] Like *ERTA* exclusivity, primacy is also founded on the broad principle of sincere cooperation. Already in *Costa v Enel*, the standard-setting case on EU law's primacy, the necessity of granting prevalence to Union law over conflicting national law is linked with avoiding jeopardising the attainment of the Union's objectives.[285] The specific duty to disapply conflicting national rules also finds its origins in the principle of sincere cooperation.[286] Both primacy and sincere cooperation find their origin and *raison d'être* in consistency: in *Costa v Enel* the Court clarified that to the extent that a Member State measure

---

282 G. De Baere, 'O, where is faith? O, where is loyalty?', 418.

283 Ibid., 418.

284 Case 106/77, *Simmenthal*, EU:C:1978:49, para. 17; Case 103/88, *Fratelli Costanze*, EU:C:1989:256, para. 33; C-10/97 and C-22/97, *IN.CO.GE*, EU:C:1998:498, para. 20.

285 Case 6/64, *Costa/Enel*, EU:C:1964:66, 593–594.

286 Case 106/77, *Simmenthal*, EU:C:1978:49, para. 24; C-298/12, *Confédération paysanne*, EU:C:2013:630, para. 37.

is inconsistent with Union law, it cannot be applied over Union law.[287] Primacy requires that precedence is given to Union law in case of conflict with national law, to the extent of that conflict and to the extent that it is necessary for the effective application of Union law.[288] The precedence of Union law therefore only applies to the extent of the conflict.[289] It does not render the contradictory national law non-existent: incompatible legislation only becomes inapplicable.[290] Exclusivity goes further in the sense that it restricts the Member States' competence: Member States are not allowed to enter into any international commitment that can affect Union competences in the first place.[291] It can therefore be argued that the negative aspect of sincere cooperation in the external sphere reflects the functioning of primacy in the internal sphere:[292] the consequence of both principles is that Member States do not lose their competence but they are prevented from acting because of a conflict with Union action, to the extent of the conflict. As such, the principle of primacy is also able to limit Member State action in the area of development cooperation policy: national development cooperation policy legislation that conflicts with Union development cooperation policy measures should be disapplied.[293]

Hence, on this basis, arguably despite the irregular shared nature of EU law in the area of development cooperation policy, it is possible – in exceptional circumstances – to encounter situations in which a duty of abstention should apply on the Member States because of a violation of the duty of sincere cooperation. On the basis of the criteria determined above, this would be the case when, considering the particular circumstances and context, unilateral Member State action would clearly contradict, undermine, hinder, or impede a specific Union development cooperation policy strategy. Such instances call for a duty of abstention on the basis of the principle of sincere cooperation. Such a situation could arise when, following the definition of incompatibility in international law,[294] simultaneous compliance with EU measures and Member State

---

[287] K. Lenaerts, T. Corthaut, 'Of birds and hedges: the role of primacy in invoking norms of EU law', 3 European Law Review, 2006, 290.

[288] G. De Baere, *Constitutional principles of EU external relations*, 37.

[289] K. Lenaerts, T. Corthaut, 291.

[290] Joined cases C-10/97 and 22/97, IN.CO.GE, EU:C:1998:498, 20–21.

[291] G. De Baere, *Constitutional principles of EU external relations*, 33, 71; P. Koutrakos, G. De Baere, 'The interactions between the European Court of Justice and the legislature in the European Union's external relations', 255.

[292] See also Arena, who argues that conflict pre-emption applies internally and externally: A. Arena, 67.

[293] See also Arena, who argues that internal conflict pre-emption applies to all areas in which the Union can adopt binding instruments: A. Arena, 34.

[294] C. Jenks, 'Conflict of Law-Making Treaties', British Yearbook of International Law, 1953, 451.

measures is impossible. Also, when a Member State action would undermine the objectives of a specific Union strategy applicable in a particular context or towards a certain third country, on the basis of the criteria determined above, a duty of abstention would apply to the Member State. By contrast, a situation which would not fall under the negative duty to abstain is when a Member State does not align itself to the Union's initiatives of positive duty of cooperation as addressed above, which remain of a voluntary nature. This also demonstrates the high threshold for applying a duty of abstention in the area of development cooperation policy, which is applicable in exceptional and particular circumstances only in case Member State action contradicts, undermines, damages, or impedes the Union's specific action. This is necessary in order to ensure that the attainment of the Union's objectives is not jeopardised in the sense of Article 4(3) TEU.

In the same light, it is interesting to note the strong relationship between the positive and the negative aspect of the duty of sincere cooperation. Evidently, it is the ultimate objective of the positive aspect of the duty of sincere cooperation to prevent that unilateral Member State action would undermine Union action. As argued above, a reinforced positive duty to cooperate applies in the area of development cooperation policy. In that regard, the presence of various positive cooperation and coordination mechanisms would prevent that Member State action contradicts or damages EU action. The boundaries of the positive aspect therefore overlap with the start of the negative duty: once a unilateral Member State action contradicts or undermines Union action, the Member States are obliged to abstain from taking that measure or are obliged to redress existing incompatibilities. While positive obligations are rather enforced in a procedural sense – translated into requirements of prior consultation and information – the negative aspect follows from the content of the Member State action and is therefore more substantively oriented: Member States are precluded from exercising their competence in a certain way because it would hinder Union action. This follows from the content of the action and not because of the action as such. This again underlines the difference between sincere cooperation and exclusivity: the latter prevents Member States from acting in an absolute sense, regardless of the content of the action and regardless of whether their actions comply with or contradict EU law.[295]

4. CONCLUSION

This chapter has analysed the vertical division of competences and cooperation mechanisms between the Union and the Member States in EU development

---

295 G. De Baere, 'O, where is faith? O, where is loyalty?', 418.

cooperation policy. As analysed in the first section, complementarity refers to two notions, which further define the legal nature of the EU development cooperation policy competence and its management. First, complementarity entails that both the EU and the Member States develop their own development cooperation policies. This refers to the legal nature of the development cooperation policy competence. Second, complementarity requires EU and Member State development cooperation policy to not only develop next, in parallel, to each other, but that they also complete each other in order to attain a coherent policy. This relates to how the principle of sincere cooperation governs the exercise of the competence.

The irregular shared nature of the EU development cooperation competence finds expression in the fact that the competence cannot become exclusive on the basis of Article 3(2) TFEU. This follows from the formulation of the specific Treaty provisions on development cooperation policy and the qualification in Article 4(4) TFEU, which clarifies that the exercise of Union competence cannot prevent the Member States from exercising theirs. Exclusivity is therefore irrelevant for the management of the vertical division of competences in development cooperation policy. Rather, the relationship between the Union and the Member States, the prevention and solution of conflicts between them as well as positive action to attain the area's objectives, takes place on the basis of the principle of sincere cooperation and, to a lesser extent, primacy.

The positive aspect of the principle of sincere cooperation is particularly strong in EU development cooperation, as it manifests itself as an explicit duty for the Union and the Member States to cooperate in Article 210 TFEU. This principle requires that the EU and the Member States take positive action by cooperating with each other and by coordinating their actions, in order to ensure the attainment of the development cooperation policy objectives and the complementarity of EU and Member State action. The enhanced duty of positive cooperation that applies in the area of development cooperation is further expressed in secondary legislation and in soft law arrangements developed in the context of development cooperation policy. This seems to confirm that the lesser the degree of preclusion of Member State action is as a consequence of the exclusion of exclusivity, the more important and the more detailed the expression of the duty of cooperation is.[296] The duty of cooperation between the EU and the Member States is moreover to a certain extent concretised and formalised in secondary legislation and soft law, a practice which has been approved by the Court in other areas.[297] The increased level of positive cooperation in development cooperation policy can be linked back

[296] M. Klamert, *The principle of loyalty in EU law*, 171.
[297] Case C-25/94, *Commission/Council*, EU:C:1996:114.

to the area's complementary or irregular shared nature. On the one hand, the enforced duty to cooperate makes the attainment of the EU's development cooperation policy objectives possible. On the other hand, a well-functioning relationship between the Union and the Member States on the basis of coordination arrangements makes complementarity possible: the objectives of the area can be attained, without the need to pre-empt the Member States in the division of competences. The aim of Article 208 TFEU is that Union development cooperation action complements Member State action and vice versa. The enforced coordination efforts in development cooperation policy, with a leading role for the EU institutions, enable this objective. This functioning of the principle of sincere cooperation in development cooperation policy moreover reflects the shift in thinking about the rationale behind the principle of sincere cooperation from unity in international representation to coherent international representation.[298]

The analysis above has demonstrated that despite the irregular shared nature of EU law in the area of development cooperation policy, in exceptional circumstances a duty of abstention is incumbent on the Member States, solely on the basis of the principle of sincere cooperation and therefore irrespective of exclusivity. This would be the case when, considering the particular circumstances and context, unilateral Member State action would clearly contradict, undermine, hinder, or impede a specific Union development cooperation policy strategy. The principle of primacy moreover requires that national development cooperation policy legislation that conflicts with Union development cooperation policy measures should be disapplied. The presence of a range of positive cooperation and coordination mechanisms, as well as the inherent link that development cooperation policy has with the political and diplomatic sphere, have arguably a positive effect on the management of the vertical division of competences in development cooperation policy, as they prevent open conflicts between the Union and its Member States from arising. However, this does not prevent that a negative duty of abstention can apply on the side of the Member States under the above conditions, in order to attain the Union's objectives and the achievement of its tasks, in accordance with Article 4(3) TEU. In this respect, the boundaries of the positive aspect overlap with the start of the negative duty: once a unilateral Member State action contradicts, undermines, hinders, or impedes a specific Union action, the Member States are obliged to abstain from taking that measure or are obliged to redress existing incompatibilities. The management of the vertical relationship in development cooperation policy is therefore based solely on the principle of

---

298 C. Hillion, 'Mixity and coherence in EU external relations: the significance of the duty of cooperation', 88–92.

sincere cooperation and primacy with exclusion of exclusivity. As such, both the positive and the negative aspect are essential to attain the development cooperation policy objectives through cooperation between the Union and the Member States and to prevent and solve conflicts between them.

6. The management of the institutional division of competences and cooperation between EU actors in EU development cooperation policy

After analysing the scope of EU development cooperation policy, the management of the area's horizontal delimitation with other related areas, and the management of the vertical division of competences and cooperation with the Member States, this chapter aims to analyse the management of the institutional division of competences and cooperation between actors in EU development cooperation policy. Also in this chapter, the central question concerns the relationship between coherence and conferral and its effect on the management of the institutional nexus and on the attainment of the development cooperation policy objectives. The inherent tension between conferral and coherence is also present in the institutional set-up. The requirement that each actor acts within the limits of the competences conferred on it, with respect for the institutional balance, is a strong requirement that flows from Article 13(2) TEU. The institutions are, on the other hand, required to cooperate and to work towards achieving the Union's objectives, particularly the aim to attain coherent external action. Coherence is an essential factor in the assessment of the functioning of institutional frameworks, as the latter affect the formulation of policies and the division of competences on the horizontal and vertical level.[1] The analysis of the institutional nexus therefore forms the completion of the analysis on the management of the legal framework for EU development cooperation policy. This chapter will analyse whether the institutional division of competences is organised in such a way as to steer or rather prevent cooperation between actors, therefore supporting or hindering coherent action. The familiar contrast in the EU's legal order applies also here: a too rigid delimitation of competences prevents the creation of synergies,

[1] S. Duke, 'The European External Action Service: Antidote against Incoherence?', 1 European Foreign Affairs Review, 2012, 46.

while responding to the need to attain coherence cannot lead to disrespecting the division of competences.[2]

The analysis of the institutional division of competences proves to be particularly interesting, as two of the most important institutional innovations brought about by the Treaty of Lisbon, the creation of the High Representative and the European External Action Service (EEAS), play an essential role in the management of the institutional division of competences in development cooperation policy. The chapter first analyses the principles governing the management of the institutional division of competences in EU development cooperation policy: the principles of conferral, institutional balance, and sincere cooperation. The next section discusses the role and competences of the High Representative. The subsequent sections of the chapter aim to address the conferral–coherence question by studying the institutional set-up of the EEAS and the Commission in development cooperation policy and their relationship vis-à-vis each other.

1. SETTING THE STAGE – CONFERRAL, INSTITUTIONAL BALANCE, AND SINCERE COOPERATION

The EU's institutional framework for external action and development cooperation policy is managed by three principles that are strongly interrelated: the principle of conferral, the principle of institutional balance, and the principle of sincere cooperation. Article 13(2) TEU brings together these principles and demonstrates how they govern the institutional division of competences. The Article holds that:

> Each institution shall act within the limits of the powers conferred on it in the Treaties, and in conformity with the procedures, conditions and objectives set out in them. The institutions shall practice mutual sincere cooperation.

The Article therefore covers both competence delimitation requirements as cooperation demands: the two essential elements to attain coherence (see Chapter 1). As such, this Treaty provision covers the existence and delimitation of competences, as well as the exercise of those competences. Competence delimitation rules flow from the principle of conferral, while the principles of the institutional balance and sincere cooperation govern the

---

[2] M. Gatti, 'Coherence vs. conferred powers? The case of the European Externa Action Service', in L.S. Rossi, F. Casolari, *The EU after Lisbon*, Springer, 2014, 242; 246.

exercise of competences. The principles of institutional balance and sincere cooperation therefore complement the principle of conferral.[3]

The principle of conferral manages the division of competences between the institutions, ensuring that each institution acts within the limits of the powers that it was granted in the Treaties. Title III of the TEU lays down these powers for each of the Union's institutions, while specific competences can also follow from specific provisions, such as in the context of the conclusion of international agreements. In accordance with Article 13(2) TEU, the assessment of whether the institution acted within the limits of its powers is determined in light of the legal basis, the applicable procedure, as well as the conditions and objectives as formulated in the Treaties.

The importance of the principle of institutional balance lies in the fact that it adds an important element to the mere respect for the allocation of competences by referring to the powers of other institutions as well. The Treaties do not refer to the notion of institutional balance, but the Court's case law has qualified it as a principle.[4] Various institutions have invoked a violation of the principle of institutional balance in a series of recent cases, in which the Court has included the principle in its analysis.[5] The Court's formulation of the principle of institutional balance has emerged as a standard definition, which reads that:

> under Article 13(2) TEU each institution is to act within the limits of the powers conferred on it in the Treaties, and in conformity with the procedures, conditions and objectives set out in them. That provision reflects the principle of institutional balance, characteristic of the institutional structure of the European Union, a principle which requires that each of the institution must exercise its powers with due regard for the powers of the other institutions.[6]

---

[3] C. Hillion, 'Conferral, cooperation and balance in the institutional framework of the EU external action', in M. Cremona (ed.), *Structural principles in EU external relations law*, Hart, 2018, 165.

[4] Case C-409/13, *Council/Commission (MFA)*, EU:C:2015:217, para. 64; Case C-73/14, *Council/Commission (ITLOS)*, EU:C:2015:663, para. 61; Case C-425/13, *Commission/Council (ETS)*, EU:C:2015:483, para. 69; Case C-660/13, *Council/ Commission (MoU)*, EU:C:216:616, para. 32; Case C-687/15, *Commission/Council*, EU:C:2017:803, para. 40.

[5] See e.g.: Case C-409/13, para. 64; Case C-73/14, para. 61; Case C-425/13, para. 69; Case C-660/13, para. 32; Case C-28/12, *Commission/Council*, EU:C:2015:43; Case C-687/15, para. 40. The principle was moreover involved in the *Mauritius Agreement* and *Tanzania Agreement* cases analysed above. In *PCA Kazakhstan*, the Court also refers to the institutional balance as created by Article 218 TFEU in the procedure to conclude international agreements: Case C-244/17, para. 24, 29.

[6] Case C-409/13, para. 64; Case C-73/14, para. 61; Case C-425/13, para. 69; Case C-660/13, para. 32; Case C-687/15, para; 40.

The importance of the principle of institutional balance therefore lies in the fact that it adds an important element to the mere respect for the allocation of competences: attaining an institutional balance not only requires each institution to act within the limits of its powers, but it equally demands that the institutional actors have due regard for the powers of other institutions and their role in the institutional framework as well. The essential difference with the principle of conferral is that it concerns the exercise of competences: in exercising the competences they have on the basis of the principle of conferral, the institutions are required to take into consideration the prerogatives of other institutions and their role in attaining the Union's objectives, in order to not negatively affect their position.[7] The principle of the institutional balance therefore reflects the delicate balance between the interests represented by each of the institutions.[8]

The management of the institutional division of competences is to an important extent also governed by the principle of sincere cooperation. Article 13(2) TEU lays down a mutual inter-institutional duty to cooperate. The duty of mutual sincere cooperation embedded in Article 13(2) TEU is aimed at the overall objective to promote the Union's values, advance its objectives, serve its interests, those of its citizens and those of the Member States, and ensure the consistency, effectiveness, and continuity of its policies and actions, as formulated in Article 13(1) TEU. The mutual duty to cooperate between the institutions is based on the duty to cooperate that applies in the vertical division of powers between the Union and the Member States. The mutual inter-institutional duty to cooperate, laid down in Article 13(2) TEU, therefore follows from and is a specific application of the general principle of sincere cooperation, as laid down in Article 4(3) TEU. The Court clarified that this entails that the same mutual duties of sincere cooperation apply in the inter-institutional context as the ones that flow from the duty to cooperate between the Union and the Member States.[9] Referring to the previous chapter on the management of the vertical division of competences, the duty to cooperate sincerely therefore covers an inter-institutional duty to assist each other in carrying out tasks which flow from the Treaties, take appropriate measures to ensure the fulfilment of the obligations arising out of the Treaties or resulting from acts from the institutions, facilitate the achievement of the Union's tasks, and refrain from any measure that could jeopardise the attainment of the objectives of the Union. As will be analysed below, the governance of the

---

[7] C-70/88, para. 21; Case C-660/13, para. 31; C. Hillion, 'Conferral, cooperation and balance in the institutional framework of the EU external action', 35.

[8] K. Lenaerts, P. Van Nuffel, 635–636.

[9] Case 204/86, *Hellenic Republic/Council*, EU:C:1988:450, para. 15–16; Case C-65/93, *Parliament/Council*, EU:C: 1995:91, para. 23.

institutional framework for development cooperation policy indeed brings about specific duties of cooperation, such as information or consultation, particularly between the Commission and the EEAS.[10] The Court held that the cooperation requirement embedded in Article 13(2) TEU is of particular importance for EU external action, as action on the external scene, even more than internal action, triggers the need for concerted action and consultation between the EU institutions.[11]

The principle of institutional balance encompasses similarities with the principle of sincere cooperation. Both the institutional balance and the inter-institutional duty to cooperate complement the conferral of competences, as they aim to ensure that the institutions exercise their powers in a way that does not affect the powers of other institutions and that, as such, is able to ensure the attainment of the Union's objectives. In attaining that objective, both principles are able to formulate procedural obligations that can limit the institutions in taking action.[12] Although the principles of institutional balance and sincere cooperation apply within the framework of the division of competences, and therefore cannot alter the division of competences, they are nevertheless able to influence the latter as they govern the exercise of these competences.[13]

The principle of institutional balance therefore relates closely to both the principle of conferral and the principle of sincere cooperation. As a consequence, the status of the principle of institutional balance as a separate principle remains the subject of discussion. Several authors have aimed to further define the principle and the consequences that it brings about.[14] The debate

---

[10] The Court confirmed the application of these specific duties of cooperation in other areas of Union external action as well. In the *MFA* case, for example, the Court tested the Commission's compliance with duties of information and consultation: Case C-409/13, para. 103–104. The resemblance between the tests to assess compliance with Article 13(2) TEU and with Article 4(3) TEU is most significant in the *ETS* case, in which the Court refers to 'concerted action'. As analysed in Chapter 5, this notion was first used in case law on the vertical division of competences: the Court determined that 'the start of concerted Union action' triggers the application of a stricter duty to cooperate (Case C-246/07).

[11] C-425/13, para. 64

[12] C. Hillion, 'Conferral, cooperation and balance in the institutional framework of the EU external action', 9, 48.

[13] Opinion AG Sharpston in C-73/14, points 98–102.

[14] See for example: C. Hillion, 'Conferral, cooperation and balance in the institutional framework of the EU external action'; M. Chamon, 'The institutional balance, an ill-fated principle of EU law?' 2 European Public Law 2015, 371–392; J. Monar, 'The European Union's institutional balance of power after the Treaty of Lisbon: visions of leading policy-makers, academics and journalists', Publications Office of the European Union, 2011; T. Christiansen, 'The European Union after the Lisbon Treaty: An

concerns the principle's definition and content, as well as how it differentiates itself from other notions, such as the principles of sincere cooperation and the separation of powers.[15] It is indeed true that while the principle of institutional balance is identified as a separate notion, the Court often analyses the principles of conferral and institutional balance at the same time, while the principles of institutional balance and sincere cooperation are also often considered together because of their overlapping characteristics that govern the exercise of competences.[16] As a consequence, it has been questioned whether and to what extent the principle of institutional balance functions as a distinct principle governing the institutional division of competences.

The added value of including the principle in the analysis of the management of the institutional division of competences would arguably be that of a 'gap-filling principle'. This follows Prechal's reasoning, who argues that the institutional balance may play an important role in the interpretation and application of EU law when the legal provisions on the relationship between the EU institutions are insufficiently clear.[17] Lenaerts and Verhoeven refer to the institutional balance as a principle of EU governance that amounts to a political rather than a legal principle. In this sense, the institutional balance requires that the EU's institutional framework is organised in a manner which allows each interest and constituency in the Union to be duly represented and cooperate with others 'in the frame of an institutionalized debate geared towards the formulation of the common good'.[18] This is linked to Advocate General Trstenjak's perspective on the institutional balance. She considers the institutional balance to refer to 'a separation of functions', which demands that the EU's functions are exercised by the organs which are best placed to perform them under the Treaties. The institutional balance therefore ultimately aims to ensure that the EU's aims are effectively achieved.[19] According to Lenaerts and Verhoeven, it then follows from the principle of institutional

---

elusive 'institutional balance'?' in A. Biondi, P. Eeckhout and S. Ripley, *EU law after Lisbon*, 2012, 226–245; J.P. Jacqué, 'The principle of institutional balance', Common Market Law Review, 2004, 383–391; K. Lenaerts, A. Verhoeven, 'Institutional balance as a guarantee for democracy in EU governance', in C. Joerges, R. Dehousse, *Good governance in the internal market*, 2002, 35–88; S. Prechal, 'Institutional balance: A fragile principle with uncertain contents' in T. Heukels, N. Blokker and M. Brus, *The European Union after Amsterdam*, 1998, 273–294.

[15] For an analysis of the latter principle: K. Lenaerts, 'Some reflections on the separation of powers in the European Community', 11–35.

[16] C. Hillion, 'Conferral, cooperation and balance in the institutional framework of the EU external action', 37, 48.

[17] S. Prechal, 277–278.

[18] K. Lenaerts, A. Verhoeven, 47.

[19] Opinion of Advocate General Trstenjak in Case C-101/08, para. 104.

balance that (i) each institution enjoys a sufficient level of independence in order to exercise its powers, (ii) the institutions should not unconditionally assign their powers to other institutions, and (iii) institutions may not in the exercise of their own powers encroach on the powers and prerogatives of other institutions.[20] Some authors have added a fourth rule to the ones identified by Lenaerts and Verhoeven, which distinguishes the institutions that reflect Member States' interests.[21] As the previous chapter on the vertical division of competences has pointed out that the Member States have a strong role to play in development cooperation policy, it seems indeed useful to also take this last element into account when assessing the management of the institutional division of competences in EU development cooperation policy.

The principles of conferral of competences, institutional balance, and sincere cooperation undoubtedly apply to institutional actors that are active in the area of development cooperation policy. This includes the High Representative and the EEAS, although they are not Union institutions as laid down in Article 13(1) TEU. The fact that they are not formal institutions of the Union does not exclude them from respecting the fundamental principles of the Union that govern the existence and exercise of competences, such as the principles of conferral, sincere cooperation, and the institutional balance. These principles are of general application in the EU's constitutional framework. Their position in the Treaties under Title I on Common Provision in the TEU demonstrates this.[22] As such, they bind all the entities that take up a particular role in the Treaties. The case law on the ESMA demonstrates the application of the principle of conferral to Union bodies, offices, or agencies,[23] on the basis of which Hillion argues that entities that 'operate in the EU context' in a specific role are subject to Article 13(2) TEU.[24] This is arguably *a fortiori* the case for actors such as the High Representative and the EEAS, who, although they are not formal EU institutions in the sense of Article 13(1) TEU, are given a specific competence and role in the Treaties. The Treaties and secondary law moreover lay down strong specific cooperation and coordination duties for the High

---

20 K Lenaerts, A. Verhoeven, 44–45.

21 M. Chamon, 378; E. Vos, 'The rise of committees', 3 European Law Journal, 1997, 223.

22 The principle of conferral is laid down in Article 5(2) TEU, the principle of sincere cooperation in Article 4(3) TEU, and the principle of institutional balance in Article 13(2) TEU. Pre-Lisbon, Case C-266/03 moreover determined that the principle of sincere cooperation was of general application.

23 Case C-270/12, *UK/Council and Parliament*, EU:C:2014:18, para. 79–80. For an extensive analysis of the role of EU agencies in EU law, see: M. Chamon, *EU agencies: legal and political limits to the transformation of the EU administration*, OUP, 2016.

24 C. Hillion, 'Conferral, cooperation and balance in the institutional framework of the EU external action', 67.

Representative and the EEAS. This is comparable with the specification and enhanced duty to cooperate as it applies in the vertical division of competences (see Chapter 5) and confirms the application of the general duties laid down in Article 13(2) TEU.[25]

The following sections will analyse how the principles of conferral, institutional balance, and sincere cooperation govern the institutional division of competences in the Union's development cooperation policy. In its analysis, the section recognises the added value of the principle of institutional balance as a separate notion. As Hillion points out, the principle of institutional balance encompasses both the principles of conferral and sincere cooperation: it reflects conferral in demanding that institutions do not encroach upon other institutions' powers, while the positive requirement that they have due regard to the power and role of other institutions requires a form of cooperation.[26] Particularly the principle of institutional balance's characteristic that the institutions should exercise their competences with due regard to other institutions' competences and their broader role in the EU's institutional framework and in the pursuit of the Union's objectives, will prove to be an important criterion to assess the management of the institutional division of competences in the Union's development cooperation policy.

2. ENTRUSTED WITH THE TASK TO ENSURE COHERENCE: THE HIGH REPRESENTATIVE OF THE UNION FOR FOREIGN AFFAIRS AND SECURITY POLICY

2.1 The High Representative's Mandate and Tasks

As is well known, one of the main aims of the Treaty of Lisbon was to strengthen the EU's external action by improving its ability to act on the international scene, in particular by strengthening the coherence of its (external) action and to speak with one voice. The creation of the position of the High Representative for Foreign Affairs and Security Policy is essential in attaining this objective. Article 21(3) TEU identifies the High Representative as one of the institutional actors that are responsible to ensure the coherence of Union external action and to cooperate to that effect, together with the Council and the Commission. The underlying rationale pursued with the creation of the post of High Representative is to integrate all elements of EU external action

---

25 M. Gatti, 251.

26 C. Hillion, 'Conferral, cooperation and balance in the institutional framework of the EU external action', 53.

into one position, in order to ensure coherence across the whole sphere of EU external action, including all relevant actors and instruments.[27] It particularly aims to connect the CFSP and the non-CFSP.[28] An important aspect in this regard is the position's intention to bridge the interests of the Union and the Member States, expressed in the aspiration to bring together the institutions that represent these interests. This aim is also reflected in the tasks that fall under the High Representative's responsibility.

The High Representative of the Union for Foreign Affairs and Security Policy replaces the former High Representative for the CFSP and the Commissioner for external relations. The fact that this new position brings together two former positions is demonstrated by the scope of the High Representative's mandate. Article 18 TEU lays down the High Representative's three main tasks, or its three hats, the so-called triple hats: (i) the High Representative conducts the CFSP, including the CSDP, by contributing to the development of the policy by launching proposals and by carrying them out as mandated by the Council, (ii) the High Representative acts as the President of the Foreign Affairs Council (FAC), and (iii) the High Representative also has the capacity of Vice-President of the Commission, which allows him to ensure the coherence of EU external action. This 'coherence mandate'[29] covers Commission responsibilities incumbent on it in external action and coordinating other aspects of the Union's external action. When acting in the capacity of Commission Vice-President, the High Representative is bound by Commission procedures to the extent that this is consistent with the exercise of its other hats.

In the area of the CFSP, the High Representative has particular functions: the function ensures the unity, consistency, and effectiveness of Union action,[30] it 'puts into effect' the CFSP together with the Member States,[31] it contributes to the development of the CFSP through its proposals,[32] acts as chair of the FAC,[33] and ensures the implementation of the decisions adopted by the European Council and the Council.[34] The High Representative moreover represents the Union for matters in the area of the CFSP at relevant level,

---

[27] The European Convention, Final Report of the Working Group VII on External Action, CONV 459/02, Brussels, 16 December 2002, 19.

[28] Article 18(4) TEU.

[29] J. Wouters, G. De Baere, B. Van Vooren, K. Raube, J. Odermatt, T. Ramopoulous, Y. Tanghe, T. Van den Sanden, The organisation and functioning of the European External Action Service, European Parliament Directorate-General for External Policies of the Union, 2013, 27.

[30] Article 26(2) TEU.

[31] Article 26(3) TEU.

[32] Referring back to Article 18(2) TEU.

[33] Referring back to Article 18(3) TEU.

[34] Article 27(1) TEU.

including conducting the political dialogue and expressing the EU's position in international organisations and at international conferences.[35] The High Representative moreover organises the coordination of Member State action in international organisations and at international conferences.[36] Article 27(2) TEU on the High Representative's external representation competences needs to be read together with Article 15(6) TEU. This Article determines that the President of the European Council, at his level and in that capacity, is to ensure the external representation of the Union on issues falling under the CFSP, without prejudice to the powers of the High Representative of the Union. Reading Article 15(6) TEU and Article 27(2) TEU together, this would imply that there is a division of tasks in external representation in the CFSP between the High Representative and the President of the European Council, based on the level on which both actors operate. In that respect, the President of the European Council represents the Union at the level of Heads of State and Government, while the High Representative ensures external representation at ministerial level, which also appears to happen in practice.[37] The Commission, on the other hand, has the task to represent the Union in matters falling outside the CFSP.[38] As regards the specific area of the CSDP, Article 42(4) TEU confirms Article 18(2) TEU on the High Representative's preparatory powers, by determining that decisions on the CSDP are adopted by the Council on the basis of a proposal from the High Representative or from a Member State. The High Representative moreover ensures coordination of the civilian and military aspects of CSDP tasks.[39]

Finally, the High Representative's relationship with the European Parliament also deserves attention. Article 36 TEU defines the High Representative's political accountability vis-à-vis the European Parliament. It requires the High Representative to regularly consult the European Parliament on the main aspects and the basic choices in the framework of the CFSP and the CSDP, inform it of the policies' evolution, while ensuring that the views of the European Parliament are duly taken into account. The protection of the prerogatives of the European Parliament has always been an essential component of the institutional balance.[40] The Court has qualified the European Parliament's prerogative to be part of the EU's legislative process as 'an essential factor in

[35] Article 27(2) TEU.
[36] Article 34(1) TEU.
[37] G. De Baere, 'EU external action', 26.
[38] Article 17(1) TEU.
[39] Article 43(2) TEU.
[40] Case 70/88, para. 21; K. Lenaerts, P. Van Nuffel, 639.

the institutional balance intended by the Treaties'.[41] Therefore, the Court must be able to maintain the institutional balance and, as a consequence, review the observance of the Parliament's prerogatives when called upon to do so by this institution.[42] In recent case law, it is indeed often the European Parliament that challenges measures and brings disagreements with other institutions to the Court. This is especially the case in external action and the disputes mostly concern the challenge of the correct legal basis, as well as the respect for the information requirement vis-à-vis the Parliament pursuant to Article 218(1) TFEU. This has been the case in several cases which proved to be relevant in the area of development cooperation policy as well (see Chapter 3 on the management of the horizontal division of competences).

The more detailed arrangements on the High Representative's political accountability vis-à-vis the European Parliament are laid down in the Declaration on Political Accountability.[43] The Declaration includes arrangements on consultation, information, and reporting. They build further on the arrangements that were previously agreed with the former Commissioner for External Relations, the former High Representative for the CFSP, and the rotating presidency. An important element covered by the Declaration is the replacement of the High Representative before the Parliament: when the High Representative is unable to participate in a plenary debate, he will be replaced by a Commissioner for issues falling under Commission competence and by the rotating presidency or one of the trio Presidencies for issues falling exclusively or principally under the CFSP. The EEAS moreover supports the Parliament, in accordance with Article 3(4) EEAS Decision,[44] while parliamentary scrutiny is further guaranteed in the programming cycle and through the Parliament's budgetary powers (see below).

It follows from the enumeration of the High Representative's tasks that the position is essential in the management of the horizontal, vertical, and institutional division of competences of EU external action, including of development cooperation policy. Nevertheless, the scope of the High Representative's mandate and its tasks have been criticised for being unrealistic. The High Representative position covers responsibilities of the executive

41 Case 138/79, *Roquette Frères* v *Council*, EU:C:1980:249, para. 33; Case 139/79, *Maïzena/Council*, EU:C:1980:250, para. 34.

42 Case 70/88, para. 21–23.

43 'Declaration by the High Representative on Political Accountability', Annex to the European Parliament legislative resolution of 8 July 2010 on the proposal for a Council decision establishing the organization and functioning of the European External Action Service (08029/-C7-0090/2010-2010/0816).

44 This is for example the case when EU Delegations support the visits to third countries undertaken by parliamentary delegations or political groups.

power and the legislative power, together with a representative role.[45] The triple-hatted High Representative function is created to increase coherence, and in theory it is able to do so. A function that encompasses CFSP tasks, a Commission Vice-President task steered towards ensuring coherence, and the chairmanship of the FAC has the potential to strengthen coherence at all relevant levels: between the CFSP and the non-CFSP, between other areas of Union action and the external elements of internal actions, and between Union and Member State external action. However, even the analysis conducted in the context of the EEAS Review admits that, from a practical perspective, it is very difficult, or not to say quasi impossible, for one person to fulfil this combination of tasks.[46] The different functions are moreover based on different applicable procedures, making the combination of roles procedurally complex or even impossible. Article 18(4) TEU encapsulates this issue by requiring the High Representative to follow Commission procedures when acting as Vice-President, to the extent that this is consistent with his other hats. This issue refers back to the impossibility to adopt comprehensive measures that are based on a dual CFSP and non-CFSP legal basis, on the basis of the legal bases' procedural incompatibility (see above).[47]

This, however, does not imply that the High Representative's Vice-President hat is subordinate to the other two hats. It is simply another reflection of the coherence–conferral contradiction at play in EU external action, in particular between the CFSP and the non-CFSP. The final report of the Working Group on External Action in the framework of the European Convention possibly provides further guidance in this respect.[48] It states that when the High Representative exercises his right of initiative in the area of the CFSP, the Commission needs to 'abstain from taking a competing initiative'. The High Representative's initiatives in CFSP matters and decisions to put them into effect 'would not be subject to prior approval by the College of Commissioners'.[49] This does not point to a subordinate relationship. It rather seems to aim to emphasise the importance for the respect for the conferral of competences and the non-affectation clause as laid down in Article 40 TEU

---

[45] M. van Reisen, 'Note on the legality of inclusion of aspects of EU Development Cooperation and Humanitarian Assistance in the European External Action Service (EEAS)', EEPA Briefing Paper 13, 2010.

[46] European External Action Review, EEAS review, 2013, 13; Council conclusions on the EEAS Review, General Affairs Council meeting 17 December 2013.

[47] Case C-130/10.

[48] H. Merket, *The EU and the Security-Development nexus. Bridging the legal divide*, Universiteit Gent, 2015, 137.

[49] The Secretariat of the European Convention, Final Report of Working Group VII on External Action, 16 December 2002, CONV 459/02, 5.

in particular: the different hats of the High Representative cannot affect each other, nor the policy areas of EU action that they represent. To further complicate the fulfilment of the triple-hatted position, the competences and mandate of the EEAS do not mirror all the High Representative's tasks, making it difficult for the service to fully assist the High Representative in all of his tasks (see further below in the next section).[50]

As a consequence, suggestions have been formulated to solve the question of the practical implementation of the triple-hatted High Representative function. A system of deputisation has been suggested.[51] This solution was put forward by various actors in the field.[52] They nevertheless disagree about the practical implementation of the deputisation and how this system should be organised concretely.[53] The difficulty, however, is that a formal deputisation would require either an amendment of the EEAS Decision or a Treaty change. A genuine deputisation, in the sense of someone else taking over the position of High Representative through a formal delegation of authority and not for mere replacement purposes, is impossible without a solid legal basis. If it would be envisaged that EEAS staff would be able to act as deputies, this would necessitate an adjustment to the EEAS Decision, providing the legal basis for this power. This would, however, not bring about a Treaty adjustment as the legal basis in Article 27(2) TEU, which states that the EEAS assists the High Representative in fulfilling his tasks, is arguably sufficient in this regard. Nevertheless, the deputies would have to constitute a special subcategory of EEAS staff with political accountability, which is not the case for traditional civil servants.[54] Granting a deputy role to EEAS staff without linking this to the necessary political accountability would negatively impact scrutiny requirements.[55] Granting the deputisation to another actor than the EEAS, for example a Commissioner, would necessitate a Treaty change, as it would bring about

50 G. De Baere, R. Wessel, 'EU Law and the EEAS: Of complex competences and constitutional consequences', in D. Spencer, J. Bátora (eds), *The European External Action Service: European Diplomacy Post-Westphalia*, Palgrave, 2015, 187.

51 J. Wouters, G. De Baere, B. Van Vóoren, K. Raube, J. Odermatt, T. Ramopoulous, Y. Tanghe, T. Van den Sanden, 32–33; S. Blockmans, C. Hillion, 39.

52 The EP has already argued in favour of deputisation before the setting up of the EEAS: Proposal for the Establishment of the EEAS, Working Document by Elmar Brok (AFET) and Guy Verhofstadt (AFCO), rapporteurs on EEAS, Updated Version, 20 April 2010, pp.4–5.

53 J. Wouters, G. De Baere, B. Van Vooren, K. Raube, J. Odermatt, T. Ramopoulous, Y. Tanghe, T. Van den Sanden, 32.

54 Ibid., 33.

55 M. van Reisen, 'Note on the legality of inclusion of aspects of EU Development Cooperation and Humanitarian Assistance in the European External Action Service (EEAS)'.

a reshuffling of competences, particularly as regards the CFSP aspects of the position. This type of deputisation is therefore different from the deputisation for the Commission President, as laid down in Article 22 of the Commission Rules of Procedure.[56] The EEAS Review itself prefers to further formalise the arrangements that are currently applied to replace the High Representative, rather than to create a formal deputy position.[57] These replacement practices involve the Presidency, Commissioners, or senior EEAS and Commission staff, as well as Special Representatives. President Juncker indeed stated that the Commissioner for Neighbourhood and Enlargement Policy and other Commissioners were able to deputise for the High Representative in areas falling under Commission competence.[58]

2.2 Commission Vice-President Role

Article 18(4) TEU defines the Vice-President hat of the High Representative. From the formulation of the Treaty Article, it emerges that the primary aim of the Vice-President role is to ensure coherence. This is to be achieved by reconciling the matters of EU external action for which the Commission is responsible and 'coordinating other aspects of the Union's external action'. The double-hatted High Representative/Commission Vice-President function is indeed ideally placed to bridge the CFSP and the non-CFSP and to enhance the coherence of the entire area of EU external action more broadly speaking. However, the implementation of the function is essential to achieve the function's potential.

In April 2010 the Barroso Commission created the External Relations Commissioners group (RELEX), gathering the Commissioners with a portfolio relevant to EU external action: the Commissioners responsible for 'Development', 'International Cooperation, Humanitarian Aid and Crisis Response', 'Enlargement and European Neighbourhood Policy', 'Trade', and 'Economic and Monetary Affairs'. Other Commissioners could be invited on an ad hoc basis. The aim of the RELEX Group was to ensure the coherence of Commission external policies with the Union's broader external action and to function as a structure to coordinate positions in the preparation of College debates concerning the strategic guidance of external action. As the chair of the Group, empowered with the coherence mandate which also includes the

---

[56] Rules of Procedure of the Commission, OJ 2000 L308/26.

[57] EEAS Review, 13.

[58] J.-C. Juncker, Mission Letter Federica Mogherini: High Representative of the Union for Foreign Policy and Security Policy/Vice-President of the European Commission, Brussels, 1 November 2014, 4.

CFSP, the High Representative was seen as the 'primus inter partes'.[59] Despite the great potential of this coordination mechanism to steer coherence, during the first years of its functioning the group and the participation of the High Representative in the Commission structures apparently did not perform to its potential.[60] The Juncker Commission strengthened the cooperation, while the EEAS Review also supported the idea to reinforce the functioning of the RELEX Group. The High Representative and the Commission President agreed further that the High Representative would chair the meetings, while the meetings would be prepared jointly by the Commission Secretariat General and the EEAS.[61] The Juncker Presidency decentralised leadership by appointing seven Vice-Presidents at the head of clusters or 'project teams' of competence areas,[62] with the aim to overcome the concerns that the different Commission constellations worked in silos.[63] High Representative Mogherini led the external cluster, named 'A Stronger Global Actor', including the Commissioners for International Cooperation and Development, Neighbourhood and Enlargement Policy, Civil Protection and Humanitarian Aid, and Trade. With this, the Juncker Commission aimed to further strengthen the Vice-President hat of the High Representative's function[64] and to steer the coherence of EU external action.[65]

The von der Leyen Commission further intensified the importance of external action, with 'A Stronger Europe in the World' as one of the priorities of the Commission. Therein, focus is on a more coherent approach across the area of external action and increased funding for the area.[66] The High Representative is one of the eight Vice-Presidents empowered by President von der Leyen to steer and coordinate the Commission's priorities. As such, the High Representative chairs the Commissioners' Group 'A Stronger

---

59 S. Duke, 53.

60 Ibid., 32.

61 EEAS Review, 8.

62 Juncker, Political Guidelines for the next European Commission: Opening Statement in the European Parliament Plenary Session 'A New Start for Europe: My Agenda for Jobs, Growth, Fairness and Democratic Change', 15 July 2014.

63 European Commission Press Release, The Juncker Commission: A strong and experienced team standing for change, 10 September 2014.

64 J.-C. Juncker, Mission Letter Federica Mogherini: High Representative of the Union for Foreign Policy and Security Policy/Vice-President of the European Commission, Brussels; G. De Baere, R. Wessel, 179.

65 J.-C. Juncker, Mission Letter Federica Mogherini: High Representative of the Union for Foreign Policy and Security Policy/Vice-President of the European Commission, Brussels, 2.

66 Ursula von der Leyen, 'A Union that strives for more. My agenda for Europe', Political Guidelines for the next European Commission 2019–2024.

Europe in the World', which also comprises the Commissioner for Trade, the Commissioner for Neighbourhood and Enlargement, the Commissioner for Crisis Management, and the Commissioner for International Partnerships. Other Vice-Presidents and Commissioners may participate in relevant meetings of the Groups and contribute to the work upon their request or invitation by the Chairs. Interestingly, for this Commissioners' Group only, the Secretariat-General and the EEAS jointly ensure the Secretariat and the preparatory meeting for this Group is co-chaired by the Secretary-General or a Deputy Secretary-General and the Secretary-General of the EEAS or his Deputy. Also unique for the Commissioners' Group 'A Stronger Europe in the World', a monthly standing planning meeting is organised between the Secretary-General or a Deputy Secretary-General, the Secretary-General of the EEAS or his Deputy, the Cabinets of the President and of the High Representative/Vice-President, assisted by the Secretariat of the Group. The planning meeting is chaired by the Cabinet of the High Representative/Vice-President.[67] The von der Leyen Commission further embedded external action in the Commission by having a weekly update on foreign policy to the College done by the High Representative. Further, a new collegial preparatory body, Group for External Coordination (EXCO), was established to ensure a more strategic and coherent external action. EXCO brings together all Cabinets to prepare the external aspects of College meetings on a weekly basis. Its aim is to better align the internal and external aspects of policies and enhance the working relationship between the Commission and the EEAS. EXCO is co-chaired by the Diplomatic Adviser of the President and the Deputy Head of Cabinet of the High Representative/Vice-President.[68]

2.3 Chairmanship of the Foreign Affairs Council

The High Representative's chairmanship over the Foreign Affairs Council (FAC)[69] is an important steering factor for coordination with the Member States' development cooperation policies and Member State external action more generally speaking.[70] The replacement of the Member State rotating

[67] Decision of the President of the European Commission of 1 December 2019 on the creation of Commissioners' Groups, P(2019) 4.

[68] Communication from the President to the Commission, The Working Methods of the European Commission, P(2019) 2.

[69] Article 18(3) TEU.

[70] S. Duke, S. Blockmans, 'The Lisbon Treaty stipulations on development cooperation and the Council Decision of 25 March 2010 (draft) establishing the organisation and functioning of the European External Action Service', European Institute of Public Administration, 2010, 11

chair by a permanent chair is moreover an important steering factor to strengthen coherence. Using the coherence mandate that covers the entire area of EU external action, the High Representative holds a key position in the capacity of chair of the FAC to steer the coherence of EU external action and by supporting a more long-term perspective than the one provided by the rotating presidency. In that light, another element contributing to strengthened coherence is the fact that the High Representative is able to bring together the input of different actors in the area of EU external action, such as the Union Delegations, EEAS geographical desks, and EU Special Representatives.[71] The High Representative is moreover involved in the highest political and strategic decision-making through its participation in the European Council, as laid down in Article 15(2) TEU.[72]

Nevertheless, a few elements would arguably negatively influence the High Representative's potential to steer coherence as an FAC chair. First, despite the FAC's encompassing mandate with responsibility for the entire area of EU external action, covering the CFSP, CSDP, the common commercial policy, development cooperation policy, and humanitarian aid, the importance of the FAC as an actor in the development of external action is declining.[73] Second, the High Representative does not chair all Council Working Groups, while these groups are a vital actor in the preparatory work. The chairmanship of the working groups is an important position to ensure coherence: these groups are important settings to find ground for compromises and to ensure the application of the EU's overall fundamental aims and objectives in external action.[74] Some working parties with an important mandate for development cooperation policy and its related areas fall outside the High Representative's chairmanship: the Development and International Partnerships Working Party and the ACP Working Party remain to be chaired by the rotating presidency.[75]

Particularly important for pursuing coherence between development cooperation policy and the CFSP in particular is the chairmanship of the Political

---

[71] J. Wouters, G. De Baere, B. Van Vooren, K. Raube, J. Odermatt, T. Ramopoulous, Y. Tanghe, T. Van den Sanden, 39.

[72] H. Merket, *The EU and the Security-Development nexus. Bridging the legal divide*, 135.

[73] The Political and Security Committee (Article 38 TEU) and the European Council are taking up an increasingly important role in taking strategic decisions, while the internal organisation affects the role and functioning of the Foreign Affairs Council: J. Wouters, G. De Baere, B. Van Vooren, K. Raube, J. Odermatt, T. Ramopoulous, Y. Tanghe, T. Van den Sanden, 37.

[74] High Representative Ashton appoints the permanent chairs of several Working Groups in the Council, Brussels, A273/10, 22 December 2010.

[75] EEAS review, 6. List of Council Preparatory Bodies: https://data.consilium.europa.eu/doc/document/ST-10360-2021-REV-1/en/pdf.

and Security Committee by a representative of the High Representative. The Political and Security Committee, as the main decision-making body on the areas of CFSP and CSDP, is a crucial actor in the achievement of coherent EU external action. According to Article 38 TEU, the Committee monitors the international situation in the CFSP and contributes to defining the policy by delivering opinions to the Council at the request of the Council or of the High Representative or on its own initiative. It also monitors the implementation of the policy, without prejudice to the competences of the High Representative.[76] It moreover has an important role to play in crisis management operations. For the preparation of its work it receives input from advisory and preparatory bodies on civilian and military crisis management, political and military affairs, and geographical groups. Considering its composition and position in the decision-making process, it is an essential actor in developing the CFSP and the CSDP. The chairmanship exercised by the High Representative is necessary to ensure coherence with the other, non-CFSP elements of EU external action and to ensure overall coherence.[77]

It follows from the analysis above that the triple-hatted High Representative function carries a tremendous potential to increase the coherence of the Union's external action. Article 21(3) TEU explicitly refers to the High Representative as one of the institutional actors that are responsible to ensure the coherence of Union external action and to cooperate to that effect, together with the Council and the Commission. With hats that cover CFSP and non-CFSP competences, the position is able to function as a bridge between these two distinct areas of Union external action. The third hat as chair of the Council Foreign Affairs Council allows the High Representative to also increase coherence in the vertical division of competences. The High Representative thus finds itself at the crossroads of the horizontal, vertical, and institutional division of competences. However, the implementation of this function is essential to assess whether the position is able to live up to its expectations. While the practical implementation of the triple-hatted function remains a concern, it is an important coherence steering factor that the High Representative's role is further strengthened in the current Commission in structures that aim to realise its coherence mandate.

---

[76] Article 24(3) TEU.

[77] A. Weston, F. Mérand, 'The EEAS and crisis management: The organisational challenges of a comprehensive approach', in D. Spencer, J. Bátora (eds), *The European External Action Service: European Diplomacy Post-Westphalia*, Palgrave, 2015, 330.

3. THE COHERENCE–CONFERRAL QUESTION: THE EUROPEAN EXTERNAL ACTION SERVICE AND THE EUROPEAN COMMISSION

The Treaty of Lisbon has created a new actor in the EU's external action: the EEAS. An analysis of the institutional framework that governs EU development cooperation policy demands an examination of the EEAS's role and competences, as well as its relationship with the Commission. They are both active in related areas and the establishment of the EEAS triggered the transfer of staff and tasks from the Commission. The two actors are therefore closely related, while their successful functioning is essential for coherent action in the area of development cooperation policy and its related areas. An analysis of the relationship between these two actors demonstrates how the conferral–coherence question is managed in the institutional division of competences in EU development cooperation policy.

3.1 Delimitation of Competences: The EEAS as a New Actor in External Action

Article 27(3) TEU concisely holds that the High Representative is assisted by a European External Action Service, which works in cooperation with Member States' diplomatic services and which contains staff from relevant departments of the General Secretariat of the Council and of the Commission as well as staff seconded from national diplomatic services of the Member States. Apart from this explanation, the Treaties are further silent on the service's legal set-up, detailed composition and organisation, tasks, and competences. As defined in Article 27(3) TEU, a Council Decision, based on a proposal from the High Representative, obtaining the consent from the Commission and after consulting the Parliament, needed to determine further the functioning and organisation of the service. The Declaration on Article 27 demanded that the preparatory work would start immediately after the adoption of the Treaty of Lisbon.[78] The Council adopted the final decision on the organisation and functioning in July 2010 with its Decision 2010/427/EU ('the EEAS Decision').[79]

---

[78] For a detailed overview of the discussions leading up to the launch of the EEAS, see: L. Erkelens, S. Blockmans, Setting up the European External Action Service: An institutional act of balance, CLEER Working Papers 2012/1, 1–32.

[79] Council Decision of 26 July 2010 establishing the organisation and functioning of the European External Action Service, OJ 2010 L201/30.

3.1.1 The EEAS's legal nature

Article 27(3) TEU refers to the EEAS as a service, which might suggest that it is attached to or dependent on another institution.[80] However, the EEAS Decision clarifies that the service is established as a functionally autonomous body, separate from the General Secretariat of the Council and from the Commission, under the authority of the High Representative, but with the legal capacity that is necessary to perform its tasks and attain its objectives.[81] This set-up seems to be a compromise between the establishment of the EEAS as an intergovernmental body closely related to the Council and a body with a strong affiliation with the Commission.[82] The European Parliament was in favour of integrating the EEAS into the Commission's administrative structure,[83] whereas the Council argued that the EEAS should hold a *sui generis* nature separate from the Commission and the Council Secretariat, while development cooperation policy and trade should remain with the Commission.[84] This is arguably a clash of views between the need to protect the Community model from too much intergovernmental influences on the one hand and the perspective that the EEAS is established as the best suitable actor to promote a new vision on a coherent and comprehensive approach to EU external action.[85]

As a body functionally autonomous from the Council and the Commission, the EEAS has been referred to as a *sui generis* inter-institutional body 'equidistant' from the Council and the Commission[86] with 'quasi-institutional features'.[87] Although the term '*sui generis*' was eventually excluded from the final EEAS Council Decision,[88] its characteristics and nature can still be described as such.[89] Blockmans and Hillion have argued that the EEAS is only functionally but not organisationally autonomous. This specification is indeed relevant, as it implies that the EEAS is autonomous in carrying out its func-

[80] M. Gatti, 248.

[81] Article 1(2) EEAS Decision.

[82] G. De Baere, R. Wessel, 176.

[83] Report on the institutional aspects of setting up the European External Action Service, EP Committee on Constitutional Affairs, Rapporteur Elmar Brok, para. 7.

[84] Presidency report to the European Council on the European External Action Service, 2009, DOC 14930/09, para. 6; 16.

[85] S. Duke, S. Blockmans, 1.

[86] B. Van Vooren, 'A legal-institutional perspective on the European External Action Service', 488.

[87] M. Gatti, 248.

[88] The Council Presidency report on the EEAS had used this term: Presidency report to the European Council on the European External Action Service, 2009, DOC 14930/09, para. 16.

[89] B. Van Vooren, 'A legal-institutional perspective on the European External Action Service', 482.

tions but that is not autonomous from an organisational perspective. The latter follows from the fact that the service needs to respect the Staff and Financial Regulations, its accountability vis-à-vis the European Parliament, and its operation under the authority of the High Representative.[90] Nevertheless, the fact that the EEAS cannot be seen as an EU institution outside this particular context does have some consequences: it not only influences the EEAS's political weight but it also to a certain extent affects its competences and capacity for legal enforcement.[91]

3.1.2 The scope of the EEAS's mandate and its tasks

The EEAS's tasks are described in a detailed manner in the EEAS Council Decision. As already pointed out, the Treaty itself merely indicates that the EEAS is to assist the High Representative. Article 2 EEAS Decision lays down the service's tasks. First, the EEAS is to support the High Representative in fulfilling his different mandates, as reflected in Articles 18 and 27 TEU. This includes conducting the CFSP and the CSDP (Article 18(2) TEU), ensuring the consistency of the EU's external action (Article 18(4) TEU), presiding over the Foreign Affairs Council (Article 18(3) TEU), and acting as Vice-President of the Commission. The latter capacity not only includes responsibilities incumbent on the Commission in external relations but also coordinating other aspects of the EU's external action (Article 18(4) TEU). Second, paragraph 2 of Article 2 EEAS Decision specifies that the EEAS is also to assist the President of the European Council, the Commission, and its President in the exercise of their respective functions in the area of external relations.[92] The tasks laid down in Article 2(1) EEAS Decision are in accordance with the EEAS's Treaty-based task: Article 27(3) TEU requires the EEAS to assist

---

90 S. Blockmans, C. Hillion, 12.

91 Its affected capacity for legal enforcement for example implies that the EEAS is not a privileged applicant before the Court (Article 263 TFEU), while it also lacks the competence to start an infringement action against the Member States (Article 258 TFEU). The EEAS has nevertheless already acted as defending party in several cases before the Court, particularly in staff cases, see for example: Case C-501/13 P, *Page Protective Services*, EU:C:2014:2259; Case T-611/16, *Trautmann/EEAS*, EU:T:2017:917; Case T-585/16, *Skareby/EEAS*, EU:T:2017:613. On the basis of the *Les Verts* case law (Case 294/83, *Les Verts*, EU:C:1986:166), the EEAS could arguably moreover have active standing before the Court, in particular to defend its prerogatives. Its active standing is also undisputed when it is the addressee of a certain act. For a detailed analysis of this issue, see: M Gatti, 'Diplomats at the bar: The European External Action Service before EU courts', 5 European Law Review, 2014, 664–681.

92 A further specification of this task can be found in Article 5(7) EEAS Decision: Union delegations shall have the capacity to respond to the needs of other institutions of the Union, in particular the European Parliament, in their contacts with the international organisations or third countries to which the delegations are accredited.

the High Representative in fulfilling his mandate. The tasks as defined in paragraph 2 of Article 2 EEAS Decision, which require the EEAS to assist the Commission and its President as well as the European Council President, are not based on the Treaty and were added during the negotiations on the proposal for an EEAS Decision. Both the Commission and the Council considered these additional tasks to be in favour of steering coordination and coherence between different areas and actors of EU external action.[93]

Article 3 further lays down the cooperation tasks which the EEAS has to fulfil vis-à-vis several actors. Following the importance of positive cooperation to attain coherence, as discussed above, the EEAS's cooperative duties are essential for the service to fulfil its bridge function in ensuring coherence between different EU actions.[94] Its cooperation tasks concern that (i) it should support, and work in cooperation with, the diplomatic services of the Member States as well as the General Secretariat of the Council and the services of the Commission, in order to ensure consistency between the different areas of the EU's external action and between those areas and its other policies; (ii) the EEAS and the services of the Commission are to consult each other on all matters relating to the external action of the EU in the exercise of their respective functions, except on matters covered by the CSDP, and the EEAS is to take part in the preparatory work and procedures relating to acts to be prepared by the Commission in this area;[95] (iii) it should attribute appropriate support and cooperation to the other institutions and bodies of the EU, in particular the European Parliament; and (iv) the Union delegations are to work in close cooperation and share information with the diplomatic services of the Member States.[96] In the initial draft, a reciprocal obligation to share information was provided, but this reciprocal duty is absent in the final draft. However, on the basis of the principle of sincere cooperation, laid down in Article 4(3) TEU, a two-way obligation would apply between the EU Delegations and the Member State diplomatic services to share information.[97] Although there is no explicit cooperative duty included vis-à-vis the Council, it can be argued that a duty of consultation and cooperation applies on the general basis of the

93 Council of the European Union, 'Presidency report to the European Council on the External Action Service', doc. 14930/09, Brussels, 23 October 2009; L. Erkelens, S. Blockmans, 4.

94 S. Blockmans, C. Hillion, 28, 32.

95 The particular duty of cooperation that is applicable in the relationship between the Commission and the EEAS will be analysed further below in detail.

96 Article 5(9) EEAS Decision.

97 This issue was already analysed in Chapter 3 on the management of the vertical division of competences between the Union and its Member States.

principle of sincere cooperation.[98] Finally, the EEAS also has a specific role in the programming of development cooperation policy and other external action instruments. According to Article 9 EEAS Decision, the EEAS prepares the strategic aspects of the programming of the financial EU external action instruments. This issue will be discussed in detail further below.

Merely on the basis of Article 27(3) TEU, it might be argued that the EEAS is to support the High Representative solely in the area of the CFSP: the Treaty Article forms part of the Treaty provisions concerning the CFSP, and the two other paragraphs of Article 27 TEU relate to the CFSP function of the High Representative. However, Article 27(3) concisely lays down the EEAS's task to assist the High Representative, without further specifying what this task entails. After examining the tasks which are incumbent on the EEAS as laid down in the EEAS Council Decision, it becomes clear that the EEAS's mandate goes beyond the CFSP. It follows from Articles 2, 3(1), and 9(2) EEAS Decision that the service is to assist the High Representative in all of his tasks.[99] As such, the tasks of the EEAS reflect the same bridging function and coherence mandate as is attributed to the High Representative.[100] When determining that the EEAS supports the High Representative in fulfilling his mandate, Article 2(1) EEAS Decision refers explicitly to both Article 18 and Article 27: the former refers to his function as Commission Vice-President and chair of the FAC, while the latter covers his CFSP tasks. The EEAS Decision therefore clearly defines the EEAS's task in light of the High Representative's triple-hatted function, pursuing coherence in CFSP and non-CFSP matters, without establishing a hierarchy between the different functions.[101] It has moreover been argued from the start by several EU institutions that the mandate and tasks of the EEAS should cover both CFSP and non-CFSP aspects.[102] Deciding otherwise by limiting the EEAS's mandate to assist the High Representative merely in CFSP matters would make it impossible for the High Representative to fulfil his mandate of ensuring overall coherence.[103]

Interestingly, the Decision does not explicitly lay down the EEAS's objectives. In order to enforce its mandate, a revised EEAS Decision, or even

---

98 G. De Baere, R. Wessel, 178.

99 M. Gatti, 249.

100 P-C Müller-Graff, 'The European External Action Service: Challenges in a complex institutional framework' in I. Govaere, P. Van Elsuwege, E. Lannon, S. Adam (eds), *The European Union in the world: essays in honour of Marc Maresceau*, 124.

101 S. Blockmans, C. Hillion, 17.

102 European Council Conclusions, 16 September 2010, Annex I para f; Council Presidency; Commission and High Representative, Issue paper on the European External Action Service, Annex II to Council doc. 9956/05, para. 7.

103 M. Gatti, 249.

a revised Treaty, could more clearly define the EEAS's ultimate objectives, steering the EEAS's work towards the attainment of these objectives.[104] Certainly, these would cover the strengthening of the coherence of EU external action as the main or overarching objective of the service's actions: as an actor autonomous from both Member State intergovernmental and Commission EU interests, the EEAS should be able to organise its work towards pursuing the objective of coherent EU external action.[105] As an actor that is active in the area of development cooperation as well, reference could also be made to the pursuit of the development cooperation policy objectives, which would ensure the mainstreaming of these objectives in the EEAS's activities (see further below).

3.2 Ensuring Coherence: Cooperation and Coordination Arrangements Between the Commission and the EEAS

3.2.1 Duty of cooperation

The previous section on the EEAS's mandate and tasks already referred to the EEAS's cooperation tasks, as laid down in Article 3 EEAS Decision. On the basis of these duties, the EEAS is to cooperate with several institutions. The cooperation duties are essential for the successful functioning of the EEAS: as a functional autonomous body, the EEAS's successful cooperation with other actors is essential in order to ensure both coherent action and institutional division of competences.[106] The division of competences between the EEAS and the other actors is not always entirely straightforward, which holds the risk of causing disputes or so-called turf battles between these actors.[107] These disputes can be averted through establishing strong cooperation arrangements. The EEAS's strong cooperative duties also emphasise its nature as a service, indicating that it is in the first place to work with and for other actors in order to perform its tasks.[108] On the other hand, cooperation is essential in

[104] S. Blockmans, C. Hillion, 13.

[105] B. Van Vooren, 'A legal-institutional perspective on the European External Action Service', 492.

[106] S. Duke, 51. See on building trust 'within' and 'in' interaction with the EEAS: S. Blockmans, R, Wessel, 'The EEAS at ten: reason for a celebration?' European Foreign Affairs, 2021, 8–11; P. Vimont, S. Blockmans, C. Hillion, 'From self-doubt to self-assurance: the European External Action Service as the indispensable support for a geopolitical EU', CEPS/SIEPS/FES, 2021, 10–16.

[107] J. Wouters, G. De Baere, B. Van Vooren, K. Raube, J. Odermatt, T. Ramopoulous, Y. Tanghe, T. Van den Sanden, 33.

[108] S. Blockmans, C. Hillion, 26. In this context, reference can be made to the EEAS's functional but not organisational autonomy (see above).

order to attain the coherence objective.[109] The specific duty of cooperation between the EEAS and the other actors and institutions, as laid down in the EEAS Decision, is a specification of the general duty of mutual sincere cooperation, as laid down in Article 13(2) TEU and in Article 4(3) TEU. The cooperation duties are linked to the objective of ensuring coherent EU external action: Article 3(1) EEAS Decision holds that the cooperation that the EEAS establishes with the diplomatic services of the Member States, the General Secretariat of the Council, and the services of the Commission is set up in order to ensure consistency between the different areas of the Union's external action and between those areas and its other policies. As already argued before, the objective of ensuring coherence could be more persuasively underscored as the main objective of the EEAS's tasks.[110] The link between the EEAS's duties of cooperation and the objective of ensuring coherent EU external action refers back to the link between the principle of sincere cooperation and the principle of coherence (see above).

The EEAS's cooperative duties, as laid down in Article 3 EEAS Decision, cover several specific duties of cooperation. First, paragraph 1 requires the EEAS to 'support and work in cooperation with' the Member States' diplomatic services, the Council General Secretariat, and the services of the Commission. Second, in accordance with paragraph 2, the EEAS and the Commission are to 'consult each other' on all matters relating to the external action of the Union in the exercise of their functions, except on CSDP matters. The EEAS moreover takes part in the preparatory work and procedures relating to acts to be prepared by the Commission in this area. Third, paragraph 3 explicitly allows for the conclusion of service-level arrangements, while paragraph 4 determines that the EEAS is to extend 'appropriate support and cooperation' to other institutions and bodies of the EU, particularly the European Parliament. In turn, the EEAS can benefit from the support and cooperation of the same institutions and bodies. Apart from Article 3 EEAS Decision, which covers the general cooperation duties, more specific duties of cooperation are enshrined in other articles which address specific issues. In accordance with Article 9 EEAS Decision, this is particularly the case for the programming of the external action instruments, where the EEAS is involved in the strategic steps of the process (see below). It therefore seems that the specific duty of cooperation that the EEAS needs to respect depends on the institution vis-à-vis which the EEAS needs to respect a certain duty of cooperation. The strongest duty of cooperation would then exist in the relationship between the EEAS

---

[109] C. Hillion, 'Tous pour un, un pour tous! Coherence in the external relations of the European Union'.

[110] M. Gatti, 261.

and the Commission, while the duty to support and work in cooperation with the Commission and with the Council General Secretariat and Member State diplomatic services still seems more compelling than the duty to extend this support and cooperation to the Parliament. The reference to 'appropriate' support seems to indicate that the cooperation with the Parliament is less automatic than with the Commission, the Council, and Member State missions.[111]

The duty of cooperation between the EEAS and the Commission is the strongest and the most important one to analyse when evaluating the management of the institutional division of competences in the area of development cooperation policy. The issues concerning the Commission–EEAS relationship follow the central paradigm of this book: both competence questions and cooperation duties are essential in managing the relationship between these two actors. Concerning the material scope of application of the duty to consult, it has been questioned whether the duty to consult between the Commission and the EEAS, as established in Article 3(2) EEAS Decision, also applies to the external aspect of internal policies and exclusive competences, such as for example the CCP.[112] Arguably, the duty to consult covers indeed the whole sphere of EU external action, including areas of exclusive competence and all external aspects of internal policies. Deciding otherwise would negatively impact the objective of ensuring coherence. The obligation formulated in Article 3(3) EEAS Decision following which the EEAS and the Commission are required to consult each other on all matters relating to EU external action explicitly excludes this duty in the area of the CSDP. It is important to notice that the CSDP is specifically excluded, which would confirm that the duty to consult does apply to the non-CSDP parts of the CFSP. Nevertheless, the explicit exclusion of the CSDP is another expression of the distinction that still exists in EU external action between the CFSP and the non-CFSP. Excluding the CSDP from the specific cooperative duty between the EEAS and the Commission undoubtedly affects the management of the security–development cooperation policy nexus, as it creates an extra institutional hurdle to attain coherence in the relationship between the CFSP and development cooperation policy. Nevertheless, on the basis of the general duty of cooperation and in light of pursuing coherence, a duty of *information* could arguably apply, as the EEAS Decision merely excludes a duty of *consultation*. This would be the case especially in instances where development cooperation policy and CSDP elements are strongly linked.[113] The duty to consult is there-

---

[111] S. Blockmans, C. Hillion, 32.

[112] Ibid., 51.

[113] B. Van Vooren, 'A legal-institutional perspective on the European External Action Service', 498.

fore a comprehensive duty of cooperation, covering all areas relevant to EU external action, except for the CSDP.

The duty of cooperation between the Commission and the EEAS is further specified and concretised in soft law arrangements, which are agreed between the two actors (see in parallel, Chapter 5 for the concretisation and formalisation of the duty to cooperate between the Union and the Member States). In 2011 the Commission developed a Vademecum on Working Relations with the European External Action Service.[114] These set out arrangements on each actor's competences, planning, coordination and decision-making, inter-institutional relations, participation in summits and visits, and briefing and reporting procedures, as well as external representation. In 2012 the EEAS and the Commission agreed on detailed working arrangements that apply between the actors in external relations issues.[115] They focus on laying down the principles and practical implementation of the relationship between Commission DGs responsible for external action and the EEAS. In that context they cover arrangements on (financial) management in delegations, issuing of briefings and preparation for visits, media and communication, and detailed arrangements for cooperation in the programming and implementation of external action instruments, further specifying the general arrangements as laid down in Article 9 EEAS Decision. The importance of these arrangements, which focus on coordination and communication between the actors, is demonstrated by the fact that often a lack of direct contact between the Commission and the EEAS is both a source of and the consequence of disagreements and turf battles between these actors.[116] The 2012 Joint Decision of the Commission and the High Representative on Cooperation Mechanisms concerning the Management of Delegations of the European Union[117] further establishes a Steering Committee for Delegations, which is to ensure cooperation and consultation between the EEAS and the Commission for all issues relating to the management of Delegations.

The working arrangements agreed and concluded between the EEAS and the Commission can be qualified, pursuant to Article 3(3) EEAS Decision, as service-level arrangements.[118] Referring back to the analysis on the vertical

---

114 SEC(2011)1636.

115 Working Arrangements between Commission Services and the European External Action Service (EEAS) in relation to external relations issues, SEC(2012)48.

116 EEAS review, 11; House of Lords EU Committee 2013, 22–23, para. 51.

117 Joint Decision of the Commission and the High Representative on Cooperation Mechanisms concerning the Management of Delegations of the European Union of 28 March 2012, JOIN(2012) 8 final.

118 B. Van Vooren, 'A legal-institutional perspective on the European External Action Service', 493.

division of competences in Chapter 5, these arrangements can be seen as a specific formalisation and concretisation of the duty of cooperation between the Commission and the EEAS in soft law instruments. As argued there, the Court accepted the concretisation and formalisation of the duty of cooperation in informally concluded inter-institutional agreements and recognises their binding effect.[119] It could be questioned whether their qualification as 'arrangements' was deliberately used to explicitly differentiate the arrangements from inter-institutional agreements and hence to argue for their lack of legal effect. On the basis of earlier case law in the *FAO* case, however, it can be argued that a violation of these arrangements would constitute a violation of the principle of sincere cooperation.[120] Analysis of the working arrangements agreed between the Commission and the EEAS proves that these arrangements focus rather on means to enhance positive cooperation and coordination than on division of labour to pursue the development cooperation policy objectives.[121] Also in this respect a parallel can be drawn with the management of the vertical division of competences in EU development cooperation policy, where positive cooperation arrangements rather than more negative divisions of labour and abstention duties proved to be essential in managing the division of powers.

3.2.2 Union Delegations in third countries

What also emerges from the working arrangements is the importance of the EU Delegations in managing the relationship between the Commission and the EEAS. With their presence on the ground in third partner countries, their activities encompassing the whole range of EU external action and their diversified composition, they are crucial in strengthening the coherence and continuity of EU external action.[122]

The Delegations are part of the EEAS[123] and operate under the authority of the High Representative.[124] They are located in third countries outside the EU, where they represent the EU and work in close cooperation with Member State missions.[125] Some Delegations represent the EU at international organisations. With the Treaty of Lisbon, the Union Delegations replaced the

---

[119] Case C-25/94, para. 50; P. Eeckhout, *EU External Relations Law*, 246.

[120] B. Van Vooren, 'A legal-institutional perspective on the European External Action Service', 495–496.

[121] S. Duke, S. Blockmans, M. Broberg, R. Holdgaard, 'EU development cooperation post-Lisbon: main constitutional challenges', 2015 European Law Review, 367.

[122] S. Hayes, 'EU Delegations: Europe's link to the world', in K.E. Jorgensen, K.V. Laatikainen, (eds), *Routledge Handbook on the European Union and International Institutions*, Routledge, 2013, 27–39.

[123] Article 1(4) EEAS Decision.

[124] Article 221 TFEU.

[125] Article 221 TFEU.

former Commission Delegations and took over the role of the former local Presidency tasks relating to responsibilities of local coordination with the diplomatic missions of Member States and external representation. Because of their transformation from Commission Delegations to Union Delegations, they now represent the Union in its entirety and not only with regard to the TFEU competences.[126] This implies that the EU Delegations are the lead coordinator in different coordination bodies and meetings, from institutionalised coordination structure to informal coordination meetings. In their role and through their presence in third countries, the Delegations are the 'mouth, eyes and ears'[127] of the High Representative and of the Union in general. An important aspect of the Delegations' liaison task in this regard is policy reporting between headquarter and Delegation level.[128] The Working Arrangements aim to strengthen the coherence of policy reporting and information flow by requiring that the EEAS geographical desks at headquarter level are systematically copied on all reports and information that is relevant for the country under their responsibility.[129] Pursuant to Article 32(3) and 35 TEU, the Delegations also have specific tasks in the formulation and the implementation of the common approach agreed on CFSP. As referred to in Chapter 5, the success of these coordination and cooperation efforts also depends on the specific circumstances.[130]

The structure and composition of the EU Delegations are interesting from the coherence–conferral perspective. In accordance with the transfer of staff principles as laid down in the Annex to the EEAS Decision, EEAS staff at Delegations work on political and security affairs, information, communication and press, as well as public diplomacy. The Head of Delegation, the Deputy Head of Delegation, their support staff, and the administrative staff are also EEAS staff. Commission staff at Delegations comprise staff with budget implementation competences and staff active in areas which fall under Commission competence. As will be discussed below, staff involved in budget implementation tasks are necessarily Commission staff, as budget implementation is a Commission competence pursuant to Article 17(1) TEU. The latter covers mainly development cooperation policy, while Commission staff at Delegations can also comprise staff working on other Commission

---

126 J. Wouters, G. De Baere, B. Van Vooren, K. Raube, J. Odermatt, T. Ramopoulous, Y. Tanghe, T. Van den Sanden, 62.

127 Ibid., 63.

128 Working Arrangements between Commission Services and the European External Action Service in relation to external relations issues, 3.

129 Working Arrangements between Commission Services and the European External Action Service in relation to external relations issues, 3.

130 J. Wouters, G. De Baere, B. Van Vooren, K. Raube, J. Odermatt, T. Ramopoulous, Y. Tanghe, T. Van den Sanden, 64.

competences, such as trade or energy. EU Delegations are generally structured on the basis of the distinction between Commission and EEAS staff and their respective competences: the Delegations usually consist of an administrative section, a political section, and a cooperation section in developing countries or a trade section in developed countries. Although Delegations consist of both EEAS and Commission staff, all staff fall under the authority of the Head of Delegation for all their activities. The Head of Delegation is in turn accountable to the High Representative for the overall management of the Delegation's work and for securing the coordination of all EU actions.[131]

In the past concerns were raised about the division and level of cooperation between Commission and EEAS staff in their aim to attain coherence. An important concern is, for example, the difficulty to align Commission development cooperation policy principles and instructions and political considerations and priorities formulated by the EEAS.[132] In this sense, their difficult relationship is illustrative for the challenges that other actors in EU external action generally face when avoiding contradictions and steering coordination.[133] Article 5(3) EEAS Decision determines that the High Representative and the EEAS can issue instructions to the Head of Delegation, who is responsible for their execution.[134] Nevertheless, the Commission can also issue instructions to Delegation staff on matters that fall within the scope of its competences, which are executed under the overall responsibility of the Head of Delegation. To remedy concerns regarding contradictory instructions issued by the EEAS on the one hand and the Commission on the other hand, the working arrangements go further into detail on the competence to issue instructions to Delegations.

3.3 Putting Development Cooperation Policy Objectives Into Action: The Programming and Implementation of EU Development Cooperation Policy

Pursuant to Article 9 EEAS Decision, both the EEAS and the Commission are involved in the management, and in particular the programming, of the external action instruments. Article 9(1) EEAS Decision determines in that regard that the management of the Union's external action cooperation programmes is under the responsibility of the Commission, but this is without prejudice to

---

131 Article 5(2) EEAS Decision.

132 J. Wouters, G. De Baere, B. Van Vooren, K. Raube, J. Odermatt, T. Ramopoulous, Y. Tanghe, T. Van den Sanden, 66–67.

133 R. Wessel, B. Van Vooren, 8.

134 The Head of Delegation is de facto an EU ambassador: J. Wouters, S. Duquet, 'The EU and international diplomatic law: new horizons?' 1 Hague Journal of Diplomacy, 2012, 31–49.

the respective roles of the Commission and of the EEAS in the programming, as set out in the following paragraphs of Article 9 EEAS Decision. This paragraph therefore indicates what this section will discuss: first, the roles of both the EEAS and the Commission in the programming of external action instruments and, second, the role of the Commission in the management or implementation of the instruments. Assessing their respective roles in the programming and implementation of development cooperation financing instruments is important in view of the fact that the programming and implementation of the instruments is how development cooperation policy and its objectives are put into concrete action.

3.3.1 The programming and implementation cycle

Article 9 EEAS Decision grants the EEAS a leading role in the strategic steps of the programming process. The EEAS Decision also clarifies that this is so with a view to attain coherent Union action. In that regard, Article 9(2) EEAS Decision explicitly recognises the involvement in the external financial assistance instruments as a means for the High Representative to ensure the overall political coordination of the EU's external action, as well as the unity, consistency, and effectiveness of the Union's external action. The preamble to the EEAS Decision moreover clarifies that the EEAS should ensure that the external cooperation programmes fulfil the common external action objectives as laid down in Article 21(2) TEU, and in particular the objective to foster the sustainable economic, social, and environmental development of developing countries, with the primary aim of eradication poverty as laid down in Article 21(2)(d) TEU. The same recital further requires the EEAS to respect the development cooperation objectives in line with Article 208 TFEU and to promote the fulfilment of the objectives of the European Consensus on Development.[135] This underscores again the importance of the poverty eradication aim as the primary objective of development cooperation policy, as well as the importance of policy coherence for development (PCD): the EEAS is required to pay specific attention to the attainment of the development cooperation policy objectives in developing external actions and programmes.

Article 9(3) EEAS Decision clarifies the EEAS's role in the programming: the EEAS is responsible for preparing the Commission Decisions relating to the strategic, multiannual steps within the programming cycle, namely the country allocations, the country and regional strategic papers, and the national and regional indicative programmes. Paragraphs 4, 5, and 6 provide further details on the preparatory steps and the role of Commission and EEAS services, as well as the responsible Commissioners, distinguishing the European

---

135 EEAS Council Decision preamble, indent 4.

Development Fund (EDF) and the Development Cooperation Instrument (DCI), the different thematic programmes, the European Neighbourhood Instrument (ENI) and the Partnership Instrument (PI), and finally the CFSP budget. The EEAS Decision, which was not amended, therefore still refers to the financing instruments under the previous multiannual financial framework (MFF). Yet, the division of tasks between the Commission and the EEAS as laid down in Article 9 EEAS Decision still applies: Article 48 NDICI-Global Europe determines that it should be applied in accordance with the EEAS Decision, and in particular its Article 9.[136] In that regard, the NDICI-Global Europe determines that the references to the external action instruments in Article 9 EEAS Decision should be read as references to NDICI-Global Europe and that the Commission should ensure that NDICI-Global Europe is implemented in accordance with the role of the EEAS as laid down in the EEAS Decision.[137]

Importantly, Article 9(3) final subparagraph requires the Commission and EEAS services to cooperate in the programming process, as a reinforced duty to the duty to cooperate as laid down in Article 3 EEAS Decision. This subparagraph also clarifies that while the EEAS prepares the Commission programming Decisions, these proposals are prepared by following the Commission's procedures and are submitted to the Commission for adoption. Indeed, Article 16 NDICI-Global Europe determines that the multiannual indicative programmes are adopted by the Commission by means of implementing acts. In accordance with the general rule for adopting implementing measures, pursuant to Article 291(3) TFEU, the multiannual indicative programmes as Commission implementing measures are subject to comitology, which grants the Member States an important controlling competence over the Commission's implementing powers.[138] In that regard, Article 45 NDICI-Global Europe establishes the Neighbourhood, Development and International Cooperation Instrument Committee, which is a committee within the meaning of the General Regulation on Comitology: Regulation 182/2011.[139] Article 45(2)(4) NDICI-Global furthermore makes cross-references to the spe-

---

136 Article 48 Regulation 2021/947.

137 Recital (84) NDICI-Global Europe.

138 For a critical analysis of the comitology procedure pre- and post-Lisbon and case law in that respect, see for example: M. Chamon, 'Dealing with a zombie in EU law. The regulatory comitology procedure with scrutiny. Joined Cases T-261/13 and T-86/14 Netherlands v. Commission, EU:T:2015:671', 4 Maastricht Journal of European and Comparative Law, 2016, 714–724.

139 Regulation 182/2011 of the European Parliament and of the Council of 16 February 2011 laying down the rules and general principles concerning mechanisms for control by Member States of the Commission's exercise of implementing powers OJ L 55, 28.2.2011, p. 13.

cific comitology procedures as laid down in Regulation 182/2011, in particular the examination procedure or the procedure to adopt immediately applicable implementing acts. Pursuant to Article 11 Regulation 182/2011, the European Parliament and the Council have a right of scrutiny in case they consider that the Commission implementing act exceeds the implementing powers provided in the regulation. Under NDICI-Global Europe, the Commission is moreover empowered to adopt delegated acts, pursuant to Article 290 TFEU, in relation to certain aspects of NDICI-Global Europe, mainly in order to amend the areas of cooperation under the different programmes, as laid down in the annexes to NDICI-Global Europe. In line with Article 290(2) TFEU, NDICI-Global Europe makes the delegation of powers to the Commission subject to the consultation of the expert group, in accordance with the Interinstitutional Agreement on Better Law-Making,[140] to the absence of objection expressed by the European Parliament or the Council and to the Parliament's and Council's right to revoke the delegation of powers. In relation to the programming, Article 4(7) NDICI-Global Europe provides for the adoption of a supplementing delegated act to further frame the programming documents.

The programming phase is followed by the implementation phase, where the Commission takes up the central role. In accordance with Article 9(1) EEAS Decision, the management of the external action instruments falls under the sole responsibility of the Commission, which is a specification of the Commission competence to manage programmes and implement the budget, as laid down in Article 17 TEU and Article 317 TFEU. The Commission's leading role in the implementation phase therefore follows directly from its prerogative to implement the budget as laid down in the Treaties. The implementation of the external action and development cooperation instruments takes the specific form of the adoption of implementing measures ('projects') and financial execution. Pursuant to Article 110 Financial Regulation,[141] the Commission adopts 'financing decisions', which lay down the budgetary commitment and at the same time constitute the annual or multiannual work programme.[142] Under NDICI-Global Europe, the latter take the form of annual or multiannual action plans and, depending on their nature and content, individual measures, special

140 Interinstitutional Agreement between the European Parliament, the Council of the European Union and the European Commission on Better Law-Making, OJ 2016 L123/1.

141 Regulation 2018/1046 of 18 July 2018 on the financial rules applicable to the general budget of the Union, OJ 30.7.2018 L193/1.

142 See also: T. Van den Sanden, 'Laying the foundation for a broad scope of EU development cooperation policy and its delimitation with other EU external competence: Philippines Border Management', in G. Butler, R. Wessel, *EU External Relations Law: The cases in context*, Hart, forthcoming.

measures, support measures, or exceptional assistance measures. Article 25 NDICI-Global Europe confirms that these plans and measures are adopted by means of implementing acts, which are subject to comitology. The Article further determines certain categories and thresholds, which are exempted from comitology. These acts should still be communicated to the European Parliament and to the Member States through the committee within one month of their adoption. In line with the Financial Regulation, the Commission implements the funding under NDICI-Global Europe either directly, by Union Delegations or by executive agencies, or indirectly through the entities listed in Article 62(1)(c) of the Financial Regulation.[143] The delegation of budget implementation entails a controlling role for the Commission to ensure the sound financial management of the Union's funds. Also in the case of budget delegation, the Commission remains responsible for budget implementation in accordance with Article 317 TFEU and cannot delegate those tasks to third parties that involve a large measure of discretion implying political choices.[144]

The fact that it is the Commission's prerogative to manage programmes and implement the budget has an important impact on the division of tasks between the Commission and the EEAS and, subsequently, on the organisational structure of the Union Delegations and in headquarters. This prerogative, which follows directly from the Treaties, ensures the Commission's leading role in the adoption of programming documents and in the implementation phase. Concretely, it entails that only the Commission and its (delegated) staff can implement operational external action budget. Article 8(1) EEAS Decision confirms in that regard that while the EEAS implements its administrative budget, in line with the Financial Regulation, operational expenditure remains within the Commission's budget and competences. At headquarter level this has led to the creation of the Service for Foreign Policy Instruments (FPI), which is a peculiar actor in the EU's external action organisation and whose mandate is linked to both coherence and conferral. It is a Commission service that works under the direct authority of the High Representative in his capacity of Commission Vice-President. It is co-located with the EEAS but remains separate from the EEAS in administrative and functional terms: as the FPI is responsible for the financial execution of certain instruments, it is to remain a Commission service, which is independent from the EEAS. Pursuant to Article 9(6) EEAS Decision, the FPI manages the implementation of the CFSP budget and certain parts of NDICI-Global Europe that correspond to the previous instruments laid down in this paragraph. As a Commission service that is closely related to the EEAS and its competence areas, even co-located with

143 Article 26(1) NDICI-Global Europe.
144 Article 62(3) Financial Regulation.

the EEAS, it holds arguably an important role in steering coherence.[145] The Commission's competence to manage programmes and implement the Union budget also governs the organisation of the Union Delegations. Pursuant to Article 5(3) EEAS Decision and in accordance with Article 221(2) TFEU, the Commission can also issue instructions to delegations in areas of Commission competence, to be executed under the overall responsibility of the Head of Delegation, who has authority over all staff in the delegation. The delegation staff indeed comprises EEAS staff and Commission staff, as clarified by Article 5(2) EEAS Decision, where appropriate for the implementation of the Union budget and Union policies under Commission competence. As set out above, as a result of this, Union delegations usually comprise a political section, with EEAS staff, and a cooperation section, with Commission staff, under the authority of a double-hatted Head of Delegation. Commission staff's activities also cover the management of projects. In that regard, the Head of Delegation implements operational credits in relation to the Union's projects in accordance with the Financial Regulation.[146] In light of this, pursuant to Article 60(2) Financial Regulation, the Commission delegates its powers of budget implementation concerning the operational appropriations to Heads of Delegation, who, when acting as authorising officers by sub-delegation of the Commission, apply the Commission rules for budget implementation and are subject to the same duties, obligations, and accountability as any other authorising officer by sub-delegation of the Commission. Under Article 76 Financial Regulation, specific duties, and in particular a duty to cooperate closely with the Commission, apply to the Head of Delegation in order to ensure the legality and regularity of financial transactions and the respect for the principle of sound financial management.

3.3.2 Evaluation of the role of the Commission and the EEAS in the programming and implementation cycle in light of conferral and coherence

After the EEAS's creation, the role of the EEAS in development cooperation policy and in its programming in particular has caused a controversial debate.[147] This debate concerned both the extent of the EEAS's legal competences going beyond the CFSP and in the area of development cooperation in particular and, from a more political perspective, the blurring distinction between development cooperation policy and security policy, linked to the fear

[145] J. Wouters, G. De Baere, B. Van Vooren, K. Raube, J. Odermatt, T. Ramopoulous, Y. Tanghe, T. Van den Sanden, 56.

[146] Article 5(4) EEAS Decision.

[147] B. Van Vooren, 'A legal-institutional perspective on the European External Action Service', 478.

that (short-term) security and political priorities would override (long-term) development objectives.[148] However, it could be argued that the EEAS's role in development cooperation policy both respects the principle of conferral and is a means to enhance coherence.

As regards conferral and division of competences, when analysing the programming process, a clear division of competences emerges between the Commission and the EEAS. The EEAS Decision defines the EEAS's role in terms of ensuring political guidance and coherence. As such, it is responsible to prepare the Commission Decisions on programming. In this regard, the EEAS is not only bound by the common external action objectives and the objectives of development cooperation[149] but also by the policy objectives formulated in the financing instruments.[150] Moreover, programming documents under NDICI-Global Europe follow from a multi-stakeholder dialogue and on the partner countries' needs and are based on the partners' national or regional strategies and development plans. NDICI-Global Europe moreover emphasises joint programming, as even the preferred approach for geographic programmes.[151] This ensures the integration and reflection of multiple objectives into the programming process. While the EEAS is responsible to contribute to the programming's strategic steps, it does so in accordance with Commission procedures and the actual decisions are adopted by the Commission as Commission Decisions, in line with the Commission's competence to manage programmes and execute the budget as laid down in Article 17(1) TEU. Therefore, apart from the political influence the EEAS can have on the programming process, legally speaking, however, the EEAS cannot adopt final measures and therefore lacks independent decision-making powers in development cooperation policy programming.[152] This is in accordance with the EEAS's competences as a service: it is involved in the preparation of decisions, which gives it an important political leverage, but it lacks the competence to take final legal decisions in the programming process. The EEAS's role is therefore to a great extent limited to a coordinating function, in line with its mandate to strengthen coherence,[153] while its competence is largely based on a procedural involvement in the process. The Commission's

[148] European Think Tanks Policy Brief, Development-proofing the European External Action Service, June 2010, http://fride.org/download/OP_Proofing_Development_Jun10.pdf

[149] Recital 4 EEAS Decision.

[150] Article 9(3) EEAS Decision.

[151] Article 12–14 NDICI-Global Europe Regulation 2021/947.

[152] B. Van Vooren, 'A legal-institutional perspective on the European External Action Service', 491; 493; M. Gatti, 255.

[153] M. Gatti, 256.

competence, by contrast, amounts to actual decision-making, in accordance with its prerogatives.[154] Both actors act consequently within the limits of their mandate: the EEAS is involved in drafting the strategic and political guidelines, which contributes to its task of ensuring coherence between the CFSP and the non-CFSP, while the Commission takes the decisive decision, in line with its task to manage programmes and implement the budget. As such, the EEAS's role in the programming process does not amount to a violation of Article 40 TEU.[155] In *Small Arms and Light Weapons*, the Court clarified that, in light of then Article 47 TEU, its role was to ensure that CFSP acts which, *by their nature are capable of having legal effects*, do not encroach upon the powers as they follow from ordinary EU external action.[156] Following the fact that the EEAS's role relates to the strategic guidance to prepare decisions on programming to be adopted by the Commission, these decisions cannot violate Article 40 TEU, as they do not correspond to the criterion of acts capable of having legal effects. The powers of the Commission in the programming process are therefore not affected in the meaning of Article 40 TEU.[157]

The involvement of both the EEAS and the Commission is moreover in accordance with both actors' Treaty-based task to ensure overall coherence of EU external action, as laid down in Article 21(3) TEU. The ultimate aim of the EEAS's role in the programming process would indeed be to contribute to coherence. Granting the EEAS the competence to co-act in the programming process allows both the High Representative and the EEAS to fulfil the tasks entrusted upon them, mainly to enhance coherence between the CFSP and the non-CFSP. Article 9(2) EEAS Decision explicitly links the High Representative's role in the programming process with the aim of ensuring coherence: involvement in the external action instruments is a means for the High Representative to attain overall political coordination of the Union's external action, ensuring the unity, consistency, and effectiveness of the EU's external action. It is the EEAS's task to assist the High Representative in all his functions, which would explain the EEAS's role in the programming process as well. In that regard, the enforced duty to cooperate in the programming process is also relevant: referring to the EEAS's more general task to cooperate as laid down in Article 3 EEAS Decision, pursuant to Article 9(3) EEAS Decision, the EEAS and the High Representative are required to cooperate with the Commission. This requirement is therefore formulated as a legally binding obligation and as such it is a specification in the programming context

---

154 M. Broberg, R. Holdgaard, 'EU development cooperation post-Lisbon: main constitutional challenges', 367.

155 S. Blockmans, C. Hillion 9.

156 Case C-91/05, para. 60–61.

157 S. Blockmans, C. Hillion, 8.

of the general duty of cooperation applicable between the Commission and the EEAS.

Arguably, the EEAS's role in the programming of development cooperation is positive for the attainment of coherence and the development cooperation policy objectives. The integration of more strategic considerations in the preparation of the programming decisions, yet with a clear primary focus on the development cooperation objectives and a clear division of tasks, could benefit the development cooperation objectives and PCD in particular. In that regard, the involvement of the EEAS could constitute an enhancing factor to mainstream development cooperation policy objectives.[158] That would be particularly the case considering the strong link and the need for coherence between the CFSP and development cooperation in particular, as well as the crucial role of the Union Delegations as a coordinator with other donors and international actor, the partner country, and the Member States. Still, the reference to PCD and the attainment of the development cooperation objectives could be further strengthened in Article 9 EEAS Decision.

The dual involvement of the EEAS and the Commission in the programming process therefore strikes a balance between both the Commission's Treaty-based duties and competences and the duties and competences of the High Representative and the EEAS, as well as the duty to ensure coherence, incumbent on both the High Representative and the Commission.[159] The EEAS's role in the strategic part of the programming cycle represents a more far-going type of cooperation and coordination than the general coordination arrangements: on the basis of a clear delimitation of competences, coherence is pursued by integrating both the Commission and the EEAS in the programming cycle. This arguably reinforces the pursuit of the development cooperation policy objectives and principles, as it has indeed been argued that the mere cooperation between the Commission and the EEAS is insufficient to effectively attain and strengthen coherent EU external action, which is the rationale behind the EEAS's formal role in elements of development cooperation policy.[160] The dual involvement of the Commission and the EEAS carries an important potential to enhance coherence, both in the specific development cooperation–CFSP nexus and within the broader area of EU external action. The advanced form of cooperation established between the Commission and the EEAS in development cooperation policy, particularly in its programming, demonstrates two things: (i) the importance of development cooperation policy in the broader area of EU external action and (ii) the significance of attaining

[158] S. Duke, S. Blockmans, 11–12.
[159] S. Duke, S. Blockmans, 8; M. Gatti, 255, 261.
[160] M. Gatti, 261.

coherence in the area of development cooperation policy for the overall coherence of EU external action.[161]

4. CONCLUSION

It follows from the analysis in this chapter that the management of the institutional division of competences in EU development cooperation policy is governed by principles that have proved to govern the management of the horizontal and vertical division of competences as well. These include expressions of the continued distinction between competence areas, and between the CFSP and the non-CFSP in particular, the importance of cooperation and coordination to attain coherence, and the significance of soft law and pragmatic arrangements in this respect. The central question in this chapter is whether and how the Union's institutional framework is able to attain the development cooperation policy objectives, considering the tension between the principles of conferral and coherence.

A first conclusion concerns the delimitation of competences. In the area of development cooperation policy, two newly established actors are active: the High Representative and the EEAS. It follows from the analysis of the competences and tasks granted to these actors that the scope of their mandate raises some questions. The feasibility of the triple-hatted function of the High Representative has particularly been questioned. The High Representative's coherence mandate requires him to be active in the different institutions that hold key positions in external action, which raises questions about the feasibility to achieve this. The EEAS has the task to assist the High Representative in his functions. As such, the scope of the service's mandate is very broad as well. It can therefore be argued that some of the initial inherent structural complexities of the EEAS partly follow from the attribution of such a wide scope of tasks to the EEAS.[162] Also, in development cooperation policy in particular, the attribution of tasks to the EEAS is rather far-going: while the Commission was previously responsible for the entire programming and implementation process, the EEAS has been granted a formal role in the strategic phase of the programming cycle. A close examination of the programming procedures, however, demonstrates that the Commission remains the lead actor. The EEAS is involved in the preparation of the strategic steps of the programming but it is the Commission that takes the final legally binding decisions and which remains in control of the implementation process. The latter is a consequence

---

161 S. Duke, 56.

162 J. Wouters, G. De Baere, B. Van Vooren, K. Raube, J. Odermatt, T. Ramopoulous, Y. Tanghe, T. Van den Sanden, 18.

of the Commission's budgetary powers as laid down in the Treaties. It therefore seems that this division of tasks respects the principle of conferral and the institutional balance by granting each actor a specific role in accordance with its mandate, competences, and expertise: the EEAS is involved in the strategic programming phase in order to ensure overall coherence, while the Commission takes the final decisions in the programming and the implementation of development cooperation policy. It needs to be emphasised, however, that the EEAS's role should be limited to offering strategic guidance on the basis of considerations of overall coherence and not on the basis of specific EU political or security interests. The latter would amount to subordinating development cooperation policy to political and security interests.

Like in the management of the vertical axis, in attaining coherent action, cooperation and coordination play an essential role. Cooperation ensures that all actors act within their own competences, while the cooperation and communication between the actors steers coherence.[163] The High Representative finds himself in a unique position to be able to attain coherence. The triple-hatted function allows him to influence the horizontal, vertical, and institutional division of competences, as he is active across the different institutions that play a key role in EU external action. His broad mandate that covers the entire area of Union external action functions as a bridge between the CFSP and the non-CFSP, his Commission Vice-President role further steers his coherence mandate, while his chairmanship of the FAC connects him with the Member States. The EEAS is subject to strong cooperative duties that are a specific expression of the general duty to cooperate. These duties further underscore the EEAS's mandate as a service. The cooperation arrangements are particularly important vis-à-vis the Commission, including in development cooperation. While the EEAS Decision focuses on a division of competences in the programming and lays down a duty to cooperate for the Commission and the EEAS, both in general under Article 3 EEAS Decision and in the programming in particular pursuant to Article 9(3) EEAS Decision, the cooperation arrangements focus further on positive cooperation and communication arrangements. The cooperation arrangements are laid down in soft law instruments that offer a flexible way to govern the relationship between the Commission and the EEAS. As such, the Treaties and the EEAS Decision leave enough room for the actors to agree on their cooperation methods in a flexible and pragmatic way.[164] Cooperation is therefore an essential steering tool to balance the division of competences on the one hand and the attainment

---

[163] M. Gatti, 250–251.

[164] B. Van Vooren, 'A legal-institutional perspective on the European External Action Service', 486–491.

of coherence and the development cooperation objectives on the other hand. In this respect, a parallel can be drawn with the management of the vertical division of competences: the management of this nexus too involved cooperation arrangements laid down in soft law instruments that govern the relationship between the Union and the Member States in a flexible and pragmatic way. Indeed, it is through the effective functioning of the EU institutions and their strong relationship vis-à-vis each other that synergies need to be created that steer coherence and that, in turn, have positive effects on the management of the horizontal and vertical division of competences and the attainment of the development cooperation policy objectives.

7. Conclusions

The previous chapters have provided a comprehensive legal analysis of EU development cooperation policy, examining the interaction between the principle of coherence and the principle of conferral in the attainment of the EU's development cooperation policy objectives on the horizontal, vertical, and institutional level.

Chapter 1 discussed the multidimensional and complementary character of EU development cooperation, from which follows the need to ensure coherence. Coherence in the EU's development cooperation policy is a crucial objective, both from a policy and from a legal perspective. The chapter has clarified that the coherence notion in the EU does not merely entail a negative consistency principle, which is focused on limiting contradictions and gaps: it also aims to attain positive coherence, in the sense of creating synergies. In development cooperation policy, this coherence aim is expressed in the notion of policy coherence for development. The need to take account of the objectives of development cooperation policy in conducting policies that are likely to affect developing countries is not only a policy notion, but is also a requirement of primary law, as it follows from Article 208(1) TFEU.

However, a broad nature of the development cooperation policy competence and its objectives entails the risk of interpreting them too broadly, which might lead to the situation where this policy potentially covers nearly every action taken related to development cooperation policy or taken vis-à-vis a developing country, potentially invading any area of Union external action.[1] The development cooperation policy competence therefore also involves the risk of violating the principle of conferral by going beyond the limits of its scope. There is, hence, a contradiction inherent to the development cooperation policy competence. A limited interpretation of the competence and its objectives would contradict the requirements for coherence, would obstruct the attainment of the area's objectives, and would hollow out the competence. On the other hand, it is clear that the competence covers the risk of having a too broad scope, potentially leading to the situation where this competence invades other areas of EU external action, causing problems under the principle of conferral.

1 Cf the Opinion of AG Mengozzi, Case C-377/12, point 29.

The analysis in Part I on the scope of EU development cooperation policy and its delimitation with strongly linked competences has, however, demonstrated that the case law largely succeeds in finding a balanced scope that ensures coherence and respects conferral at the same time. The Court confirmed the broad scope of the EU development cooperation objectives not to be limited to measures directly related to fight poverty, but that it also pursues the objectives referred to in Article 21(2) TEU, in accordance with Article 208(1) TFEU.[2] The Court's two-step test to assess the scope of EU development cooperation is a specific application of the centre of gravity test that takes into account the aim and content criterion in a balanced manner.[3] As regards the aims, the Court confirmed that EU development cooperation's objectives are broad enough for measures required for their pursuit to concern a variety of specific matters. Second, as regards the content, the characterisation of a development cooperation agreement has to be determined having regard to its essential object and not in terms of individual clauses, provided that these do not impose such extensive obligations concerning the specific matters referred to that those obligations in fact constitute objectives distinct from those of development cooperation.[4] Therefore, as a centre of gravity, the development cooperation policy competence is able to cover other areas of cooperation on the basis of its predominant character. When the other competence areas are no longer subordinate to the development cooperation policy competence, they can no longer be covered by the latter. As such, the case law on the scope of EU development cooperation would also balance coherence and conferral. The test on the scope of EU development cooperation allows for the integration of other specific matters into development cooperation, while, as soon as the other specific matters go as far as to become distinct objectives, they no longer fall under development cooperation as the centre of gravity and they would require the addition of their own legal basis.

This was further tested by examining the delimitation between EU development cooperation on the one hand and environmental protection, the CCP, and the CFSP on the other hand. The analysis of the different nexuses demonstrated that the delimitation of development cooperation with environment and with CFSP is in line with the test on the scope of EU development cooperation. The findings on the development–environment nexus demonstrated that the development cooperation policy competence indeed covers and absorbs

---

2 Case C-91/05, *Commission/Council*, EU:C:2008:288; C-377/12, *Commission/Council*, EU:C:2014:1903; Case C-180/20, *Commission/Council*, EU:C:2021:658.

3 Although not a relevant criterion for the specific case, the Court also confirmed in *CEPA Armenia* the context as a relevant criterion: Case C-180/20, para. 54–55.

4 Case C-268/94, para. 37-39; Case C-377/12, para. 39; Case C-244/17, para. 46, Case C-180/20, para. 45.

environmental matters unless they constitute obligations so extensive that they are to be considered as distinct objectives. As regards the development cooperation–CFSP nexus, while the Treaty framework still very clearly separates the CFSP as a distinct area of EU law,[5] the Court's case law has normalised the delimitation by applying the traditional rules on choice of legal basis, the centre of gravity test,[6] and the test on the scope of EU development cooperation[7] in particular, to the nexus. As such, the Court recognises the importance of the CFSP as a separate and distinct area that is to be equally protected, in accordance with the Treaty framework, and normalises the delimitation between CFSP and non-CFSP by applying the traditional rules on choice of legal basis. The delimitation between development cooperation and the CCP, by contrast, would not be in accordance with the test on the scope of EU development cooperation and would be characterised by an imbalance of coherence and conferral. This is due to the fact that the CCP's dominance over the development cooperation policy competence by being omnipresent as a legal basis does not follow from the test on the scope of development cooperation policy but is rather to be explained by the CCP's nature and by historical reasons.

Part II assessed the division of competences and cooperation between actors. In that regard, Chapter 5 analysed the interaction between coherence and conferral in the nature of the EU development cooperation competence and the division of competences and cooperation between the EU and the Member States in EU development cooperation. Here, the notion of complementarity reflects the legal nature of the EU development cooperation policy competence and its management. First, complementarity entails that both the EU and the Member States develop their own development cooperation policies, which relates to the irregular shared nature of the development cooperation policy competence. Second, complementarity requires EU and Member State development cooperation policy to not only develop next, in parallel, to each other but to also complete each other in order to attain a coherent policy. This relates to how the principle of sincere cooperation governs the exercise of the competence. The irregular shared nature of the EU development cooperation competence finds expression in the fact that the competence cannot become exclusive on the basis of Article 3(2) TFEU. This follows from the formulation of the specific Treaty provisions on development cooperation policy and the

[5] See Article 24 TEU for the specific rules and procedures applicable to the CFSP and Article 40 TEU on the specific delimitation between CFSP and non-CFSP. Additionally, the CFSP has lost its specific objectives, which were previously laid down in former Article 11 TEU. See also: G. De Baere, T. Van den Sanden, 106.

[6] Case C-263/14.

[7] Case C-244/17; Case C-180/20.

qualification in Article 4(4) TFEU. Exclusivity is therefore irrelevant for the management of the vertical division of competences in development cooperation policy. Rather, the exercise of the Union's competence in development cooperation and the management of the division of competences between the European Union and its Member States in this area is governed by the principle of sincere cooperation.

As formulated in Article 4(3) TEU, both the positive and the negative aspect of the principle of sincere cooperation govern the exercise of competence between the Union and the Member States in development cooperation. The positive aspect of the principle of sincere cooperation is particularly strong in EU development cooperation, as it manifests itself as an explicit duty for the Union and the Member States to cooperate in Article 210 TFEU in order to ensure the attainment of the development cooperation policy objectives. The enhanced duty of positive cooperation that applies in the area of development cooperation is further expressed, and therefore concretised – and to a certain extent formalised – in secondary legislation and in soft law arrangements, a practice which has been approved by the Court in other areas.[8] The increased level of positive cooperation in development cooperation policy links back to the area's complementary or irregular shared nature. On the one hand, the enforced duty to cooperate makes the attainment of the EU's development cooperation policy objectives possible. On the other hand, a well-functioning relationship between the Union and the Member States on the basis of coordination arrangements makes complementarity possible: the objectives of the area can be attained, without the need to pre-empt the Member States in the division of competences. This would confirm that the lesser the degree of preclusion of Member State action as a consequence of the exclusion of exclusivity, the more important and the more detailed the expression of the duty of cooperation is.[9] The aim of Article 208 TFEU is that Union development cooperation action complements Member State action and vice versa. The enforced coordination efforts in development cooperation policy, with a leading role for the EU institutions, enable this objective.

Still, despite the irregular shared nature of EU law in the area of development cooperation policy, in exceptional circumstances a duty of abstention is incumbent on the Member States, solely on the basis of the principle of sincere cooperation and therefore irrespective of exclusivity. This would be the case when, considering the particular circumstances and context, unilateral Member State action would clearly contradict, undermine, hinder, or impede a specific Union development cooperation policy strategy. In such a case,

---

8 Case C-25/94, *Commission/Council*, EU:C:1996:114.

9 M. Klamert, *The principle of loyalty in EU law*, 171.

a duty to abstain is necessary in order to attain the Union's objectives and the achievement of its tasks, in accordance with Article 4(3) TEU. In this respect, the boundaries of the positive aspect overlap with the start of the negative duty: once a unilateral Member State action contradicts, undermines, hinders, or impedes a specific Union action, the Member States are obliged to abstain from taking that measure or are obliged to redress existing incompatibilities.

Chapter 6 demonstrated that the inherent tension between conferral and coherence is also present in the institutional set-up. The requirement that each actor acts within the limits of the competences conferred on it, with respect for the institutional balance, is a strong requirement that flows from Article 13(2) TEU. The institutions are, on the other hand, required to cooperate and to work towards achieving the Union's objectives, particularly the aim to attain coherent external action. Likewise, the analysis in this chapter confirmed that the management of the institutional division of competences in EU development cooperation policy is governed by principles that have proved to govern the management of the horizontal and vertical division of competences as well. These include expressions of the continued distinction between competence areas, and between the CFSP and the non-CFSP in particular, the importance of cooperation and coordination to attain coherence, and the significance of soft law and pragmatic arrangements in this respect.

The division of roles between the Commission and the EEAS in development cooperation proved to be particularly interesting. The EEAS is involved in the preparation of the strategic steps of the programming, but it is the Commission that takes the final legally binding decisions and which remains in control of the implementation process. The latter is a consequence of the Commission's budgetary powers as laid down in the Treaties. Hence, this division of tasks respects the principle of conferral and the institutional balance by granting each actor a specific role in accordance with its mandate, competences, and expertise: the EEAS is involved in the strategic programming phase in order to ensure overall coherence, while the Commission takes the final decisions in the programming and the implementation of development cooperation policy. Like in the management of the vertical axis, in attaining coherent action, cooperation and coordination play an essential role. Cooperation ensures that all actors act within their own competences, while the cooperation and communication between the actors steers coherence.[10] The cooperation arrangements are laid down in soft law instruments that offer a flexible way to govern the relationship between the Commission and the EEAS. As such, the Treaties and the EEAS Decision leave enough room for the actors to agree on their cooper-

[10] M. Gatti, 250–251.

ation methods in a flexible and pragmatic way.[11] Hence, in this respect, a clear parallel emerges with the management of the vertical division of competences.

Indeed, across the different chapters, the positive coherence notion, in the meaning to steer synergies, is expressed in the horizontal, vertical, and institutional axis of EU development cooperation policy. At first sight, the legal framework, and in particular the Treaty framework, seems to mostly lay down delimitation rules. To a certain extent, this follows from the nature and characteristics of the legal sphere. Delimitation rules that aim to eliminate contradictions and gaps are an expression of the rule of law, which is one of the essential principles on which the EU's legal framework is based.[12] In that regard, the adoption of acts must be in conformity with the rules laid down in the Treaty.[13] Legal frameworks therefore tend to focus more on delimitation rules than on positive coherence. The negative notion of consistency is a static concept: rules and frameworks are consistent or they are inconsistent. The positive notion of coherence, by contrast, is more a matter of degree. In that regard, overstepping competences is arguably more easily enforceable than a lack of cooperation.[14] The ambiguous character of the Treaty framework embodies this: while it is formulated towards the attainment of Union objectives and the need to attain coherence, its rules are, at the same time, to an important extent focused on competence delimitation.

In the competence delimitation between development cooperation and other related areas, the broad legal scope of development cooperation policy allows for the integration of specific matters into the development cooperation competence. As such, EU development cooperation can provide for in-depth cooperation. While this is conducive to positive coherence, the Court's case law on the scope of EU development cooperation finds the balance between coherence and conferral. With its case law on the delimitation between CFSP and development cooperation in particular, the Court contributes to coherence between the different areas, while respecting the principle of conferral and the CFSP as a separate but equal area of EU law, in accordance with the Treaties. Interestingly, in the *Tanzania Agreement* case, the Court confirms the importance of the principle of coherence to EU external action and to the CFSP in particular. It emphasises that the cooperation requirement between

---

11 B. Van Vooren, 'A legal-institutional perspective on the European External Action Service', 486–491.

12 Article 2 TEU.

13 M. Cremona, 'Coherence through law: what difference will the Treaty of Lisbon make?', 15.

14 R. Wessel, 'The inside looking out: consistency and delimitation in EU external relations', 1150.

the institutions in the context of concluding international agreements aims to ensure coherence.[15]

Positive coherence indeed not only follows from synergies between instruments; it necessarily requires that actors create synergies. In that regard, strong cooperation can also soften delimitation rules. At the vertical and the institutional level, the legislative and Treaty framework lays down an explicit legal duty to cooperate. Article 210 TFEU determines that the Union and the Member States have to coordinate their policies on development cooperation and consult each other on their programmes. Article 21(3) TEU identifies the Commission and the High Representative (as well as the Council) as the institutional actors that are responsible to ensure the coherence of Union external action and to cooperate to that effect. Pursuant to Article 3 EEAS Decision, the EEAS needs to cooperate and support other actors, while Article 9 EEAS Decision lays down the role of the Commission and the EEAS in the programming and implementation of the external action instruments. The definition of the duty to cooperate at the vertical and the institutional level therefore remains quite general, while the further implementation of the duty to cooperate takes place on the basis of soft law. The general duty to cooperate is at both levels further specified in cooperation and coordination arrangements, which address specific aspects of coordination and cooperation, such as communication, information-sharing, division of roles, or joint actions. In that regard, the cooperation arrangements in both the vertical and institutional axis focus on positive means to enhance cooperation and coordination rather than on division of labour to pursue the development cooperation policy objectives.[16] Those positive cooperation and coordination arrangements are mostly laid down in soft law instruments. As such, EU primary and secondary law leaves room for the actors to develop and organise their cooperation and coordination arrangements, which makes it possible to organise cooperation and coordination in a flexible and pragmatic way that is adapted to the particular context.

Hence, the legal framework would arguably support a broad development cooperation notion and positive coherence, necessary for the attainment of the development cooperation objectives. The Treaty framework, secondary law, and case law provide for a broad legal scope of development cooperation, for an enhanced demand for coherence with other competence areas and for an enhanced duty to cooperate. Such lays the firm basis for the relevant actors to translate their duty to cooperate into cooperation arrangements that are

---

[15] Case C-263/14, para. 72.

[16] S. Duke, S. Blockmans, M. Broberg, R. Holdgaard, 'EU development cooperation post-Lisbon: main constitutional challenges', 367.

flexible, pragmatic, and adapted to the specific context in order to ensure the attainment of the development cooperation objectives.

Index